# The Abused
# & The Abuser

## By Brenda Lee

*Inspiration for helping resolve abusive situations*

Princess Lee Publishing Co.
P.O BOX 72012
OAKLAND, CA. 94612- 8212

The' Abused and The' Abuser   By Brenda Lee
Human Biography: BASED ON LIFE EXPERIENCES
Inspiration for helping others,

Second Edition

Library of Congress Cataloging in Publication Data


The' Abused and The' Abuser is a Biography based on Family
Relationships and how abuse can destroy a perfect family. It
Includes self help information in case things don't work out.
It provides guidance on how to gain a perfect relationship and
Prevent abuse before it starts.

Princess Lee Book
ISBN: 0-9649571-6-7        CIP 98-92785

10% proceeds- helping
                    abusive situations

# TABLE OF CONTENTS

ACKNOWLEDGEMENTS

ABUSE IN OUR TIME

INTRODUCTION: THE BEGINNING OF LIFE

WORDS FROM THE AUTHOR

1. START OF LIFE
   POEM: CONTINUING TO ABUSE
2. CONTINUING TO ABUSE
   POEM: MY HUSBAND WENT TOO FAR
3. FOLLOWING THE LINE OF ABUSE
4. FACING THE PROBLEM OF ABUSE
5. DEALING WITH AN ABUSIVE PERSON
6. WORDS FOR THE ABUSER
   POEM: TO THE ABUSER
7. FALLING IN LOVE AGAIN
8. HAPPY FOREVER
9. HOW TO PREVENT A WAY OF ABUSE

   HAVING SELF ESTEEM

   SEEKING OUT OTHERS

   ALWAYS BE GRATEFUL

   INVESTIGATE

   NEVER BE AN INSTIGATOR

   BUILD BRIDGES

   ENJOY ONE ANOTHER

   NEVER MAKE THE PAST YOUR FUTURE

   SET LIMITS ON HOW FAR TO GO

   MAKE SOME DIFFERENCE IN YOUR RELATIONSHIP
10. IN NEED OF HELP?

## ACKNOWLEDGEMENT

This edition of *The Abused and The Abuser* was but together in memory of those who suffered unto death because of abuse and to those living an abusive life and can't find a way out. This book is dedicated with peace and joy to all those who love their abuser:

We can never take for granted that relationships are perfect or that they will one day become perfect. That love comes by patience and peace.

Child abuse is an un-formulated sense of anger, an ability to learn comes from making mistakes. Anger that leads to abuse can be controlled, seek help so that your children won't grow up being abusers in their environments.

A very special gratitude goes toward the advisors, may it inspire you to help those that are in need, to exclude abuse in their surroundings.

With love to my family and friends and those who gave special advise and lots of patience.

Special thanks to Lord above for giving me the wisdom and knowledge to express the world's most difficult problems.

MAY GOD BE WITH YOU:
*THE ABUSED AND THE ABUSER*

## ABUSE IN OUR TIME

In our time abuse has taken over the system, and it's becoming a nation-wide problem. Abuse has been ignored for so long it has gotten out of hand, and no one seems to care - it's as if it's just another problem on the table. Abuse should be considered the number one crime in America and around the world. In America it has gotten out of hand to the point where husbands are killing their wives and parents are killing their children. Abuse is so overlooked that women are abandoning their children, leaving them home by themselves with no one to care for them, no food or water available, leaving them in the complete dark. It seems that women can't keep up with their babies, leaving them for dead in garbage dumpsters or wherever they can dump them off.

Abuse has taken a toll on our lives. In America we seem to ignore this problem if it's not in our households or in our neighborhood, and we blindly think that we don't have to deal with this problem of abuse. Some people act like it doesn't exist in our society, but it does, it's in our world and we must find ways to help prevent this problem of abuse.

Abused children really suffer the most, because they have nowhere to run, and if they run, more trouble comes their way. They have nowhere to hide, because someone will find them, and it won't be the right person. And of course they have no one to talk to, because who would listen to a child when he's crying out for help? These kids are left all alone with their abusive parents; these kids need someone to reach out to when this comes about in their lives. Most of them end up dead, and no one really cares or wonders how or what happened and how they even got there.

Abuse in our lifetime has no end: it continues on forever, especially for those who don't seek out help. In reality, abuse is not considered a crime. No one goes to jail or people are rarely even punished for abusing someone else. Abuse is a crime and it should be treated as one, maybe then abuse would go away.

We should look at abuse like we look at gold, and see what kind of outlook it could bring about in our lives. Abuse in our lifetime doesn't look good at all.

This story it tells about abuse and some ways of preventing it, if we could only follow some guidelines in helping us to prevent abuse. Maybe someone we know might need advice for those times when abuse comes their way; or maybe they're experiencing abuse and need a way out. This book doesn't have all the answers, but maybe it can help you find a way out of the situation that you are in, because no one can really "beat abuse" once it gets started. Maybe in America we can get together and try to solve this problem of abuse in our time.

## WORDS FROM THE AUTHOR

Abuse should not be taken for granted in any aspect. I hope this book can be as helpful as counseling. It's more like words of wisdom to those who are in need. It is written for those who are looking for some great reading material. It is also for those who are looking for a great story or a thought on what abuse is about and how it actually feels to go through an abusive situation. The author has taken great pride in writing this book, solely for others to enjoy. Try reading it with care so that you too may experience some of the feelings that occur.

Abuse is like a flower that has no life
it's colors of fading without any strife
it's like the rain that never stops flowing
it's like the grass that never grows
Abuse is sorrow, pain, and heartache
it's like darkness of the living dead
you cannot tell, whether it's for the good or the bad
Abuse has no name, no friend, or family
it's like no life when there's no one to help you
it's like black, purple, and dark blue
it's lost all of it's feelings and the way to the truth
it seems as if, there's no way out
locked in a shell and that's what abuse is all about.

## INTRODUCTION

## THE BEGINNING OF LIFE

In the beginning it was thought spanking your child was a form of discipline. It seems that discipline in our society became more of a cruel insulting solution or treatment for raising your child. People began losing their minds, started something that could not be stopped, or no longer controlled. This story is about the beginning of abuse in a family. It starts at the time of fertilization when a woman becomes pregnant and the fetus begins to grow inside the woman. The mother becomes sensitive, easily irritated and worries about having a healthy baby. The woman becomes tired and very worn out with the weight of trying to conceive a healthy baby. In spite of the happiness of being pregnant, the wait becomes long and anxious. The father, his mind filled with anxiety of the moment, becomes depressed. He wonders if and when this baby is coming, and ignores the anxiety of the mother. Finally the baby is born, a beautiful baby boy. The mother and father of this new baby are happy; happy that the anxiety and the fear of waiting for a healthy baby is over. They're happy to have a child to love, cherish, care for, and teach forever. They're happy to carry the burden that they have to bear in guiding this baby into a perfect ongoing life and becoming a perfect man - this is the way it was supposed to go until something went wrong in this family!

Before the baby was born, this couple had the perfect marriage. This man loved his wife, caring for her and treating her with the utmost respect from the first day of their wedding ceremony. They promised to be with each other until death parted them, through sickness and health, for richer or poorer. When one failed the other would fall and together both of them would go through hell, because they took their marriage to be as one complete whole, and that's the way it went for this particular family called the English family.

# THE
# START
# OF
# LIFE

# 1

The baby was born, beautiful, soft precious baby, as innocent as a baby can be; the parents were very happy. Then finally it came time to take the baby home, home to his beautiful, lovely room, freshly painted in natural colors of white and yellow with matching accessories. Pat continued to hold the baby never putting him down. It got to the point that if Mike wasn't held he would cry. Pat often embraced him with love while rocking him in his chair, sitting along side the window in his room, where the green leaves framed parts of the window. Mike began to cry. He began to cry all night long and all day long. Widening his brown eyes, as tears flowed deeply onto his Caramel brown skin. Grabbing his soft curly hair, crying for attention, continuing to cry all day and night long. As the coloration of his sight settled in. When Mike hadn't seen his mom for long hours, he cried his way to sleep all alone. Pat suffered from postpartum (after birth effects) Pat being still vulnerable from Mike's birth, could no longer handle his crying. She began to leave Mike in the room alone. Shut in behind the closed doors. She would no longer have to hear him crying; instead he cried louder, enough to drive her in sane. No matter what Pat tried, he was getting louder, nothing could stop this baby from crying. This distraction decreased her everyday activity.

Cuddling missed, Mike wanting a little attention, something she had stopped doing. She withheld the attention he deserved. Her abuse! Pat never experienced the trauma of being abused and she had no understanding the spanking (nearly beating) was very harmful to her precious baby.

As my baby grew, he was innocent, not knowing how to react to my hysterical ways, doing what babies do best—crying to get attention; his only way of communicating. His instant demands sent me into a mental state where shaking him wouldn't help, in vehement attempt while shaking the baby, telling him to be quiet. My nerves began to take its toll on my mental health, (slamming doors) while turning up his musical toys became a normal activity. Sometime it seemed to help, until he figured out my system. Mike screams led to an obnoxious point, I found myself locking him in his room, hoping this would solve the problem, but he continued to cry! My anger continued to grow. Trying to exercise the extra excess left from the stretching of my baby. He cried and cried and nothing seemed to calm him down. This problem could not be solved.

At the toddler stage, Pat tried to make Mike understand that he was crying too much for her to handle. She began to lock Mike in the room, thinking that this would solve the problem. The problem just got "worse and worse," and as time went on and baby Mike began to crawl while trying to walk, exploring his surroundings, destroying and eating everything that touched his hands.

Pat began to spank Mike. Day after day, the spankings got out of hand turning his brown legs red, Pat spanking were becoming increasingly brutal her hands were uncontrollable. Mike became fearful of her whenever she touched him he feared, she would hit him and he screamed. Caressing Mike became uncomfortable for my baby, my appearance made him cry although my love was much greater than imagine, constantly afraid of the pain my touch may have caused him. While his father was away working and had no knowledge of what was going on, the constant hitting became part of the baby's daily routine.

The problem between my baby and me continued to grow. As time went on, the abusiveness of Mike got way out of control, continuing in my mental state. As Mike began to start school, he became annoyed by his surroundings. Not knowing anyone but his parents, he was afraid to participate in any of the school activities. Fearing if he'd touch anything, anger would strike and the teacher would spank him and spank him hard, like the spankings that he received at home on a daily basis.

Mike's fears grew increasingly worse, annoying his teacher, Mrs. Morgan with her long straight black hair and yellow skin. Wore a continuous stern look abruptly across her face, after Mike spent two years with Mrs. Morgan she was compelled by Mike's attitude; how it hasn't changed in over five years-avoiding his surroundings, Mike was an isolated child. Fearing the pain from others, this disturbed Mrs. Morgan dramatically, seeing Mike's reaction toward the other children. He was growing into a paranoid kid, retaliation grew as Mike assumed all people were mean, nervously confused about how to handle this situation of Mike's. Mrs. Morgan tried hard to reach his parents calling until she finally reach an answer.

*Hello! Mrs. English*

Yes, this is Mike's teacher, were having difficulties, problems with your child. silence fell through my mind, as this strange teacher explained her experience of handling my child. Mrs. English, be here tomorrow with your spouse for a parent and teacher conference to discuss your child future.

*Sure, we'll be there bright and early*

Staring through her glasses with a concerned look on her face, Mrs. Morgan began telling Pat and Bill about her present experience with Mike, how he wouldn't participate and her closeness makes him tremble in fear. My job as a teacher, she continues to say, to insure the safety of the children and keep them healthy, I'm suggesting that your child be checked out by a physician. Its been several months since school started and he still hasn't adjusted to our simple daily routine. He cries; this is unusual for someone his age. My nervous mouth began assuring the teacher, Mike had never been around other kids, and it will take time for him, "It's all in your mind I began to say, Mike's only been in school a couple of years and he's a little skeptical about things." Constantly speaking in a manner she wouldn't understand, but she gave me an odd look, in questionable to what was going on. Speaking loudly, "He's learning and I can assure you there's was nothing wrong with him."

Bill agreed, while scratching the bald part of his head looking very worried unaware of the abusive situation between mother and child. When we arrived at home, Bill followed me into the room feeling the soft touch of his beautiful brown hands rubbing my shoulders, thinking how much I really love this person Bill began asking, "Why is he always so jumpy? He's such a quiet kid? I know that he doesn't bother anyone, maybe the teacher's right, we should let the doctor check him out."

The problems were at hand that Mike suffered from, nervously shaking, while trembling appeared in my voice, he continued to rub my shoulders speaking loudly, There's nothing wrong with him. Maybe the teacher had our kid mixed up with another kid. I mean, we only have one child and he plays alone at home and that's why he probably doesn't want to play with other kids.

*"You're probably right! Pat, Then maybe we should have another baby?"*

"No! one kid is enough. Besides, Mike will learn to play with other kids as time goes on. The thought of cruelty reign through out my mind about what was going on and how it was affecting my child, trying to divert myself was impossible, an addiction-which had ruled the raising of my child something that could no longer be restrained, the addiction of abusing. Stroking my permed straight hair turning away from Bill thinking how my brown skin would be pale as a goat if he ever found out the truth about me spanking our child. Immersing my mind of something that would easily vanish away knowing that this was an addictive mental problem. Brutalizing my conscience of something so simple while help is not needed, Maybe he should know my insanity about what's going on between me and our son, but then our marriage will be on edge. "At this point confusion reigned once again, nervous about the decision to tell my husband."

At this point, Pat became confused, thoughts ran through my mind, maybe it'll just go away by itself. In due time, Bill is sure to find out; but it's been a while, I'm OK.

Once again my husband continued on his job, going on long

business trips, weeks at a time, our life is based on telephone calls. If phones had feelings it would make marriages a lot more content for traveling husbands. I'm always suggesting to my husband about satellite, then we could see one another while discussing family life. Time had certainly taken its course, the room was quiet while Mike was understanding my point about crying. He was growing so big and beautiful, his image was exactly of my strong genes, as I stared at him smiling, my beautiful boy of six years old.

Quietly driving and peeking at Mike, playing happily with every toy Johnson & Johnson had to offer, listening to the sounds of his imaginary thoughts as his voice carries throughout the car. Driving my way to the nearest department store, maneuvering my mind through the store, concentrating only on the items I needed to purchase. Just when the thought of abusing was cleared from my mind, While picking up a large amount of items, Mike grabbed a toy that he liked and began to play with it, it reminded him of a toy that a kid at school had been playing with. Mike became attached to this "Big red fire truck with action toys attached (refusing to buy it) Mike began to cry so loud that everyone could hear him screaming and throwing toys off the shelves. Mike was getting out of control, trying viciously and unsuccessfully to calm him down. People began to gather around watching from every where, running from the other isles their I was seeking a solution to my problem, grabbing Mike, shaking him, pulling and dragging him to the car, leaving all items behind, hurrying out of sight of these watchful people mattering in my life, rushing to open the car door and physically threw him in, locked the door. Then Proceeded back into the store  purchased my items.  Driving very angry from the embarrassment, upset at Mike, "You've done it this time! I'm going to teach you to act up! I'm going to spank you, you deserve it! Every bit of it! Yelling at Mike as if he was three miles  away. 'How could you do this to me? After all, you have enough toys to play with at home! That horrible scene! You embarrassed me in the store in  front of all those people!

Insane and growing angrier by keeping this little incident on my mind of Mike's behavior in the store. Quickly stomping on the brakes, pulling over to the side of the road, yanked Mike out of the car while repeatedly saying, "I'll make sure you don't embarrass me any more in a store!"

By this time Mike had forgotten all about what happened in the store. As we were standing on the road he kept playing with the toys as if he didn't hear me, uncontrollable my hands, hitting him and hitting him hard, telling him, "Don't ever do that to me again! This Mike; you will understand! Once I'm done."

Viciously beating this child of mine and Bill's, not realizing that the abuse was starting over again, hurting my six year old child, all poor Mike could do was cry; crying silently, with no one to help him.

The Spankings became beatings and Mike began to have bruises on his back and legs. From the constant and daily beatings that my vicious hands performed on him, because insanity had taken control (unable contain myself) This continued for several years, it became a normal habit, apart of our every day life.

Mike tried to express to his father in certain ways about what Pat was doing to him, but he failed every time. Bill was very business minded, Mike way of expressing his problems to Bill, he was ignored, he was silently showing Bill his bruises, but Bill never took notice.

Bill's absent led to a speechless relationship between him and Mike. Communication was on level zero it never went as far as to say hello or good bye. Locked in abuse-Mike was unable to express his pain caused by his birth mother "Mike growing pains increased. "Still unable to have friends afraid of what others might say, not wanting to be teased because of his mother foolishness. Mike was a child afraid to explore being around others Mike was a growing child, experiencing the changes off a twelve -year -old, like women go through menopause. Starting his life as a teenager in a new environment.

Moving into his seventh year in school where every thing appeared so different even his PE class had its advantage, Mike was all excited! Comparing himself to others every one on the same accord the changing of clothes made Mike very happy for the first time, the kids were really nice treating him like one of them, he felt alive for once in his life, as if someone loved him, even if they weren't family he felt loved.

He was really happy, but as he took off his regular clothes there was a problem, a problem with his skin. Something was different from the other boy's legs; Mike's legs were mottled with different colors everywhere purple-red clots fading his skin color which was no longer brown. Focused on his legs with disgust, one of the boys screamed out, "Mike! What happened to your legs?"

"Nothing! None of your business, mind your own business."

The boy then proceeded to get the teacher, telling her that something was wrong with Mike's body. "You should go and see he's different colors all over, I saw it!

By the time the teacher got there, Mike had left and gone home. When he got home, he explained to me about what happened at school. Urgently grabbing my purse, to find a solution to my on going-problem searching to buy sweat pants for his PE class. As we were shopping for sweat pants,

Mike screamed, "Mom! Please buy this sweater!"

Mike, I screamed; "We just came for a few items.

Please don't ask for anything else."

He continued to throw a fit,

Extremely embarrassed by the scene Mike was making in the store.

"Please don't act like this, No! I said in a low harsh tone, Mike got louder and louder, No choice, we purchased the items that Mike wanted so badly.

But when we returned home he was warned, if he ever did that to me again that he was going to regret it. As we walked into the house trying to avoid hitting, him but my anger was to aroused so I viciously grabbed him around the neck and said "Don't ever do that again. Do you understand Mike?" while vigorously choking him.

"Yes, Pat! I'm sorry. I'll never do that again. Please don't hurt me, Pat!" he cried out.

Pat continued to beat Mike, not paying attention to what he was saying, not listening to him pleading for her to stop, to leave him alone because he was tired of getting what she thought he deserved simply because of embarrassment. Mike had no where to turn. Mike knew his mother would abuse him again if he told someone what she was doing to him, he was afraid of that horrible pain. Six months later Mike came to school with a black eye and his face very, very swollen. When the PE teacher Miss Tate asked Mike what happened, he just said, "I got into a fight with my brother."

Miss Tate reminded Mike that he didn't have a brother, that he was an only child. She quietly took Mike to the office to find out who did this to him. When she began to ask Mike questions, he started shaking and getting nervous and afraid. Fearing his mother would find out and do something else to him, he got up and ran out of the office. The teacher tried to catch him, running down the hall after him and calling his name. There was no answer; Mike was out of sight. He went straight home. Miss Tate called Mike's house and Pat answered the phone. She began to tell me about what happened in school growing in to a nervous state) slowly interrupting the teacher, stating, "There's nothing wrong with my child. He probably got into a fight with another kid I'll take care of it. Speaking to her as if we've met I've never seen this woman in my life but she calls to tell me about how my son looks to her, he's fine to me after all its my problem anyway! *Thank you for calling and have a nice day. Good bye!"*

After hanging up the phone, Miss Tate called another teacher into the office to discuss Mike's problem, wanting to know how long he had been coming to school with bruises. Absent minded to Mike's problem. Mr. William sat down and asked, "Is there a problem?"

"Yes, there is with Mike English. He's had a lot of bruises on him lately and I was wondering if you had any information about this."

"Well yes, he told me that he got into a fight with his brother."

"He doesn't have a brother."

"That's what I thought, but I had no way of verifying that. Assuming he had a stepbrother or maybe a play brother; somehow I would of not imagined it to be someone other than another kid."

"Well," Ms. Tale said, "will have to investigate if he comes to school with more bruises on him. This has been going on for too long, every since school started he's been coming here with bruises on body and hiding. He even wears sweat pants while the other kids wear shorts, and it just doesn't seem right,"

*"Well, did you call his house?"*

"Sure did, and his mother seemed very angry saying; There's nothing wrong with my son, then she hung up the phone really fast, before I could response, I just wanted to let her know that this has been going on for a very long time. His mom hung up real fast..

"Where's his father? He should know something about this problem. How can you live in a house without knowing the existing problems with your child? He must know something, unless he's the one performing this horrible act!

"Well, we've got to find out what's going on before it gets worse."

Thoughts ran through my mind about why Mike would tell his teacher that his brother beat him.

Maybe Mike said my mother; but I'm was fairly sure he said my brother. "What am I'm going to do? Questions ran through my mind, I've got to stop this before someone finds out, but it's so hard, needing serious help, there's nothing wrong with me, I'm just spanking my child, teaching him right from wrong what could be better? Someone has to keep him in control and I'm always home to face the problems that occur."

After all I'm just doing what's right: just simply spanking my child. Along with spanking. Pat abuse has taken its toll on hurting Mike. When Mike returned to school he was called into the office immediately by the Ms. Tale, and by Mr. William's to discuss the problem. When he sat down at the table, they were waiting for him. Mr. William's began to say softly to Mike, "We know there's a problem at home and we brought you in here to see if we can help you. We talked to your mother about this, now we need to hear the truth from you about your father, is he abusing you, molting your body?"

Mike screamed out, "No! My dad would never do anything to hurt me, he loves me a lot."

"Well, who's doing this to you Mike? We're only trying to help you so you won't have to go through this any more."

Mike began to say again, "My brother did this to me, we got into a fight..."

"Are you sure?"

"Yes. I'm sure."

"Okay, you can go to class now."

Mike got up and left the office. Ms. Tale and Mr. William's began talking. "He doesn't want to tell us what's going on, so there's nothing that we can do. We already talked to his mother about this problem, and she says there's nothing wrong at home so maybe he's getting into fights with other kids in the neighborhood." They concluded their conversation without further investigating or having Mike examined by the school nurse.

While doing my spring cleaning pulling out every thing in Mike's room, noticing a pile of papers sitting neatly behind his chest drawer, stacks of papers! My thoughts were, to scam through them before throwing them away, Yes! Shaking my head, his homework (angered flared) waiting for him to return home, holding my stick, Mike calling softly, he came running up the stairs and I swat him across the shoulder and pushed him down the stairs.

Two weeks later Mike returned to school unable to have PE class because of his broken arm. I'd pushed him down the stairs because he forgot to do his homework once again he'd been warned several times before that the situation would be much worse. While Bill was away on a business trip and Pat knew he would be gone a little longer than two weeks plenty of time for Mike's arm to heal. Mr. William's asked; what happened to your arm,

Mike said; "I fell off my bike real hard and ran into a car." Mr. William's felt that there was something wrong, so he said to Mike, "I know that you didn't fall. Tell me the truth. I won't tell anyone Mike, that's a promise and no one will ever know."

Mike just stare scornfully, feeling hurt, wanting to discuss this problem of his mother, fearing what will happen next if he told.

Miss Tate grabbed Mike and hugged him, saying its all right Mike I know its your mother, Mike pushed himself away as if to run but Miss Tate grabbed his arm so he couldn't he get away, figuring his first thoughts, (while holding his arm) "Please tell me! Who is doing this to you? Just tell me is it your mom? Mike, who's doing this to you?"

"No!" shouted Mike, "leave me alone, please."

Then Miss Tate asked; "Where's your father?"

"I don't know. He's out of town. He's gone on a trip and he won't be back for a while."

"May I call your mother and talk to her about this?"

"No! She knows I fell off my bike."

"Did you really fall, Mike?"

"Yes Ms. Tale, I really fell."

So Ms. Tale allowed herself to be convinced, and believed the story that Mike told her, his family was pretty much well off and abuse couldn't be possibly have occurred in this family. They lived in a well set community where everything appeared perfect.

Miss Tate called Pat anyway, for clarification of Mike story.

"Hello! Pat answered the phone.

"Hi! This is the teacher at Mike's school. He missed two weeks of school and I was wondering if every thing is okay, because he returned to school with a broken arm. He was gone so long that he missed lots of work. Why was he absent for so long?"

"Mike has been sick with the flu and he was unable to return to school. As for the broken arm, he was sleepwalking and fell down the stairs, it was pretty dark in the house."

*"Oh my God!*

*"Are you sure that's what happened, Mrs. English?"*

"Yes, I'm sure about what happened. He's my son and I should know what goes on with him. Thank you for your concern, now good bye." Slamming down the phone not realizing that they knew the truth about me abusing my son. In fact, he'd driven me to the point where it didn't matter, just continuing my daily abuse teaching him what I thought he deserved.

As time went on and Mike began to start high school the beatings continued and became much worse and very serious. Mike's father was still unaware of what was going on between his son and his wife. He believed Pat when she said that Mike was getting into fights with other kids, boys older than himself. Bill had no idea who was abusing his son. At 14 years of age, Mike was suffering from an abusive past, one that his mother had forced upon him. He was unable to concentrate fearing that one day his action or his words would offend Pat and she would continue to beat him like always.

His abusive mother would suddenly start it again. Mike's greatest fears in life, was that strike, that punishment to the body, known by a word he learned in school and looked up in the dictionary; the word he couldn't bring himself to saying. It was something he was experiencing; something that coursed through his body, it was P A I N and it hurts so bad, it seemed like something that would never go away.

At age 14, Mike had something far worse to fear than any bullies at school; it was his own precious mother Pat, whom his father promised to love and cherish until death parts them. Mike wanted so badly to alert his father about Pat, her hatred toward him, he was afraid! That his father would misjudge him about his loving wife, afraid that Pat would find out. She constantly warned Mike while Bill was present, constant fear, afraid of the pain and hurt his mother was active in performing.

Mike began his young adult life, he began to mix with others kids his age who were somewhat like him. Mike was trying to blend in and cope with the new society while feeling great that he was finally growing up. He would move far away from his parents, someplace where his mother could not find him or even call. Matching up with the other kids showed Mike that something was wrong, very wrong with his life. He was different, and he began to search for answers while being afraid open to up to his father about what was happening, about his fears, about his mom and why she didn't love him, why she hated him so much –Mike wanted to discuss all the things his father never knew. He was absent minded always on business trips. Mike actually thought; Pat performed these horrible acts because his father never came home. Lots of unconditional things ran through Mike's mind. While searching for reason Mike was wrong about his father involvement, Pat had a serious problem and that was her reason for beating him, an addiction and very uncontrollable a beast of her own kind. Mike finally decided that he was going to act his age and start hanging out like the other kids. Mike daily instructions were to report straight home after school while the other kids had after school activities. He stayed out too late one evening, having a little fun an urge he always wanted to experience. Being out with the other kids away from his mom, for not a little while, but for a long time, without his mother and father's permission having no idea of Mike's presents, Mike stayed out past nine o'clock. There I was setting around and waiting as my thoughts were crooked when he didn't return home to say where he was, worry settled in that Mike had ran away because of me. Knowing that one day Bill will discover all the things that had been done to our son.

Sitting and waiting drinking lots of coffee arousing my nerves because he didn't call, leave a note, or ask me about going out, my thoughts open up of his punishment when he came home. Obstructing my nerves I could no longer contain myself pacing the floor telling myself, "If he doesn't come home soon I'm going to go crazy!

"Where in the world could he be, staying out late knowing

that school is an important factor in our lives, another problem, as a mother I have to deal with my child hanging out at night, for getting the concept of school, I found myself staring out window, nervously waiting!

*Anger captured my mind, pacing the floor telling myself,*
*"If he doesn't come home soon I'm going to go crazy!*

It's 11:00 Mike still isn't home. As my thoughts were at hand the door slowly creep opened, Mike sneaking into the house, thinking that I would be fast asleep and hoping that my knowledge was vague of where he had been when not returning from school.

In a shocking surprise, out of the blue, grabbing Mike throwing him against the wall, frantically shaking him and screaming through my lungs sending him into complete shock, while he's imagining his body turning a course of colors blue, red, green, and purple all over. Unable to contain or stop myself he began screaming loudly, fearing what his mother, this lady, his father's wife was going to do to him. Out of nowhere came a "flying board" which hit him across the back and legs, knocking him down. Hitting him until he could no longer see, then he passed out on the floor. He was out for hours.

Fear swept through my body I've never gone this far before now something was horribly wrong. "Mike!" She called, "Mike, wake up!"

When he didn't wake up, she screamed again, "Mike! Mike! Wake up, please, wake up!"

When he didn't wake up, her screams appeared louder, "Mike! Mike! Wake up!"

He couldn't move, not for his sake, not for mine; he couldn't move for anyone. He was out cold, running to hide the board so Bill wouldn't find out what really happened, calling the hospital, trying to do so before Bill came home.

It was too late, he was pulling up in the garage. Frantically running to the door as if the moment had just occurred and having no knowledge of what happened to Mike, Mike was out cold Calling, "Bill! Bill! Something happened to Mike!"

Bill ran into the house, picked up Mike and said, "Call 911!"
"I called. They should be arriving in a moment, as my tongue was sponging to released its pressure, as the ambulance pulled up in the driveway. Nervously running to open the door. When the medical team saw Mike laying on the floor not moving, they started asking questions about what happened, what happened he yelled! Who beat this child? Staring waiting on an answer, barley grasping my teeth as they watched my every moved deepening the color of my eyes,, I said; he yelled out who did this! Trying to kill this child, which one of you? Bill looked amazed at what he was asking, then spoke out, he's our son, and will find out, just help him while the other medical personnel asked, if Mike had been in a fight after school.

Responding immediately, "Yes! Yes! That's where he was. He just came home and passed out on the floor. He never said a word."

Bill looked up at Pat, saying, "Since when did our son start getting into fights at school?"

"I think he started today. He didn't come home from school today, and when he came home he just passed out, you can plainly see that for yourself."

They took Mike to the hospital; he was unconscious for two days. When Mike woke up and saw his father and, of course, his mother standing over him, he began to cry with anguish over the pain she caused him."

Bill holding Mike's hand, saying, "It's going to be all right son. Don't worry, we'll find out who did this to you. I promise you, who ever did this, will pay for what they have done to you."

*"My eyes widened as usual at Bill's words, speaking softly saying; "*

"When you came into the house I was so afraid, you fell right to the floor. I called your father right away when he was pulling up into the garage. Pat nervous said; Confused and disturb.

Mike looked at his mother in fear, knowing that she was lying, and that she was trying to cover up what she had done.

"But why, he thought, was his father was trying to comfort

him by telling him that all kids go through this and that you will be okay so don't worry?" Mike began telling his father that no kid should have to go through this and he wanted to move far away and fast.

Bill just said, "Hey, you just got into a big fight at school. Don't be upset because all the rest of the kids are probably dealing with the same problem. You just need to rest, so we're leaving. We'll be back to get you in a couple of days."

"No! Dad, please don't leave me. As Mike was screaming out a nurse was standing by ready to comfort him, tears rolled down his smooth brown face, barely able to speak because of his swollen lips, Please! May I move in with my aunt and uncle-away from you and Pat. You're no longer my mother and father.

Bill then looked shocked at what Mike was saying, wondering why his child was talking in this manner. He thought he was the perfect father, he turned to look at Pat and asked, "What is this? Why is our son speaking so sorrowful?"

Pat wasn't able to answer. Lips barely moving giving Mike a long hard stare as fear swept through my body, fearful that the time had come for me to confess, fearful of a divorce, fearful from my horrible act of beating Mike, all these years fear of the lies I've been telling my husband but he deserve it, he was a bad kid and he'll appreciate me later in life. A smile appeared on my face grabbing Bill soft brown hands, honey! He needs to rest, the medicine is taking over.

"Honey, I don't know what's wrong," Pat answered.

"Maybe the school has some answers. Maybe he has a problem in school and teachers know about it. Someone has to have some answers,," Bill pondered.

Bill, this isn't necessary, every thing will be all right and he'd probably just had a bad day at school. Bill agreed, believing in his wife how she was so honest and faithful, making sure that every thing in the home was taking care of .

Holding my hand not doubting  me one bit,  hugging me telling me, "I can count on you to take care of things while I'm gone and not having to worry. " continuing to smile, assuring Bill, that every thing was in control.

"I will honey, you can count on me to take care of everything."

As we were driving home in our beautiful Cadillac of emerald green exterior and off white interior wondering about life being so great with my husband while staring at him and smiling, Honey! It will be okay, I'll take care of everything, don't worry!

After spending five days in the hospital Mike finally arrived home, insinuating the action of what could happen warning him that if he ever told his father about me he would regret it for the rest of his life. Mike just look at her with hatred, not saying a word. He got up and went on with his business, staying in his room most of the time while his father was away because he didn't feel comfortable around his mother. After school he would go straight to his room. Sometimes he avoided eating dinner because he didn't want to be around his mother whom he hated so much.

Every time she tried to talk to Mike he would just ignore her. Mike couldn't live a normal teenage life, couldn't join after school activities, he was always expected home at a certain time. Out of fear, Mike just never got involved. Pat kept close tabs on Mike, making sure only what she consider proper words would slip from his mouth. Mike got apathetic, not caring if he had to stay in his room the rest of his life, just as long as Pat no longer beat him. Pat gained control of herself after he was hospitalized and his father began questioning her involvement. She seemed to have calmed down.

Two years passed by and Mike began to rebel against his mother and father. Bill felt pretty bad about Mike's suffering so he decided he'd throw Mike a sixteenth birthday party to soften his young adult hood.

Bill allowed him to have this party, he invited all the teenagers he possibly could. After running out of invitations he alerted every one by word of mouth Mike wanted to invite every kid he came in contact with. Finally his dad was agreeing to his way of life, as usual Bill was away on a Business trip. The party still continued as planned.

The music was playing and all the kids were having a great time congratulating Mike and thanking him for such a great party. Pat stood and watched his every move, Mike lost the thought that she even existed and continued to act in his school age manner-amazed she'd never seen him so happy and of course silly.

The silliness was driving me crazy grabbing my cup and slamming it down hoping he would get the message but he just ignored me and continued having fun, pacing the floor wanting to grab Mike, throw him in the closet, lock the door and hide the key. Anger rolled over me like lightening my eyes were turning red like fire while no one watched or acknowledge my existence I hurriedly ran over to the stereo, threw it on the floor grabbed and pushed Mike over the table and loudly yelled, Get out! Get out! Right now, picking up what was ever in sight, throwing items at these kids invading my privacy, then quickly grabbing Mike's cake and threw it at him yelling stupidity, stupidity! You immature brat! Get over here violently screaming at Mike, right now! Mike was shaking and crying of embarrassment of my actions he ran out the door and slammed it! My thought were crocked, the deepness of the caffeine had settled in from the eight cups of express-o I allowed my self to drink, looking through the windows searching for Mike but he was no where to be found, eyeing the bottle of sleeping pills to calm my nerves urgently rushing six pills down my throat to overcome this caffeine high.

Mike was watching his mom through the window having no where to go, or nowhere to hide afraid that Pat was waiting, so he sat out side the window waiting for her to sleep. Pat sat at the table nodding waiting on Mike, dozing until she passed out, her face was position right in the table, still afraid, Mike took off his shoes creeping up stairs trying not to awake Pat, for she was out cold-from the pills. Mike had woke up very early trying to leave before she took notice that he was in the house, as he walked around down stairs noticing that nothing had been cleaned the mess which was left over from Pat's angry actions, Mike began cleaning, scrubbing, washing dishes putting things back into place it took him hours, while Pat was still sleeping in the same place from the amount of pills she had taken Mike then went off to school, ready to face the embarrassment of others, teasing and rumors from the kids, shame pierced Mike's life as he walked into the school with his head down and face half way covered until a group of kids approach him with comfort explaining to him it was all right, one girl softly said; do not be ashamed it wasn't your fault while someone handed him a flower and candy, they were all very supportive and this eased the heart ache of Mike's horrible life.

(When kids interact with one another in the manner of kindness it dissolve all unloved and unwanted heartache instead of adding to the problem and making it worse.)

Mike felt better he felt relived that sometimes, caring can make a difference in other people lives.

He thought that his father knew all about what his mother had been doing to him. It seemed to Mike that his father had to know about Pat's craziness how can you be part of an household and not know the existing problem, creating more problems Mike began to talk back to his parents, ignoring everything that they said to him. Pat tried talking to him but this didn't work because he would yell out how much he hated her. Threatening her if she touched him, He was going to run away and never come back. Pat anger grew in a matter of minutes and Mike quickly changed his attitude, cursing her every thought, Pat's anger was very uncontrollable. "Calling Mike, into the room, saying to him, , "Sit down honey, so we can talk."

"Mike was alert to what was going through her mind, he said; "No! I'm leaving."

As Mike started to leave, my first instinct was to grab his arm, yanking him, saying' "You're not going anywhere at all" repeating the question, as he gave me a sorrowful look Mike, "I'm in no condition to hit you, it's your behavior with your father and me we need to discuss, you're getting out of hand" We can't understand this problem that you're causing, but you should stop it before it gets completely uncontrollable. Please! Don't, let this to go any further. Do you understand? We can no longer handle you Mike, this problem will be taken care of!

Mike began to have flash-backs about when she brutally beat him the last time, how she was really serious about getting to the bottom of situations.

"I'm sorry Pat, I didn't mean to be rebellious and act bad," he said nervously.

Pat said, "Its too late. I warned you already." Quickly rushing to get my stick which was hiding in the closet, the stick that was used whenever Mike got out of hand which was setting away collecting dust. Please don't cause me to use my options you've been really bad and your attitude is getting worse.

Pat backed Mike into the corner and began beating him. She could not control herself, she was beating him so hard and fast that he didn't have time to scream for help. Pat beat Mike striking him in all angles making sure she covered all parts of his body beating him for about an hour until she got tired, until she could no longer hold herself up, beating him in the face and everywhere.

***When Pat was finished she asked, "Mike do you get my point?"***

Sore by the affliction, unable to move, as tears drowned his face Mike starred at Pat directly in the eyes for all that it was worth, then replied

"Yes, Pat! Please... Don't!" He got up and ran into his room where he stayed for two days without going to school. When he came out of the room he was badly bruised. Mike's face was so swollen that he could not see. Pat couldn't look him in the face. She was ashamed about what she had done to her son, but she had no way of controlling herself and no one to respond to her wrong doing. Pat finally went to apologize to Mike. When she approached him he backed up and started calling her names, telling her to stay away from him. Enraged, she grabbed him by the throat and started choking him and asking him, what are you saying!

*"Stay away!"*

"What can you do about it?" She began choking him harder and harder, calling him really bad names.

Bill came home unexpectedly and heard weird noises, like someone was crying. He quickly ran upstairs to find out what was going on, and there was Pat, choking Mike with all her might. Bill screamed out,

*"Stop! Stop!*

*Get your hands off my son! What on earth do you think you are doing? What's the matter with you?"*

Pat just stood there and looked at Bill, not moving her hands off Mike. Bill took her and pushed her down on the floor. Pat just looked at Bill, fearing what he was going to do next, daring him to touch her; Instead of hurting her, he grabbed Mike, hugged him and asked, "Are you okay? Why is she doing this to you? Look at your face, who on earth did this to you?"

Mike pointed at Pat, then he said, "I thought you knew about this."

"About what?"

"Her beating on me!"

"She's been beating on you?" Bill cried out.

Mike could not say another word; he just cried. Pat began to say, I'm fixing the problem we have with Mike, he was getting out of hand, you don't have to worry any longer.

Bill said, "What's going on? What are you talking about? Bill was shocked, by Pat's anger lifeless she appeared, confusion ran through Bill's mind, where had he gone wrong, how could something like this occur. Bill said; "Why! Why! What on God's earth do you think you're doing?

Speechless-aggravated by the deadness of my conscious, turning to Mike, fearing that he might say something about the years of abuse. Bill began to ask once again in a demanding manner, "What's going on?"

Still there was no answer, silence reigned in the house. Fear pierced Pat. Mike stood trembling, aching and fearing more reprisals. No one was saying anything. Bill was getting madder and madder, not knowing what to do or how to react. He asked; Mike to please leave the room so he could have a private conversation with his wife.

"I want to find out what was going on. I need some answers. This silence is not going to work. Beating our son, putting bruises on him and trying to choke him to death isn't normal. This is no way to discipline a child."

*As Mike left the room Bill said to Pat "I'm waiting for an answer. Where in the world did you get such an idea?"*

Silently unable to speak, confused, lost, maneuvering in a different state of mind focusing on a wild colorful pitcher, trying to avoid the roughness of his question, while all along he was never home wondering where to begin.

This had been going on for a very long time.

"I'm waiting for an answer."

Bill said harshly,

Different thoughts ran through Pat's mind while Bill was waiting for her response. Pat had nothing to say; she stood there feeling guilty and ashamed about being caught in the act. Bill got tired of waiting for her answer. He just sat there thinking about the bruises, black eyes, and Mike's swollen face through the years. He thought about how the teachers had complained and how he had listened to his wife, believing her stories that other children were hurting his son. All the time it was his wife, his wife who was abusing his son. There was child abuse in his own house, and he thought that everything was so perfect. Hadn't he been the perfect husband and father? He had worked so hard to give his family a good life, to make sure whatever they needed they had. He wondered how this could have happened and where he had gone wrong. Bill started feeling sad, thinking that this was his fault. If only he hadn't gone on so many business trips, maybe this would not have happened. Bill turned to look at Pat, stung by what he was thinking. He could no longer contain his anger, he could no longer think. He could feel his blood rushing through his body to his head, thinking about how his son had been living in so much pain. Bill could not have imagine anyone putting a child through something so horrible. All of the lies began to take a toll on Bill. The more he thought about this situation, the madder he got; even the word abuse made Bill as mad as hell. "My wife is abusing my son," he began to sink under this knowledge, feeling as though he was falling into the tunnels of the earth, there was just no way out. Bill was in another world, deep in thought about this situation.

Pat began to call his name "Bill! Bill! Honey, can you hear me?" Still in shock, imagining Mike's fears and pain, Bill did not hear his wife call his name.

Bill ran out of the room, out of the house, and down the street. "Far away," he thought, "I have to get away, far away. But where can I go? Mike is my son, I can't leave him. I love him very much." He had to walk, and walk for hours and hours. What would his wife say to him about the abuse of their son?

Pat knew what she had done was wrong, but she didn't know that Bill would take it the way he did. Pat went into Mike's room and started saying; "Look what you've done now you upset your father. Now you are really going to pay for this. When he comes back, he'll see what I'm talking about, how you upset people, and he'll start beating you, too. Mike, you deserve everything that's coming to you and I'm going to help him beat you."

Mike didn't say a word, he just looked at her, and turned his head as if he didn't hear a word. Pat turned, went back into her room, and closed the door. She began crying because she knew she had made a big mistake but she didn't know how to control herself or seek help.

Bill was gone for three days trying to clear his mind. Finally returning home. Pat had been concerned about where Bill had been, waiting and crying as if she never cried before. She knew he had to cool off but she was in doubt about his thoughts. The sight of his son molted skin turned his stomach the abuse had taken its place since infant stage.

Bill, still in shock, didn't ask Pat any questions, instead he went directly to Mike room.

Mike jumped up off the bed and started backing up toward the wall, thinking that Bill was going to start hitting on him.

"Come here, Mike. Don't be scared, I'm not going to hurt you!
"Pat said that you were going to beat me when you came home.
I'm really sorry, Dad, I didn't mean to upset you."

"Don't worry. I'm not upset at you, come here so we can
talk."

Mike sat down on the bed next to his father and Bill began
holding him and telling him how sorry he was, "I didn't know
what was going on."

He asked Mike, "Why didn't you tell me about this?" explaining to Mike he had not known the real cause of his bruises.

Mike began to hug his father back while crying and telling
him, "Dad I hope it's over. Please don't let her hurt me any more,
Dad, please! I love you Dad."

Bill heart was sunken by Mike words, and said;

"I will not let anyone else hurt you, I promise, as long as I
live. I told you that whoever was doing this to you would regret
it; that's a promise I made to you, I will not let you down. You
need to go in for a check up."

Bill took Mike to the hospital to have him checked out and
the wounds cleaned up. While at the hospital the doctor demanded that Bill press charges against Pat while the nurse was taking
pictures of Mike making sure she covered every part of his body,
his legs were so badly bruised from over the years it appeared to
be natural. Ashamed at what he saw, tears nearly escaped the
closing of his eyes.

When they returned home to where Pat was waiting. Bill sat
down next to Pat and said, "Are you ready to tell me why you
were abusing Mike?"

"He was getting to the point where he wouldn't listen and it
was hard to control him."

*"Why did you have to beat him like that?" Pat didn't have
an answer. "How long has this been going on?"*

"Since he was an infant."

"What! You've been beating him since he was an infant?"

"Yes, it began and I couldn't stop and it didn't seem like he
was getting any nicer. He's a bad boy, Bill, you'll see what I'm

talking about."

Bill couldn't believe what he was hearing, coming from his wife. "I thought about sending Mike away for a while until we straighten out this problem that we're having."

*"Where are you planning on sending him?"*

"Someplace where you don't have to worry about him being 'a bad boy.' I'll take care of my son from now on.

He'll leave in the morning when I go to work.

Pat didn't have a word to say about what Bill was doing. In fact, she couldn't say much about anything because she didn't want to make him any madder than he already was. Mike was gone and Pat was left all alone with no one at home but herself. Bill didn't say much when he came home each night, he just sat on his favorite sofa and acted like nothing ever happened. Bill sat there night after night, brooding about all the things that Pat had done. He never said a word to her. She thought that he had forgotten all about what happened and she never brought it up. Bill began to feel hatred for Pat. He couldn't make love to her. He couldn't have a direct conversation with her. He hated talking to her, hating the sight of her and could no longer take being around her. But she was his wife and there was nothing he could do about it.

Bill made sure that whatever he had to say to her would be blunt and short. He got so fed up with the sight of her that he no longer wanted to sleep with her. He didn't want her touching him, so he put her out of the room that they shared together. He began eating in restaurants to avoid dinnertime conversation. Bill grew bitter, he no longer trusted Pat, because of her lies and her abuse, their son no longer could live at home. He missed him. Bill's bitterness continued to grow.

Pat thought Bill had another woman. The way he was turning away from her she knew that sooner or later that he wouldn't have a need for her, and she would have to go live somewhere else. She decided that she would stay until he actually told her to leave. Not wanting to see Pat at all, Bill started coming home later and later. Pat realized how Bill felt, so when she heard him come into the house, she would go into Mike's room where Bill made her sleep. Pat would stay there until Bill left. Two years past when Pat decided to break the silence. Bill accepted the truth and let Pat back into the room without an argument, feeling a little relieved knowing that he still cared about her and that he still loved her despite her past actions.

Pat apologized for tormenting Mike, Bill assured her, "Nothing in this world and no amount of apologies can make up for what was done. It's still hurting me and I can't seem to get it out of my mind. I want you to know and understand what I'm going through. No one can take that hurt away, what's done is done and there's no way to change it. I know that you haven't learned your lesson, but you will, in due time you will, and that Pat I can promise."

Bill was very bitter, always thinking about his son's swollen face and deadly bruised body. He thought, "If I'd never taken him to the doctor, his body would have remained a mystery to me. How terrible, how could someone do something like that?" Bill could not clean these thoughts out of his head, and he hated Pat for what she had done. Bill could not forgive her, it was stamped away in his brain forever.

# CONTINUING TO ABUSE

SHE ABUSED MY SON, FOR NO REASON AT ALL
SHE MESSED UP HIS MIND
AND GAVE HIM BROKEN BONES.
SHE LIED AND TOLD ME IT WASN'T HER AT ALL
MY WIFE, I CALLED HER
SHE'S LOWER THAN THE EARTH AT FAULT
MY SON WAS ABUSED; IT HURT ME SO MUCH
UNTIL ONE DAY I FELT IT WASN'T ENOUGH.
I PROMISED HIM, THE ABUSE WOULD END
FOR HE WOULDN'T HAVE TO WORRY
WORRY NO MORE, FOR THAT WAS THE END
THAT SHE WHO ABUSED HIM, I WOULD SURELY LET HER KNOW
MY SON WAS HURTING AND HURTING ALL OVER
FOR SOMETHING I DIDN'T KNOW, OR EVEN LOOK OVER
AND HAD NO TIME TO DISCOVER
HOW BAD I FELT, ABOUT WHAT SHE HAD DONE
ABOUT ABUSING MY ONLY LOVED SON
PAY BACK I CALLED IT! I WHISPERED IN HER EAR
YOU WILL SURELY PAY FOR ALL THOSE ABUSIVE YEARS
SHE DIDN'T QUITE UNDERSTAND, EXACTLY WHAT I MEANT
SO I HAD TO SHOW HER, JUST WHAT,
PAY BACK DEFINITELY MEANT!

# CONTINUING TO ABUSE 2

Two years later, Bill being emotional started drinking, having a drink here and there, never forgetting what his wife had done to his son. Her abuse was always on his mind. He could no longer think or function properly because he was constantly thinking about the abuse Mike had experienced through the years from childbirth to adulthood. Bill's drinking worsened, it got to the point where he no longer had control.

Before Bill found out about the abuse, he would almost never drink, no matter what the situation was. This painful thing that happened to his son drove Bill to drinking. It wasn't long before he turned into an alcoholic. While he was working, he learned to contain himself. Bill worked very hard and long hours. When Bill left work, however, his first stop was at the bar. There he had to have a strong drink before he returned to his home where the wife he no longer respected lived.

This went on day after day, and month after month. The alcohol began to direct his thinking, until it became a mental and dangerous state of mind which could no longer be controlled. Stumbling in the house after dark, slamming doors making sure Pat was alert, Bill was drunk and full of alcohol calling Pat into the room. Pat did not answer. He called to her again screaming out loud, "I'm coming!"

"You're taking too long," Bill said. Pat finally went into the room where Bill was sitting, and he began speaking in a sorrowful tone, telling her how much he really loved her and said, "Why didn't you tell me you couldn't handle our son?"

*When Pat didn't say a word, he said, "Why! Pat, just tell me why!"*

Pat replied, "Honey, you're drunk, you smell really bad."

Anger aroused in Bill, "You dummy! Answer me! Why, tell me why, did you do that to my son?" Pat stood up. "Sit back down! I really want to know."

Pat didn't have an answer. She began to cry and he said, "You didn't cry when you beat my son, so don't cry now."

"Maybe I did cry, and you just weren't here to hear my cry. It hurt me just as much as it hurt Mike. I told you that he was a bad kid and he deserved it, and you're making too much of it. Bill, it's over, honey! Don't get worked up over nothing. It's been two years now, let's go on with our lives."

"Who gave you the right to beat my son?" Pat didn't answer, she just got quiet. Bill, in his drunken state stood up, lost his balance and fell to the floor. Pat tried to help him up off the floor but he told her to get away from him, so she went to bed. After hours of sleeping on the floor Bill got up and went upstairs, calling for Pat. Knowing that he was still drunk, Pat tried to ignore Bill, but he got louder and louder as he stumbled up the stairs.

Bill said, "I can see now that you're treating me like you treated my son. I never knew that you were dirty like this."

Pat continued to ignore him and went on to sleep. Bill passed out at the top of the stairs. After he was out for a while Pat got up to see where he was; and there he was laid out on the floor. She didn't bother to touch him or even wake him up. Pat went back to bed and slept. Bill woke up in time to go to work, wondering why he was still on the floor. "Pat," he muttered, "you didn't have enough brains to put a cover over me." He got dressed and left.

Day after day this went on, Bill stumbling in drunk and passing out on the floor and Pat just leaving him there as if he didn't exist, walking right over him. Bill was so drunk he didn't see what was going on, he didn't understand how cruel his wife was being, not caring one bit about what he did.

Bill began to blackout, forgetting the things that went on while he was drinking, waking up on the floor and wondering why he was there. He had gotten used to drinking and it was taking a great toll on him. Bill began to really curse Pat, using all kinds of profanity. Pat began to get scared, fearing that one day he was going to hit her like she hit Mike when she abused him. Bill began screaming at Pat all the time. It seemed that she couldn't do anything right; her cooking was no longer good enough. If he thought it wasn't worth eating he would throw his plate on the floor and make her clean up the mess. Her cleaning was no longer perfect. Bill would make Pat clean the house while he stood and watched. If she missed a spot he would gladly make her clean it over scrubbing as hard as she could scrub.

Bill began to call his wife by anything other than her name. He would call her anything he could think of, daring her to comment on what he was calling her. Pat never said a word or talked back to him. She was afraid he would start hitting her. After all it was heading that way anyway. Bill didn't care about Pat anymore and he promised her that she would pay for what she had done to his son. Bill began to accuse Pat of things she had never done. He would make up things just to see what kind of reaction he would get from her. Pat thought Bill was going crazy and she was sure that the alcohol was eating up his brain and that he had no way out. He used to consider her the perfect woman better than anyone else he had ever known, but now she was flawed and nothing she could do was right. Every time Bill talked to her he would put his finger in her face and dare her to move it out of the way.

Time after time he would start a conversation with her and would never let her say a word. When she did talk he told her, "Shut up. You're not supposed to talk, I just want you to always shut up because you have said more than enough."

At this point Pat couldn't say anything and couldn't ask for anything. She started to feel really closed in, separated from his world. Not only did she feel like she didn't exist but she felt like a complete dummy when he was around. Pat finally suggested that they seek marriage counseling because the situation was getting worse. She swore from her heart that she loved him and she didn't want their marriage to go bad.

Bill asked, "What are you talking about? Our marriage went

bad when you started beating on our son." "We really need to go and talk to someone!" Bill grabbed Pat by the throat choking her, asking her if she remembered this, "This is the only therapy you will ever get!"

He threw her on the floor then picked her up and began slapping her until she turned colors and she fell again to the floor. Pat feeling, were very harsh toward abuse knowing that one day Bill would explode. My time was at hand when he slapped me experiencing the trauma that Mike suffered from, being hit was a different experience for me. He was starting to abuse me, knowing that one day he would hit me again, because he was bitter and hurting so badly. So now it began, the "abuse of the next abuser being abused."

On a daily basis, as Bill's drinking continued, he began to get more violent, and each time he remembered what he saw of his son and the abuse that occurred, he was getting worse, thinking about the failure of his wife, Bill  thoughts rolled deep into his mind and turned into a mental nightmare which alluded  violent reactions. .When stepping into the house, the first sight of Pat would turn his stomach so much that his hatred would increase, Bill despising her in all ways.

**One night a drunken Bill called for Pat, "Pat come in here!"**

Yelling, from the top of his lungs;

No answer; He called again, "Pat, come here."

Running quickly to Bill's calling;

As Pat entered into the room he was hiding behind the door, he grabbed her, threw her to the floor, Bill! Screaming loudly but my screams were unheard, he picked me, over and over throwing me every where, rushing to the phone screaming loudly someone has to help me!  Pat picked up the phone urgently trying to dial, Bill snatched the receiver in one hand  and grabbed my throat with the other tightened his grip, hitting me with the receiver and pushing me to the floor, Bill snatched the whole phone out of the wall and threw it at my head, asking me, "Who are you calling? Ho, ho," he said, "are you going to call the police or your mother? Tell me, who! are you going to call? Maybe I can help you, Pat."

"What's wrong with you, Bill? You act like a madman! What has gotten into you? You're drunk."

Bill picked up the phone again and threw it at Pat's head, hitting her hard and causing a lump to appear right away. He picked her up off the floor and threw her up against the wall saying, "Does this hurts? Tell me, Pat does it hurt? I really want to know, right now!"

Speechless, my mouth was shut, making sure he wouldn't hit me again, because he was very drunk and he didn't know what he was doing.

Bill started to grab me again but instead he turned and walked away. He went away sad, sad in his heart that he had promised his son that he would repay whom ever it was that was beating him. It was a promise he had to keep.

The next day Bill decided to fix Pat since she picked up the phone to call for help. He had the telephone turned off for any out-going calls. He made sure that she wouldn't pick up the phone again. When Bill got home from work, I informed him that something was wrong with the telephone, it wouldn't dial out, were only getting incoming calls. "I think maybe we should have the telephone checked out?"

"The telephone is working, but it's not working for you. Don't you even think about picking up that telephone as long as you live in this house that telephone is not for you to use," Bill replied.

"But why! What is going on? Why are you doing this to me?" Pat asked.

Bill grabbed Pat by the throat and said, "I want my dinner and I want it right now and don't ask any more questions."

Running into the kitchen to get Bill's dinner. Trying to sit down next to him but he stopped me and said, "You are not worthy to sit next to me. Sit on the floor."

Amazed by his actions, Bill snarled,
"I said sit on the floor!"

"Honey, I'll go wash the dishes."

Pat got up to go into the kitchen and he grabbed her and said, "Sit down on the floor." Continuing to ignore his demand of her sitting on the floor like some animal. She wouldn't sit, so he grabbed her by her hair and threw her on the floor now. "Scoot over here by me and don't move." Scooting suspiciously over by his leg and said, "Honey, if you want an animal, we should buy one." Leaving Pat on the floor and not saying a word Bill put on his coat and left. He went to the bar to drink and drank for hours until his friend John came in.

John with his hazel brown eyes and chocolate brown skin, clean shaven out of the forties nearly wearing a part in the middle of his head sat next to Bill.

John and Bill has been friends for several years. He sat next to Bill and begin talking to him about going fishing and asked him if he and his wife would like to come and stay the weekend with them. John's wife was named Joan and she worked as a nurse for battered women. Bill knew that she was a nurse, but he didn't know where she worked. John began to tell him all about her job and about the women that came in to get help, but Bill interrupted, "That's nice, John, but I've got to go. I'll give you a call later about the trip and let you know whether or not we'll be able to go."

When Bill returned home from the bar he walked into the kitchen looking for Pat. She was not sitting in the same spot on the floor where he had left her. She had moved, thinking that he wouldn't remember that he told her to sit on the floor or anything that had gone on. Bill started calling Pat again, and she refused to answer, fearing what he might do to her.

***"Pat come here!"***

Pat went to see what he wanted because he wouldn't stop calling her name. As she went into the room he grabbed her asking her "Who told you to get up off the floor?"

***"No one, I had to clean the kitchen!"***

Bill began hitting, slapping and punching her in the face until she turned blue, saying, "Who told you to get up!"

"Please Bill! Please! Don't hurt me, Bill! I'm sorry for getting up."

Bill kept hitting her and throwing her around the room, making sure she understood what he said. Bill was getting very vicious and mean. He could no longer control himself when he was drinking, but Pat still loved him and thought he needed her. She told herself that he was just upset about Mike, that he would get over it and this would be over. She was just fooling herself. Every time he beat her, Pat would delude herself.

Pat was too embarrassed to leave her home because she was often covered with bruises which sunglasses couldn't cover. When Pat would go to the grocery store people would stare at her and whisper about the way her face looked. She couldn't accept that people were talking about her every where she went. Kids laughed at her, making remarks about the lady with the purple face. Pat felt totally disgraced. She was so bruised and wounded that babies would cry when she got near them because she looked so scary.

Pat was so humiliated by the actions of others she started going shopping early in the morning when the stores were empty and no one was around. Pat was really getting tired of Bill beating her. The beatings would go on every day. He no longer had control over his actions because the alcohol had taken over his mind. Bill was as resentful as he could be. He couldn't get over the idea that Pat had abused his son. This made him hate Pat even more. Somehow however, mingled in with the hatred were remnants of love. Somewhere in his heart he still loved her, but he felt it was his responsibility to teach her how much abuse could hurt another person.

He wanted her to feel it inside and out, and he didn't care if she felt embarrassed in front of other people. He actually felt pretty good about what he had done to her. Every time he abused her, he felt a tiny bit of bitterness about what she had done to his son vanish away. He was bitter and it would take a lot for him to get over Pat's abuse of Mike. Unfortunately, Bill was so full of spite he was becoming meaner and meaner to Pat. It was very dangerous for her to be around him because he couldn't stand the sight of her. Even though he loved her. Pat was his wife and Bill wanted her around, he had lost all trust in her and believed that she needed to be punished. He had made that promise to his son. Day after day he taught her lessons thinking that it would prevent her from ever hurting Mike again.

John called Bill to confirm their fishing trip. Bill had forgotten about the trip and had not told Pat about it. While Pat was discussing the trip with John over the phone, Bill stumbled into the house drunk, and shouted "WHAT ARE YOU DOING ON THE PHONE! GET OFF THE PHONE!"

Pat dropped the phone on the floor shocked, staring at him wordlessly.

*"Who is that on the phone?"*

Pat just stood with her mouth open, fearing what he was going to do next. Bill picked the phone up off the floor. "Hello! Who is this, and what do you want?"

"It's John, your friend."

"Yes, and what do you want with my wife?"

"Nothing. I called to remind you about the fishing trip that I planned for a weekend and I was wondering if you would still like to go."

"Sure, when?"

"How about this weekend, Bill?"

" Okay, John I'll give you a call ." Bill hung up the phone and turned to Pat to tell her about what was going on and that she had better be ready.

Pat was glad to hear that she was finally getting a break from Bill, thinking that he wouldn't hit her in front of his friends. Bill went up to bed, for once not hitting Pat, trying to hide the abuse which was occurring behind closed doors.

As the fishing trip began, Bill caught a big fish. It was on the hook fighting its way off. Bill called for Pat because he no longer wanted to tangle with this fish. Happily approaching Bill, he told her to reel in the fish, (her smile faded) She just stood there looking at him, "Are you serious, Bill? I can't reel in that fish. . . it's too big."

He just looked at her. Pat nervously grabbed the rail and tried to reel in the fish, but when she couldn't Bill said, "Pull it in right now!"

"I'm trying!"

He kicked her in the butt and said, "Try harder, You idiot."

He began calling her all types of foul names that the other people found offensive. Everyone looked shocked at what they heard and saw, not knowing the full extent of Bill and Pat's situation. Pat began to pull the fish in, but it was larger than she could handle and it pulled her into the water. Bill just sat and watched. While others screamed for him to help her, Bill just sat there. He calmly watched while she fell deep into the ocean.

John quickly jumped into the water to save her. He had a hard time because Pat was fighting the water not knowing how to swim and he had never rescued anyone before. After tugging a while they finally got back into the boat. Bill continued to ignore them. John refused to ask any questions about what was going on because he didn't want to hear anything Bill had to say. Instead, he just looked at Bill and sat down next to him wondering what Bill had to say. Bill said nothing.

Bill started drinking, as usual he started thinking about Mike. This wasn't a good place for Bill to start drinking. Once he started the alcohol too control became so drunk, stumbling around the boat looking for Pat, but Pat was hiding, hiding from Bill, and from the embarrassment of being hit or thrown around in front of Bill's friends. Pat had became acquainted with, they seemed really nice. She wondered why Bill had never introduced her to them, she had never known about these friends during all of their years of marriage.

One of the ladies approached Pat, telling her that Bill was looking for her. Pat went up on the dock although she already knew that he was drunk and wanted to beat her like he had been beating her at home. She knew then that he would never leave her alone, that it would never go away because he didn't want to stop. Pat knew what she had done to their son was wrong. She knew that she would never forget it because Bill wouldn't let her forget. Every time he beat her, he reminded her about her past. Bill didn't care if he hurt her or embarrassed her anymore. He no longer cared about how she felt.

When she got to where he was standing, he grabbed her and stuck her head in between the ropes on the side of the boat. He picked up a paddle and began beating her and kicking her real hard in the head and asking her, "Does it hurt? Does this hurt Pat? Tell me, does it hurt or does it feel good? Tell me, Pat, I really want to know."

He began viciously beating her. Pat began screaming loudly but by the time the others on the boat reached them, Pat was flat out on the floor, begging for help from Bill's friends, her face drenched with blood. As they approached her, Bill stopped them saying, "I dare anyone to touch her. She is my wife and I'll do whatever I please to her. I own her. I take care of her and I will continue to beat her whenever I want to."

"Can't you see that she bleeding badly? She needs to go to a hospital, Bill. Let us help her!"

"I told you to stay away from her. I'll take care of her."

So they went back downstairs, not wanting to argue with Bill. Pat got up and started to run and Bill caught her by the hair, "And where do you think you're going?"

"Downstairs to get help, didn't you hear them? I need to go to the hospital, Bill."

He didn't answer. When she turned around to look at him, Bill hit her in the head with the fishing rail and she passed out cold. He left her there by herself and went to his sleeping quarters and passed out from the alcohol. While Bill was out cold, John and his wife went to help Pat, cleaning her up and carrying her downstairs. Joan started telling her that she needed help and when they arrived home that she was welcome to stay with her and John.

"Oh, no. I can't do that. Bill will come and get me and it will be much worse. Everything is all right. He just had a little too much to drink. He'll be different in the morning. You'll see,

Joan, he was just drunk. It's really not that bad."

Pat stayed up all night, looking at her face. It was all swollen up and badly bruised. She just couldn't sleep she was in so much pain from the beating she had received with the paddle. When the morning arrived Joan decided that she wanted to go home, saying she wasn't feeling well because she could not stand another night in hell with Bill beating Pat and Pat making excuses for him. They pulled up to land and John thanked Bill and Pat for coming, although he was upset with Bill he was very polite about it.

The next day Bill came home drunk and he began to accuse Pat of spoiling the fishing trip. Pat began to argue, calling him a liar and saying she was tired of his abuse. While she was arguing with him, he took off his belt and started beating her with the belt buckle, leaving deep gashes in her skin. He beat her as if there were no tomorrow. He began to strike her really hard, then he stopped as she scooted over to the corner screaming and screaming. He just looked at her and told her to take off her clothes. Pat just looked at him, wondering why he wanted her to take off her clothes, "Take off your clothes," he shouted.

***Pat, with her eyes red would not take her clothes off.***
***"Why? Why do you want me to take my clothes off?"***

"If you don't take your clothes off, I will take them off for you."

Pat got up and took off her clothes, confused and wondering why he wanted this. When she got them all off he started beating her again, cutting into her skin even more with this very hard belt. Bill went upstairs to run very hot water with baking soda in it. He dragged Pat into the very hot water, so hot even Bill couldn't stand to put his hands in it. The heat burned her open wounds, causing a tremendous amount of pain. She began to scream with the pain of being burned, Bill asked her how she felt. "Don't you feel great knowing what it's like being abused and how painful it feels?"

Pat just sat and cried but Bill had no sympathy for her at all. He kept talking and saying, "Cry, baby, cry, cry, cry! Just keep crying, cry all you like because I don't care. It's not over yet, there's still more to come and there's no way out for you so don't even think about it. You're going to feel all of it I promise you."

Pat didn't say a word, she just wanted to get out of the hot water because it was more painful than anything he had ever done to her. He kept running more hot water into the bathtub, making sure she got what she deserved. Bill then got up, he didn't say a word, he walked sadly away and went to bed. Pat got up and went into Mike's room, she had not stayed in his room since Bill let her back into the room with him.

While she was in Mike's room she began to wonder how she was going to get away from Bill. Maybe she could leave before Bill got home from work. After all, Joan did invite her to come over and stay, but she didn't have Joan's phone number. She couldn't call Joan anyway because she couldn't make any outgoing calls, thanks to Bill.

"What am I going to do? I've got to get out of here before he ends up killing me or seriously hurting me."

Pat's nights were sleepless, filled with concern about her life, fearing that Bill was going to kill her and that he didn't love her any more. She had no one to talk to. She was in this abusive world all by herself trying to figure out how to stop this situation. Pat thought really hard, afraid to come out of the room, fearing that she might wake up Bill, something she didn't want to do.

All of what she had considered was a waste because when Bill got up to go to work, he woke up Pat and she looked up in fear. He looked at her then said, "Get up right now."

Pat jumped up saying, "Where are we going?"

"Downstairs to breakfast."

"Breakfast? We never had breakfast together, why would you want to have breakfast?" Pat replied nervously.

Bill turned and went downstairs. Without any more questions, Pat followed him, still in her nightgown. When they got downstairs there was no breakfast anywhere to be found, the kitchen was clean. Pat started to wonder about the abuse; maybe it was over, maybe he wanted to talk, maybe he was tired of beating her. "I'm so glad he sees that what he is doing is wrong and that he could seriously hurt me. I knew he still loved me."

As Pat thought all these things he told her to sit down and she sat down in the chair. "Not in the chair, sit on the floor!"

"Why would you want me to sit on the floor?"

"Just sit on the floor under the table."

Pat looked very confused, "The floor?"

"Yes, the floor. And be quick about it, I have to go to work."

Pat refused to sit on the floor so he grabbed her, threw her on the floor, pushing her under the table by the legs. He swiftly chained her legs to the table and locked it with a dead bolt. He tied her legs to the other end of the table and he told her, "I'll make sure you don't go anywhere until I'm finished with you, and I'm not nearly finished with you. Did you think you were getting off that easy? You'll pay for what you've done to my son: I promise you, you will pay, Mrs. English."

Bill packed a suitcase full of clothes. He was going on a business trip for five days. As he was leaving, he turned up the radio so loud that no one could hear her scream for help. As he was leaving with his suitcase Pat said, "Please don't leave me here, Bill."

Bill just turned and looked at Pat. He walked away and left her with raw open wounds all over her body. He left her tied to the table with ropes and chains and a dead bolt. As Pat sat on the floor with no water, she had plenty of time to think about what she had done and what was being done to her. She felt sorry only for herself. Sorry about what she had done to her and her family, how she had driven her husband to drinking and messed up his life. She thought about how she was living in misery, living in pain, how her body was aching, aching and bleeding badly from last night, with only her gown to wipe away the blood.

As she was sitting and thinking chained to the table, the phone rang and rang. "The phone never rings when Bill isn't home. Who could that be and why are they letting the phone ring so many times?"

There was no way she could get to the phone. More than any

thing she wanted to get off the floor because the chains hurt so bad. Pat spent the whole night under the table, wondering what Bill would do to her when he returned. The next day there were loud noises outside the house. People were working on their house while Bill was gone. Pat started screaming as loudly as she could but no one could hear her because Bill had turned the radio up so loud. The people worked for two days outside the house.

"I wonder what these people are doing? Maybe he's having the house painted  my favorite color, or maybe he's having it painted red to remind me what blood looks like. Why is he doing this to me? I really don't deserve to be treated like this, he's really hurting me."

Two days later a different noise began, "Someone's trying to get in, someone's coming to help me finally; but why would someone try to help me when no one knows I'm here? No one will ever know. What if Bill doesn't show up? What if he never comes back and just leaves me here like this, chained to the table. I'm going to die  there's no food or water."

Pat had a lot of thoughts while chained to the table dehydrated, needing water badly. As the days went on all Pat could do was think about food and water.

***"How could someone be so mean and uncaring?"***

A little later there was a knock on the door and Pat started screaming, "Help! Help me! Please!"

Whoever was at the door couldn't hear her because the radio was up so loud. The knocking and all other noise that was around the house finally stopped. Pat was very, very sad. No one could help her. She was dying of starvation and growing very weak and stiff. For five days Pat stayed under the table, crying and screaming for help. Screaming and bleeding and hurting with the chains biting into her skin.

Finally, the locks started turning on the door; Bill had returned. Pat could barely move. She couldn't even turn her head she was so weak. It was late, and poor Pat was still in the same spot where Bill had left her. Bill went and stood over her, thinking that she was asleep. He didn't bother touch her, he just said,

"One more night won't hurt you, right, Pat?"

He went upstairs and began changing the locks on his room door. He took all of her clothes and put them in Mike's old room. He no longer wanted to be near her, but he still wanted to make her pay for what she had done to his son. With the locks changed Bill went back down stairs and got a bucket of cold water and threw it on Pat. All she could do was scream.

"Here's your shower! Now dry yourself off," Bill said.

He went back upstairs and went to bed, leaving her soaking wet. Pat was so thirsty that she began sucking the water out of her gown from being dehydrated of spending five nights chain like an animal to Bill's table. Pat continued to suck on her wet gown all night long. When Bill got up in the morning he didn't feel any remorse about abusing Pat. Bill's anger increased forming numbness, therefore Pat became a loss cause meaning less to Bill.

Pat woke up and started screaming, her dehydration lead to memory loss of Bill's present. Hearing the loud horrible screams, Bill quickly ran down the stairs. Pat looked up in shock at Bill's present, sorrowfully crying. Staring at Bill, increasing her screams. "Please! Bill I'm sorry, please! Unchain me, I'm hurting all over. Can't you see? Look at me Bill, I'm all wet. Help me!"

"Please Bill,

"Is there a problem, Pat? Is something wrong with you? Why are you crying? There's nothing wrong, I hope. You look okay to me, and you also look pretty good down there on the floor. You should stay like that; I think I like you better, just- like -that." Chained in the course of pain!

"Please, Bill! I can't take it anymore!"

"That's right, beg, and beg real hard Pat"

"Let me go. I won't leave Bill, please! I'm sorry about what I've done to Mike, please help me."

"I told you it wasn't over yet and it's not."

Bill went back upstairs and got dressed and left for work, leaving Pat chained to the table. Pat continued crying and screaming, thinking that he was still in the house. But Bill had left, he was gone for hours. Bill finally returned home from work he went into the kitchen and unchained Pat from the table. (Bill quietly walked away listening through the walls of her reactions.

Pat dragged herself to the sink to get water washing the tears the flowed down her face forcing Bill's cold food that was left on the counter over night. Standing there watching he rushed over to Pat and snatched the food out of her hands, spit in her eyes and sadly walked away and went back upstairs and locked his room door.

Pat cleaned herself up, standing in the mirror examining her bruises with regret every moment of telling Bill the truth about her abusive ways. Walking into the door, it was locked and she couldn't get in. She needed her clothes so she began banging on the door calling Bill's name, kicking the door hard. Bill came out, forcefully grabbed her and threw her into Mike's room, "There are your clothes and don't bother me anymore."

Pat, crying as usual started putting her clothes in Mike's drawers. As she laid down on Mike's bed trying to sleep, she thought, "Oh I need some air maybe I'll go for a walk. I need to see the outside, see some trees. I really need to see what the outside looks and feels like. I need to talk to some people, someone outside this house, someone that Bill doesn't know."

When she got to the door it wouldn't open, something was wrong, the door was locked. She went to the window and the windows had bars on them; she was locked in, she couldn't get out!

Fear swept through Pat's body with cold chills"

*"Bill, he did this to me! What was on his mind? Is he going crazy?"*

Pat began to break down. She was in fear of her life, fearing that her husband was going to kill her because he was as mad as hell at her. "We really need help, but I have no contact with anyone."

Pat went to the room where Bill was sleeping. The door was locked so she went back into her room and slept until the morning.

When Pat awoke Bill had already left for work. Pat went into his room searching for the telephone, but Bill had taken the telephone to work with him, he made sure that Pat's contact was completely cut off.

"Oh my God, help me!" she cried out but no one heard her. No one could possibly have heard her because no one ever came to the house to visit. "I should have friends, at least one friend. Where have I gone wrong? Where are my friends and family?"

***After work Bill continued his daily trip to the bar. While he was sipping away John walked in and asked, "Is this seat taken?"***

"I don't think so, go right ahead and sit yourself down."

"How's Pat?"

"She's okay, why?"

"I was just wondering."

"Joan tried to call your wife, but it seems she didn't get an answer."

"Well, maybe she didn't want to answer the phone, maybe she was busy her or maybe she wasn't at home. Did you ever think about that?"

"No! My wife was a bit concerned since you were out of town and your son is away. We just thought she would be lonely, is something wrong with that?"

"Pat doesn't get lonely. Her days are always busy and yes there is something much more wrong with it than you think. She's my wife and she doesn't need any friends, so mind your own business."

Bill turned around and asked for another drink, a stronger drink, stronger than before. By this time Bill was so drunk that John offered him a ride home but Bill said, "I'll walk, thank you!"

As Bill was leaving, John approached him saying again, "If you ever need to talk, give me a call. Please Bill! Or tell Pat to call Joan, then maybe we could lend a helping hand. I'm always home and ready to talk or listen to whatever you have to say. I'm your friend, why don't you take advantage of it? That's what friends are for. When you need someone to lean on, Bill, remem-

ber I'm here waiting; so is my wife. Joan wants to help in anyway she can. Just give us a call when you get tired of what you
are doing to your wife, and no matter what, we will be there. It's
confidential, no one will ever know."

Bill nodded his head and said, "Yeah, okay John," then he
stumbled on home.

John went back into the bar and started a conversation with
Jim. "You know, Jim, something is not right. I've never seen Bill
drink like this before, he only had soft drinks, something is seriously wrong."

"Well, John, when he came in he said that his wife wasn't a
very good person. She was abusing his kid while he was working and this went on for a period of almost 14 years. He never
knew it until one day she thought he wasn't at home, and he
caught her choking him to death. When he took him to the hospital, his son had bruises all over his body. Bill said he couldn't
understand why and how she began to do this. Every time he
would ask her about it she wouldn't say anything. Since then he
just comes in and doesn't talk about anything. He just asks for
the usual and sometimes something stronger. I know his son
doesn't live there anymore. He sent him away because he does-
n't trust his wife. It seems like something serious, I wonder if
he's still married."

"Yes, he's still married and I don't think it's good. He just
doesn't seem right anymore."

"Well, he gets real drunk and goes home and that's all."

Pat felt helpless. All she could do was wait for Bill to come
home drunk and beat her. It had become her life, it was all she
looked forward to day after day. Pat was getting used to these
beatings. She no longer had tears to cry with, she had cried them
all out long ago. She had no self esteem at all, she couldn't ini-
tiate a solution to the problem and if she said anything he would
just beat her.

Bill had become a real beast, one that thrived on beating her.
It had become his life. He didn't want any help and refused to
seek it until he felt that she had learned her lesson about abusing

another person. Pat now knew what it feels like to hurt all over. She never was spanked when she was a little girl. She never knew what physical punishment felt like. Now she knew how her son felt and she wouldn't wish this kind of hell on anyone. If she had to do it all over again, she would have never beat her son.

Pat thought hard while laying in bed. All she could do was lay in bed she was in so much pain. The hell that Bill putting her through was too much. Pat just wanted to fade away, to disappear off the face of the earth. She considered committing suicide but she had nothing to kill herself with. Bill had removed all necessary tools out of the house. Bill wasn't going to let her escape until he thought that she had fully paid back her debt.

Bill was serious about the things he said and he didn't hold back anything. No matter how hard Pat begged and pleaded with him he just ignored her and kept doing what he wanted. What she said it didn't mean anything to him; nothing she did meant anything to him. He was after her like a demon, a demon who had no life, had no intentions of stopping. He didn't know how to forgive and forget and just go on living. He was crazy. Crazy with bitterness augmented by the alcohol. He couldn't control his drinking, and when he was drunk he was a real beast. His eyes were constantly red, his skin unhealthy and mottled; he no longer looked human.

The anger and drinking had taken over Bill and Pat's life. Without drinking Bill would not have been able to abuse his wife, he would have been lost trying to figure out what to do with his marriage. Pat had started something she no longer had control over, something that now caused her to suffer; she had brought this situation to life. She could no longer handle this beast of a man. When she met him he had been so kind, so sweet, so nice and innocent, made in heaven for her. "But he's no longer that. He's mean, mean as can be, not perfect, not loving toward me and or himself. He's unfair, he's been unfair for such a long time, like a demon from outer space," she thought.

Pat wished she had something that would clear her mind so she wouldn't think about what was going on between her and Bill, "Maybe a drink would do, then I would be more like Bill drunk, not caring about anything and able to deal with him like he is dealing with me."

Where and how was she going to get a drink when there was nothing in the house and no way out. She had no way to get what she thought she desired the most. All she wanted was something that would numb her mind while he was beating her. Pat began to gain a desire for something she had never tasted or even experienced, thinking that it would help her solve her problem, but it would only make it worse. Pat began speaking out loud while she was cleaning up her house, "This abuse has gotten out of hand. He thinks I'm a punching bag!"

As she was cleaning up she started throwing things, making herself more upset at Bill. "He has to stop this. I can no longer take this from him."

She started messing the house up even more, throwing dishes everywhere, breaking them and leaving them right where she threw them. "If he wants this house clean, let him clean it. I'm not cleaning another thing. Oh! I need some air. I have to get out of here, I'm going crazy. I have to find a way to stop him and stop him now! Maybe I'll kill him. That's it, I'll kill my husband and then I won't have to deal with him anymore. He'll be long gone and I will personally bury him and tell every one we got robbed, .that someone robbed us. That's the only way I will get away from him, and who cares anyway."

Pat began looking for knives but she couldn't find any. Bill had taken them out of the house because he knew that she would try to do something to him. Pat found a butter knife but that wouldn't do the job. She was lost and confused, not knowing what to do. "When does the mailman come? I haven't seen the mailman he doesn't come here anymore, not even to deliver junk mail."

While Pat was looking out through the barred windows, she saw a mailman but he didn't come her way. He crossed the street and when she started screaming out the window he just kept on going. He had been instructed to keep going and not to stop at that house for any reason at all, and that's exactly what he did. He had been the mailman for twenty years in that neighborhood but he never knew Pat because she never came outside. The mailman didn't have any reason at all to go to the English house because Bill had all the mail delivered to a postal box four miles away. He wanted Pat to be completely locked in with no contact at all. He handled this pretty well, no one would ever have suspected why Bill had the mail go somewhere else instead of at his house. No one questioned him.

"How could he do this to me? I don't deserve to be locked up like I'm in jail. I'm completely locked up in here, away from the world; I'm trapped in a world of serious abuse. Bill's becoming so cold, it's like a freezer is turned on inside his head. He's frozen and there's no way of thawing him out."

Pat moved away from the window and sat on the stairs feeling sad that there was no way out. She thought about how smart her husband was and how she couldn't outsmart him. It seemed like he knew her every thought and every move even though he was gone most of the day. "This certainly feels like jail, a place where I've never wanted to be. Why can't I get help? There has to be a God somewhere; maybe I'll pray."

Pat never prayed before or had experience in praying but she had heard people talking. She started talking or rather trying to pray. " 'Dear the . . .' I know it goes something like that. But maybe it's 'Dear Father,' that's it. I think I've found help, but that's not how it goes, there has to be more to it. Maybe I'll tell Him my problem, and if there's a God, He will help us."

Pat tried again to pray for help. This was the only way she could seek help for herself and her husband. "Dear Father, I know you probably don't know me but I am Pat English and my husband is Bill English. I've never prayed before, but please can you help us? I'm really sorry for what I've done to my son, I'm really sorry. I didn't mean to hurt him and send him away, but I couldn't gain control over what I was doing. I need serious help. Please help me and my husband, both of us have lost our minds and we're out of control. Help us, please, I know you can. Please help us before my husband kills me. Thank you very much for

listening, even if you can't help. To the Father In Heaven."
Pat fell asleep on the stairs. Little did Pat know a little prayer of confession helps even though she didn't know how to pray. It came from her heart and that is all that mattered; Pat prayed from her heart with sincerity. Despite all that had happened, she still loved her husband, and she just wanted him to stop abusing her.

As Pat was sleeping on the stairs, Bill walked in drunk as usual, calling for Pat. She didn't answer, she was still sleeping soundly. Bill shouted, "Pat! Pat! Are you are trying to pretend like you're asleep. I'll teach you!"

He ran up the stairs and began dragging Pat down the stairs and she woke up screaming, "Bill stop! Stop it!"

He kept dragging her until they reached the bottom kicking her, beating her and throwing her around the room, asking her who she had been with. He began to sexually abuse her, telling her that he was going to find out who she's been with. For six long months this type of abuse continued. Pat continued her little prayer, she would say it every night because he would beat her every night and she knew one day help was going to come. She was going to leave him and never come back no matter how much she loved him. She was tired of him beating her. He didn't care at all, he just got drunk and stumbled along the way.

Bill went to the bar to have his usual strong drink when Jim the bartender finally asked, "Are you still married, Bill?"

***"What's marriage? Tell me, what is marriage, Jim?"***

"When a man has a woman and they become lovers for the rest of their lives."

"Oh yeah, just give me another drink, a strong drink, as strong as you can get it."

Jim gave Bill a drink stronger than he'd ever had before. Bill just swallowed it down and told Jim, "It took you six years to give me a real drink. Where has your mind been all this time? You must be a new Jim. Are you a new Jim?"

***Jim just laughed, "Do you want another one? "***

"Yes, give me two more of those and I just might tip you really big."

Instead of two drinks, Jim gave Bill four. "Do you think you can handle this?"

"Oh sure, I can handle anything you put out on the table."

So Jim gave him something different, something stronger, and he knew that Bill couldn't handle it. But Bill drank it anyway, and drank it quickly. "Slow down, man."

"Give me another one of those."

"I think you better get lost before you lose it. You've had enough."

"I'll get lost, all right. Right in my wife's butt, real hard!"

Jim said, "Why would you want to do that to your wife?

"Well," stated Bill, "you know how women are. They get crazy sometimes and go their own way."

"The women that I know are too good to go."

"Well, maybe I need to meet some of the women that you seem to know."

Bill began to cry knowing that his wife used to be like one of the women that he was talking about. "Give me another drink and stay away from me, far away. Make it a strong drink, or I'll call your boss."

Jim did as he was told, then went on to serve other customers. Bill was more drunk than he'd ever before. As Jim stood at the end of the bar talking to someone else, Bill fell on the floor. He got back up talking loudly, acting mean and using profanity. Bill asked for another drink. Jim just ignored him. Bill could no longer contain himself. Whatever Jim had given him really had an effect on him. He was stumbling and falling, there was definitely something very different, something that made him crazy out of his mind, something worse than he had ever experienced before. He continued to fall and pick himself up as he stumbled home.

He stumbled right into the house and there she was, Pat his wife, who abused their son. He went right for her and grabbed and dragged her up the stairs then pushed her down. She was begging for him to stop, but she sensed something different. He was so drunk that he was crazier and madder than usual. He dragged her up the stairs again and she was yelling, "I need some air, Bill. Please! Let me get some air!"

Once again he pushed her down the stairs, trying to break everything in her body. He picked her up and threw her up against the wall, punching her in the face telling her how much he hated her and asking her, "Why are you still in my life?"

He began choking her until she passed out. He went into the kitchen and got a bucket of cold water and threw it on her saying, "So you want to play games? Well! I'll give you some air."

He took her over to the window and forcefully stuck her head through the bars. He left her there and went up stairs, locked his door and went to sleep. No matter how hard she tried twisting and turning Pat could not get her head out, so she began calling for help. No one heard her as Bill he slept for two days. Pat was afraid for her life; living in fear, fear of a man she thought she knew, and that she really only knew as a brutally abusive man.

Pat was living in fear of something that a lot of woman fear today. Something that's not controllable in life, that is seemingly unstoppable, that should be unheard of; the fear of being hurt by a loved one. Pat was experiencing the double pain of being hurt by someone who should have cherished her, supported her, loved and respected her. Pat could no longer depend on her man, she had lost all faith in him, and no longer loved him. Now she was stuck in the window with her head between the bars and unable to get out or seek help.

Pat wished she had someone to talk to, someone to give her a hug, someone who would say, "I love you and everything's going to be all right." But she didn't, she didn't have anyone. She was becoming very lonely and very sad and desperately needed some-one in her life. Her son didn't call her he hated her so much but she still loved him and she wished he would come and see what his father had done to her. Maybe he would help her. She would apologize to him for all the things that she had done to him and it would be over.

During those two days, Pat wondered where Bill was and if he'd forgotten all about her. Maybe he had gone on another business trip. Pat thought how much she loved Bill, "He's all I have, all I ever wanted, all I ever need."

Just then Bill woke up. She could hear him taking a shower, brushing his teeth and shaving. Listening to him, she wondered, "What he is thinking? Did he wake up with a new mind after sleeping for two days? How can I change him? What can I say or do to stop him from hurting and controlling me like he does?"

Bill came out of the room well dressed, like nothing ever happened, like he had never taken a drink. He went downstairs to look for Pat, but when she was nowhere to be found he began calling her name. Pat started screaming ,"Please! Bill, please! Don't leave me like this."

Bill walked over to the window and said, "What are you doing in the window? Are you trying to kill yourself getting out of the window? You can't get out that way, so try something else."

He pulled her out of the window and she just stared at him. He had been so drunk he forgot that he forced her into the window. She noticed how well dressed he was, different from his usual work day attire. He normally wore a shirt and a tie but never a whole suit. "Maybe he has another woman, he has to if I'm locked up all the time." Pat was going crazy by analyzing it too much and adding more to the problem than was already there. If she were to die it would be from thinking too much.

Bill acted liked nothing had ever happened, like he had never taken a drink, and he left. Where is he going? He didn't know that he had slept for two days and that this was not a work day. As he was driving down the street he started thinking how everything seemed so empty and wondered where everybody was; didn't people work on Fridays? Little did he know it was Saturday. As he drove around he began to realize that this was no longer Friday, so he stopped to call his son at school. He went to visit his son and took him to breakfast, he planned on spending the whole day with him, something he had not done in a long time.

As they were having breakfast, Bill started telling his son, "Remember I told you that whoever put you into the hospital I was going to take care of? Well, son, I'm taking care of the problem and you won't ever have to worry anymore. That person will no longer hurt you. I promised you that and I will always keep my promise. I will never let you down son, because I love you like I love myself, I won't let anyone hurt me. I'll take care of you the same way. Anytime you need me, I will always be there for you, no matter what."

Mike started thinking about what his father was saying and said to him, "Dad, how's mom? I've tried to call several times but the phone just rings. Is everything okay?"

"Sure, everything's okay. Don't worry, I've taken care of everything, especially your mother."

"Where is she? Is she still your wife?"

"Yes, you bet she's still my wife, and she's preparing dinner for me right now, so everything is okay. She's changed, she's like a new person not the same old witch that you used to know. You have a new mother and I can promise you that, Mike. So everything's okay."

*"Did she seek help?"*

"Oh yes, she got a lot of help; all the counseling she needed and a little more. She will never do what she did to you again. She's probably begging to see you and apologize to you for all the terrible things she did. She's probably hating herself because she did that without telling someone. Don't you worry about your mother, Mike, you just continue your education and don't worry. Pat won't hurt you any more, I promise she will never again hurt you as long as you live."

Bill and Mike continued eating and went out for a ride. Bill took Mike shopping for new clothes, Bill felt really good, almost like a new person. It was almost as if that last strong drink had made him a new person. He actually smiled, something he hadn't done in a long time.

Mike returned to school where he was happily living since he didn't have to deal with Pat or even look at her. He could never forget what she did to him. He was always having nightmares about her beating him every time she felt like it. He didn't tell his father how he was still suffering from the abuse because he didn't want his father to be concerned or worried about him. He kept quiet, hoping that this would all go away someday and that he would be free from this mental anguish which his mother had brought upon him. Since his father said that his mother had gotten help, he didn't want his father upset with him or his mother.

Little did Mike know his father was abusing her every day and night to make up for what she had done to Mike. This was the only therapy and help Pat was receiving. Mike thought she had gone to see a therapist because she had a serious problem. "Well, at least when I go home to visit she won't be the same. We could probably get along like mother and son, something we never had a chance to experience and we could be a family like never before."

Mike didn't know the situation at home. He had great dreams of reuniting with his mother but she hadn't changed one bit, the table had just been turned on her. She was being abused instead of him and the whole family needed help. Bill thought that he was solving the problem, but he was only making it worse. Not only did Pat need help, but he needed help also. He had an alcohol problem plus he was abusing his wife. Bill under the delusion that everything was okay, returned home sober, looked around the house and saw that it hadn't been cleaned in five months. Broken dishes were everywhere.

*"What is going on here?" he shouted out. "Pat, where are you?"*

She came running down the stairs and stood in the middle of the floor and looked at him.

*"How come you didn't clean this house up?"*

Even though he was shouting, she noticed he was different. His voice sounded different, he wasn't drunk and he was looking at her waiting for an answer. She started cleaning up really fast, moving like she was on speed while Bill just walked away and went to bed.

MY HUSBAND WENT TOO FAR

HE SAID HE LOVED ME
HE SHOWED ME JUST THAT
WHEN WE ARRIVED AT HOME, IT WAS NOTHING OF THAT
HE LIFTED HIS HAND, ONLY TO NEVER RELEASE IT
MY HUSBAND, I CALLED HIM
WHICH MADE ME FEEL UNEASY -
HE TOOK HIS FOOT, KICKED IT IN THE AIR
IT NEVER CAME DOWN TO EVEN A COMPLETE PAIR
HE SAID, HE LOVED ME ASK ME WHY?
HE GRABBED A BOTTLE AND HELD IT REAL TIGHT
HIS GRIP WAS SO STRONG IT BROKE LIKE ICE
MY HUSBAND I CALLED HIM
IT DIDN'T FEEL NICE
HIS THOUGHTS MADE ME UNEASY, WHILE HIS EYES TURNED
BRIGHT RED
HE STARED AT ME FOR ALL IT WAS WORTH
AND EVERY STARE TURNED INTO A SCAR
MY HUSBAND I CALLED HIM
BUT MY HUSBAND WENT TO FAR

# FOLLOWING THE LINE OF ABUSE 3

For any reason, or for seemingly no reason at all, Bill abused Pat. He called it a "pay back" for abusing their son Mike. Bill felt if he could make her a prime example of what abuse felt like, to be in pain day after day that this wasn't a game. Instead of seeking help he fell into a line of abuse himself. He was getting out of control with nowhere to turn, nowhere to look for answers, and no one to talk to. Abusive Bill and his abusive wife Pat. Little did they know both of them needed serious help and fast. Things were getting out of hand, and Bill was getting to the point where he could not gain control of himself he really needed help.

What is abuse? This is something we must all think about. What is the definition of this word and where did it come from? How did it get so out of control in our society? How did this deadly disease enter into our world? Abuse is definitely a deadly disease, one that kills women, men and children. How did this creep into our subconscious and from there invade our brains to make us act in this manner? Help us! Help us! How we silently scream out for help, the abusive man and his wife, but where, where can they find help and who would believe what is going on?

Brutal abuse seems to be the American way of solving problems in a family. Something like "I'll take care of her or him" and then the beating begins. Viciously performing anger doesn't solve problems it pushes the situation out of control. There has to be another way out. Sadly, we don't even wonder where all this comes from and how it got started. Which family member hit first, how did it get carried down within the emotional interaction of the family. Like a gene which gets passed down the family tree from generation to generation. Abuse seems to flow down through the family tree as if it were something worth having or as if it were meant to be or supposed to happen, but why? Why do we have to fall into the line of abuse? This line of abuse is like entering into a new world and a different society. A world that is not understood, one that cannot easily be brought out into the open. A world that cannot easily be uprooted and done away with, a world without answers.

Where did all this come from? Who put such a demon in our minds, like an unknown beast that destroys all in its path. It seems that it started way back when the first man hit the first woman or the first woman hit the first child. Who were those first unknown people, and what were the reasons and thoughts which created such a cruel thing? Abuse is serious, some people's lives depend on whether they can overcome this very thing. Something simple, like using a spanking to discipline, can turn into something ugly and cruel, creating an environment of fear. Sometimes when one is using physical force while trying to discipline when the situation isn't in their favor their ugly vehement nature begins to grow and become uncontrollable. That demon begins to peek out and take over. It's no longer a spanking, it becomes abuse. There is no real way of defining abuse and no way of knowing about what the abusers are doing. There's no one to stop them of their horrible acts or counsel them about their behavior, because no one completely understands the abusers.

Their anger continues to get out of control, and like a very contagious disease it continues to spread all over the United States from one household to the next. Many people in the United States are catching this contagious disease of abuse. In many ways they are innocent, not knowing that beating someone is wrong, they think they're doing something right controlling, abuse not right.

Abuse takes over one's life, and whether it's physical or verbal it all becomes mental abuse and damaging to us all. Most abused victims goes through a healing process on the inside and outside. Inner pain is more difficult to see than a bruised body. It seems as though no one is really interested in listening to those whom say they have been verbally abused. Any type of abuse takes it toll on those whom has experienced it.

Pat was pretty badly damaged from the abuse she had received. In fact, the effects of the abuse would probably never go away because she was abused on a daily basis and she lived in daily terror, something which deeply scarred her mind. Bill verbally abuse her, he put his mark on her and he wanted her to remember and feel every bit of agony Mike had felt. Pat would cry for help, uselessly hoping that someone would hear her and understand. She thought that maybe then the fear would go away. She doubted that anyone would believe her, her mental state was serious. She had no real proof of what caused her bruises but she was deeply bruised. She felt there was no way out of the shell called mental abuse. Even if she tried talking it out, abuse would always remain a part in her mind, a part that wouldn't vanish away until she died. This is something that Pat had to face, that memories of this would always be part of her life and would be known as her abusive past.

Bill came to feel that abusing his wife was a real honor, a privilege that allowed him the freedom to escape the truth, wrong doesn't signify correction. This put Bill in a position of absolute control. He received no punishment for his brutality, receiving treatment could find the meaning of his actions and how to stop him. Bill fell into the line of abuse. Bill and Pat were both abusers who had no control over their actions. They fell into the path of their own brutal demon (which is called secondary abuse) and they both desperately needed treatment. Just when you think you don't need treatment is when you really do.

Bill grew anxious, feeling a need for help but couldn't find a solution to receive help. He began to ignore this feeling and no longer wanted help. In fact, he became addicted to his need for power and control. Bill extreme behavior believing that Pat would never leave as he continues to perform a lesson that turned into something seriously dangerous. Sometimes he would feel anxious about what he was doing, but it paled next to his drive to hurt his wife. Had Bill sought help when he first began abusing

Pat it would not have become such a powerful addiction. Now an overwhelming urge pierced Bill conscious into believing control was the only solution.

Abuse is not something that just goes away, it takes a long period of time, and if the problem isn't fully solved then it starts over and over again. It not only affects your loved ones, but also others in your life. There's really no end to the lure of abuse full treatment does not take place.

Bill was out of control and the idea of abuse became fused in his mind. He became like a poison to his environment and this poison affected everything in his life. Everyone in his life had to deal with it one way or the other. They either had to look at the way he abused of his wife or deal with his violent attitude when he had been drinking. Bill had caught that old disease that is still not yet understood.

Once Pat was abused, her mental pain would probably never go away. Her own son suffered from this horrible thing and the emotional impact would always stick with him. Mike would do the same thing allowing himself to commit abuse simply because of discipline, abuse can be contagious. Once you have been abused it tends to carry on to the next generation. It becomes a family thing, you feel the need to be beaten, it becomes an urge. The abuser is worse off because they don't understand the need to hurt or lash out, because there's no way out!

No way out. Pat got a glimpse of this. . .no way to get out! She was locked in  not only in the house but also her mind. Understanding that abuse is  like a ghost it continues to flow, Pat was locked behind the bars of her mind with thoughts that her situation couldn't be resolved or settled. Her situation was always on her mind but she was going nowhere. Pat was seriously locked into her own world. Pat had no one to love and no one to love her. Driven by material values refusing to associate herself with the out side became very devastating. The only way for Pat problems to escape her was through Bill. Vehement situations are based around those of an uncontrollable nature Pat was stuck in the realm of abuse, locked in her world all by herself.

Almost never send your family or friends away, for the road that life takes us on is uncertain. It's been said that you never know where you might end up or who you might need to be there for you, and that's the honest truth.

For the English family there was a way out, a way to love all over again, a way to overcome abuse in the household. Despite the problems Bill still loved his wife. Bill truly loved Pat which allowed her to escape her imprisonment of his cold berate ways by the mouth of others, death probably would have been Pat's next stop. Bill denied his loving feelings while misapplying his authority Bill was a cruel vicious and brutal abuser who had no sympathy for Pat. Most abusers are hard mental thinkers losing all sympathy for their victims, killing their sensory nerves and all feelings become void and non vital to the one they are abusing.

Bill hadn't lose his last nerve, he still had some left for his wife and some for his son, but mostly for his son. He did everything to Pat in the name of revenge, and he felt good about "paying her back." He was satisfied with what he had done. Pat often thought that their ever worsening problem would be solved, but how? She grew tired and worried wondering day after day and night after night, seeking a solution for a problem she had no control over. She became weak in her soul, drained from being beaten and feeling that her life was a lost cause. She didn't have a solution because he wouldn't listen to what she had to say. Her words became meaningless to him and every time he saw her he would get even more angry. She had no rights and her solutions went unheard. The anxiety of knowing there was a problem and not being able to do anything about it became more stressful for Pat. She wanted to leave her husband, but couldn't. Even if he let her go she couldn't leave him all by himself. She kept thinking that one day he would stop abusing her.

But that (one day) can be too late for women who can't seem to find their way out of an abusive situation. Abuse has not been quite understood because when the victims have the freedom to leave the abuser they often return, knowing this person will continue to hurt them. Abuse is abuse and there's no excuse for meltarn behavior. Pat didn't have an excuse for abusing Mike. Refusing to leave can cause a strained situation to increase. Abuse carries on to the next person, allowing yourself to be suckered into abuse it will definitely stick with you your entire life-search to overcome this line of your abusive ways before the cycle continues on, stop abusing as often said what comes around goes around. That wonderful therapy is available for you although if you promoted the problem of abuse.

Pat knew that nothing could help her escape Bills abusiveness while excepting his brutal ways for abusing their son. Pat deserves help and way of excluding abuse out of her life. Pat blamed Bill's actions on the alcohol that created danger in to believing that abuse was his only way of paying back his wife, how ever it became an goal for Bill all matters and thoughts were compelled in absent of her abuse that maybe life would continue on the alcohol was an addition for his abuse their dilemma was how Bill would overcome his anguish of Mike's abuse at the hand of his mother. The memory of Mike abuse turned over and over in his mind, like an never ending story. Anguish which grew into hatred Bill was lock in his own shell with no way out! but through Bill himself.

Pat was really depressed and halfway demented from the beatings. She was unable to put her mind at ease. She was seriously depressed and alone, nowhere to run or hide closing herself in closet, hiding from the bars of mentally disturb anguish of a home made jail. Searching the telephone book for help for her and her husband hoping to find answers. Bill ignored Pat, death by her speech, Pat was stuck in her own mind, lost and confused and without any answers. Pat needed to talk to someone who would listened, but there was no one, everyone had disappeared. She needed to find out about brutal abusers, who are they and why did it enter her world without any notice. Pat had plenty of time to get out of what she lured herself into, blinded when evil enter into our world by overlooking the bad and replacing it for good. Pat often called out for help, she even prayed that someday help would come. Help was slowly finding its way in- especially when your problem is unknown, speaking out eventually someone will rescue you. Pat needed outside friends in case she ended up back into the same situation of being abused without anyone to help her.

Most abused women feel guilty and unloved when leaving an abuser so they return back to hell, to give it what they call a second chance. Sometimes it works and sometimes it doesn't, but most women gamble their lives on abuse. Abuse is shame; Men fear seeking out help, the fear of embarrassment and degrading from others, (men therapy it the right solution).

Bill was wrong and so was Pat, but it happened and they fell into the cycle of abuse. Should they feel privileged and yet ashamed? Well, Bill felt pretty good, as Pat lived in shame. Bill felt he had completed a mission only to go on with his life and forget about what happened, Pat's forgiveness for Bill was overwhelming considering the danger he put her through commending him and blaming her self of Bill's uncontrollable nature her search became doubtless her questions still went unanswered while living in the line of abuse.

# FACING THE PROBLEM OF ABUSE 4

In the beginning when Pat began abusing her son Mike, falling into a cycle she could not control. Pat was out of hand, like most people when they abuse. Assuming she was doing the right thing spanking her son. The simple spanking turned into deadly abuse and it became a serious problem. Abuse is simple to figure out, over reacting can easily be distinguish. Pat was wrong for her abuse of not being able to handle her child, her thoughts, the cruelty that reign through her uncontrolled mind.

It started way at the beginning when she couldn't control his crying; Pat couldn't handle having kids. She began to look at the outcome of her present situation while trying mentally to accept it in her mind. Pat admitted to herself that she had gotten out of hand with Mike, and it became more clear to her why Bill couldn't stop beating her and treating her cruelly.

This stuck in Pat's mind for a long time. She regretted how she had treated Mike and she wanted to apologize to him for hurting him and sending him away from his family to live with strangers. As these thoughts ran through Pat's mind, they were making her crazy this problem of abuse was something that wouldn't go away. When all these problems began, Pat didn't have anyone to talk with to help her find a solution. She was still lost in her own world, locked away from the outside and trying to work things out alone. Pat had to figure this problem out for herself. Both she and Bill needed help. Pat began a system for herself and she called it therapy it was her way of facing and solving her problem. Hopping her home made therapy would work insinuating this would help them with their problem of abuse. She began her so-called therapy session with a prayer and meditation, hoping to clear her mind from all abuse. Speaking out loudly, "Admitting her guilt of abusing her son. I'm guilty and I'm sorry for performing a cruel thing. beating him for no reason at all; mentally destroying him. Mike was suffering a case of fear from her horrible actions. My understanding is, there is no way to clear this ``Abuse`` out of our minds. I'm really sorry. Realizing that it was wrong and painful and it has also hurt me quite a bit. I'm sorry. There's no better way of expressing myself out loud about how I feel and now I'm seriously suffering along with my family and we need help to face this problem of abuse."

Facing the problem of abuse is often more serious and difficult than performing the actual abuse, because anger strikes when the real truth comes out. When guilt has settled in the truth is hard to acknowledge. While Pat was sitting at the table trying to sort out her problem there was a knock on the door. staring at the door in shock, someone was knocking nearly beating down the door its been a long time and the sound was quite strange. The knocking became very loud and persistent, as if someone were trying to break the door down screaming,

"Help! Help me! Please!"

Running to the door banging from the inside, yelling

"Who's there? Who's knocking?"

"It's me, Mike. Open the door."

There's no way to open the door, because Bill had locked it. There was no way for me to let you into the house, screaming as loud as my lungs would allow. "Bill has the key. He is the only one that can open the door. You have to call him at work."

"Why don't you have a key?" But before she answered he looked around the house and saw that the windows were barred and the door had a dead bolt on it. "That's okay, I'll see you later." He left to call his father.

As Mike left, Pat returned to facing her problem that she had with her family. "I wonder why Mike came home? He hasn't been here in a long time. Maybe Bill told him to come home so he can beat me like his father was doing. Now both of them are going to abuse me. I have to get out of here, he is going to pay me back like his father is doing and I can't take any more of this.

My husband and now my son. . .what do they have planned for me?"

Pat began to cry thinking about the revenge that her husband and her son were planning. She was getting hysterical, not knowing that her son had come to help her, not to hurt her. "I'm sorry I beat my son. Please, don't let them hurt me."

Pat was crying out loud to herself. She had a problem that required help from an outside source, but she kept trying to face it alone by saying to herself, "I beat my son over and over again for no reason at all. I thought I was disciplining him, raising him to be a perfect kid. I wonder if he has nightmares or if he thinks about this. If he does, will he become brutal to his kids? I have to apologize to him and make him understand that what I did to him wasn't the right thing and I'm really sorry. It can be taken away and he doesn't have to suffer, he can get help from someone. I have to tell him how much I love him and how much he means to me, he has to understand that I am sorry." Pat was driving herself crazy with these notions of abuse, it has completely taken over her mind and became a part of her everyday thoughts.

Bill walked into the house with Mike. Pat jumped up and gave Mike a hug, hugging him tightly and telling him how much she loved him and how much she really missed him. She began crying and telling him that she was sorry for abusing him.

Mike hugged her back, "I love you too. Pat, you are my mother and no matter what happens you will always be my mom."

He pushed Pat away from him and took a look at her. Her face appeared to be different colors. Mike didn't say a word about her face being bruised but she noticed him staring at her and she turned her head. He began to cry, saying, "You need help, Pat. Someone needs to help you because it's been ten years and you are still feeling sorry for what happened. You need to face it and go on with your life."

Mike felt that something else was going on from the way Pat was acting. She was acting oddly and every time he would reach over to her she would jump like he was going to hit her. No question about what happened to her face, it was obvious.

"Pat I want to forgive you, but you left a bruise on my mind no matter what I'm doing the thought of your abusive ways continues to cross my mind. Sitting near a window would sometimes help me to overcome the past and start over, its really hard to continue on with flash backs, for some reason the imagination doesn't want to vanish away so by coming home I figured it would help me understand your reason for hurting me maybe the suffering would go away. This is why I came home."

Pat just sat and listened to him. She knew that one day he had to face an abusive past as an adult. He was no longer afraid of his mother, and he couldn't continue running away from the problem.. He wanted to understand it and get it out of his life. He wanted to get married someday and raise a family. Unless the problem was resolved he knew for a fact that the abuse would affect his lifestyle and he would begin to beat his wife and kids and live in an unhappy environment. Mike didn't want that, he wanted to be happy and enjoy his family. He expressed this to Pat and tried to make her understand why he came home.

But Pat had her own problems and couldn't really help him. All she could do was listen to him and feel bad about what she had done. She was in a worse situation than she had ever put him in. Mike could plainly see that she has been beaten by someone because she didn't look like herself. If he had seen her on the street he would not have known who she was. Mike asked Pat to sit while he search for a brief explanation of why she abused him.

Pat began to tell Mike how he cried too much and he wouldn't shut up. "I tried everything and nothing worked. It was driving me crazy because I couldn't control you and the demon just came over me, it took over my mind and it was something that I couldn't stop. But Mike, honey, I'm trying to face it and I'm admitting to myself that I was wrong. I haven't gotten over it."

"But why, Pat? Why me? Why couldn't you just let me cry instead of beating me? You really hurt me and the pain is still here and it won't go away. I can't stop thinking about this and every time I do I hit the wall, it's making me crazy.

"Wasn't I good enough for you Pat?

"Wasn't I?"

Pat stared at Mike speaking in an off tone voice, "You were more than good, you were wonderful, but I had to make you understand that you were wrong and I needed to beat you for you to see that."

Mike wasn't looking for that type of answer. What she was saying didn't make any sense to him, it wasn't a good enough reason, and he couldn't accept what she was saying. She had to have another reason, one she wasn't telling him.

"I became addicted to hitting you, that's the only time you would be quiet. Mike, you were a real brat, uncontrollable, no one could handle you. Even the teachers complained about you being bad and not paying attention in class. Everyone had a problem with you and I had to straighten you out. You were getting out of hand and I didn't want you to go the wrong way, I just wanted to guide you in the right direction. So what I was doing was right, you'll see. Later it will benefit you. . . it will, later."

Mike just looked stung at what Pat was saying, he couldn't believe what he was hearing. She actually thought what she had done was right.

"Mike, I know that you were probably hurt on the outside, but on the inside you felt really good about what I was doing. It wasn't so painful, it wasn't something you couldn't take or you wouldn't be here now. I thought you were faking every time you cried, just to make me stop beating you. I'm your mother, Mike, and you can talk to me anytime. You don't have to pretend that everything's okay. I know that it's not."

"Pat, you are right, you are my mom and that's why I'm here talking to you about the problem that you had with me as a child"

"But you wanted it, Mike, so I gave it to you. Even though you're blaming me, you wanted me to beat you because you would never straighten up."

"Mom, how can you say that? I never even talked to anyone. I never did anything wrong. I think you are just crazy and you need help, serious help. Pat, I begged for you to stop but you wouldn't. What are you implying Pat? You wouldn't give me a chance, you just kept on beating me, hurting me. Why didn't you seek help? Why Pat? You knew that you needed help. What was your reason? Refusing to expect the truth you lied to the teachers. Can you please be honest? Please!"

Pat just looked sad, speechless searching for an answer. She began crying, "There was no help! No one would have understood us, Mike, our problem of communicating. The problem still remains, Mike."

"What problem, Pat? You have the problem, and you alone. Instead of trying to solve our problem, you are making it worse."

Pat and Mike began to argue and argue viciously. It was getting out of hand, Pat was getting very irritated, telling Mike, "I was doing just fine before you came home. Why don't you leave and never come back. You will definitely suffer for the rest of your immature life, because you are a brat and brats never grow up. Someone else will take my place and start doing what I was doing to you because you don't listen."

Mike growing angrier at his mother briefly explaining his concern of seeking help to cure his horrible nightmares of abuse Pat was in an unstable condition making the situation worse. She needed help just as much as he did. They continued to argue. Pat being easily irritated, she grabbed Mike shaking him and telling him, shut your mouth, "Shut your mouth or else!"

*"Or else what? Are you going to beat me like before?"*

Mike took Pat's hands and threw her on the floor, Pat screaming loudly, "Please! Please! Don't hurt me. I'm sorry, please, Mike."

Pat scooted into a corner and covered up her face, Mike just stood there staring at her trying to figure out what she was doing. "Get up, Pat!"

He reached down and pulled her up off the floor and began shaking her, "I'm not going to hurt you, I just want you to realize that I'm not a child anymore. I'm a man now and you will treat me with respect."

Pat shook in fear of Mike, thinking that he came home to pay her back for what she had done to him. "Please! Mike don't hurt me, please! Let me go, I'm sorry about what I've done to you." There's no way to explain it.

Mike let her go ( screaming) "Get out! I want you out of my house, out of my life and right now. You're causing problems, Mike you'll remain the same even as an adult continuing to destroy every thing in sight. I can't handle you anymore. Please just leave before someone gets hurt."

Pat went back into the corner and huddled up as if she were insane.

"What's the matter with you, Pat? Why are you doing this to yourself? Don't act like that."

Pat wouldn't say another word so he picked her up and sat her in the chair, hugging her and telling her that he loved her in spite of everything would be all right. Pat Mike explained, I'm here to help us not cause confusion look at you Pat. She was staring back whit her swollen face. He now realizes what his father meant when he said that he had taken care of everything and not to worry, that previous problem would never occur again. Mike knew that hurting someone wouldn't solve the problem, it would only make the problem worse.

"Pat, this is not facing your problem. You still have it inside you and you need a psychiatrist, it seems as if your mind needs fixing and this abuse thing has really taken a toll on you. Just look at you, Pat. You don't look good at all and you need to be cured of this problem."

Pat began crying, knowing her son was telling the truth. "Mike, I'm sorry. How many times can I make you understand how sorry I am?"

"I can't forgive you until you seek help so that you can live with yourself. Pat, I believe that your tyrannical nature allowed you to beat me because I'm a spitting image of you and not Bill you hate yourself and that's why you beat me. You hate yourself and that's why you hated me. Stop hating yourself your beautiful even behind the molted bruises you need to start admitting to yourself the love the exist deep within then maybe you would accept me. I'm your son and you have to face reality and stop hating me and stop hating yourself.."

Mike began talking about how she had abused him. Pat refused to listen turning her head from one side to the other trying to avoid Mike sorrowful complaining for several years stamped permanent in her mind the guilt often cursed Pat barely listening as Mike was making the problem much worst.

Bill finally came into the room and asked in a hard tone, "Is there a problem? What's going on?"

*The room fell quiet, no one said a word. "Well, is there a problem?"*

"No," Mike answered, "we're just trying to over come our abusive problems helping Pat open up to her pathetic ways, look at her crumbling up in hatred losing her mind she need help look at Pat's condition, Have you noticed dad? Did you know how serious her condition was?"

"No, I never looked at her, but I totally agree with you, she does need help. She needs to go to a shelter or maybe a mental ward and live there for a while to get over her horrible ways its all your fault Pat."

Bill roughly screamed out, Your the cause of any mental problem that occurred, look she really needs help!

Pat, listening to Bill speak about her receiving help, smiled for the first time in a long time. She put such a big smile on her face that Bill looked at her in astonishment, as if he had never seen her smile before. He couldn't remember the last time she had smiled. Bill started to feel pretty good about the way she looked despite the bruises he put all over her face. Pat just looked at Bill not unable to say a word. She was as happy as can be knowing that help was finally on the way.

Pat looked at Bill but refused to speak knowing that both of them were prison into this cycle of abuse. Bill was worse because he was driven by obsession creation a home made jail locking her up for several years. Pat was frightened but she finally spoke out, "How can I seek help if I'm locked in this house? You won't even let me go outside and get air. You need to face it as well as

I do, we all need help. You are much more of a beast than the rest of us."

**Mike then asked, "What's going on?  What are you talking about?"**

"He's just as guilty as I am."

"What exactly do you mean?  My dad would never do anything to hurt anyone.  He's not an abuser."

Little did Mike know, he had another problem to face; his father's abusing his mother.  Mike could not believe this, he thought he had the most loving and understanding father on earth.

"He abuses me and continues to hurt me, he doesn't care anymore." Pat murmured.

"I can't accept this.  She's lying, isn't she dad?"

Bill said nothing.

"Isn't she lying?  Tell me, Dad, tell me the truth.  You didn't hurt her, you're not like that I don't want to believe this, it doesn't seem right.  She is just crazy and wants to blame someone else because she's the one with the problem and it's all in her mind, right, Dad?"

"Just look around you.  Look at the windows and the doors and ask where the phone is.  Pat began taking off her clothes showing her tarnished skin marks for the baking soda and open wounds see Mike, I wouldn't lie to you, he's worse off than I am." Pat cried.

Mike couldn't believe this, not his father falling into the line of abuse.  He began to get angry and ran up to his room, not wanting to believe what his mother has said or what his eyes witness of her badly bruised body.  As he sat in his room looking around he found all the answers he needed.  All of Pat's clothes and everything she owned were in his room.  He just sat and cried, telling himself that it was really true about what was going on here.  Mike knew then that his father was really abusing her and abusing her badly, to the point where she had to sleep in another room;  his room, to keep the memories alive of the beating.  He was cruel to her, very cruel.  Mike fell asleep thinking about how serious this problem was.

"Now look what you've done. You are always doing something wrong." Bill said.

He slapped Pat and threw her on the floor, walked into his room and locked the door. Pat was left with nowhere to sleep and no one seemed to care. She made a bed on the floor because Bill would not allow her to sleep on his favorite sofa. She knew if she slept there he would get very angry at her. She decided not to make him mad, hoping he would not change his mind about her seeking help. She slept on the floor, freezing all night.

Pat got up early to make breakfast for Mike. As he sat down she began thank him for everything he had done last night, he interrupted her by saying, "It's not over yet, it's just the beginning. I'm going out to find some kind of help, there has to be someone out there who can help us and I won't be back until I find what I'm looking for."

He ate the rest of his food and left. Pat just stood staring at the door; it wasn't locked anymore. . . maybe Bill was finally finished abusing her. She began to feel pretty good about herself and her son.

Mike began searching for answers. He researched the library and the hospitals. He went to see a lawyer to find out what his family needed to do to face this problem of abuse. But he didn't find any answers, he was told that if he didn't have any children there was nothing that could be done. Despondent, Mike went to the neighborhood bar, the same bar Bill allowed himself to be suckered with alcohol, Mike began discussing his problem with Jim, the bartender. Mike told him what his problem was, but since Jim didn't know who this kid was he gave him John's phone number and told him that John's wife might be able to help him or guide him to someone who could help him solve this problem.

*"Who is this Joan and what type of work does she do?"*

"She's a nurse and she works for the battered women society. She could give you some information about how the system works."

Just as they were speaking about John, he walked in and sat in his usual spot. Jim walked over to him to tell him about Mike and the problem he was having. John went over and started a conversation with Mike.

"Hi, I'm John holding out his hand for a secure hand shake of invitation. Since Jim has told you all about me and my wife, why don't you tell me a little about yourself and your problem."

"Well, it's my family. We're not getting along and abuse is floating in the air and we need help it seems like an never ending store.

"Well, Mike, I think you are doing the right thing by seeking help." Mike interrupted by saying,

"Would you and Joan like to come over for dinner and explain to us how to face this problem so we can go on with our lives?"

*"Sure Mike, when would like for us to come over?"*

Mike gave John the address then thanked Jim for his help. "No problem, that's what I'm here for. I serve the customers and it what keeps them coming back."

Mike returned home and said to his parents, "I found someone who will help us or give us information about how to find help so we no longer have to live like this. We can be a family again."

*Pat began dancing around the room and singing, "Help is on the way!"*

She was very happy and Bill was happy for her, "Did you invite them over for dinner?"

"Yes, and they're coming over tomorrow."

"Oh great!" Bill shouted out. "Then we need to prepare."

Bill instructed Mike to assistance Pat at the store making sure she doesn't disappear out of his sight because of her mental illness to buy whatever she needed to make dinner for their company. Bill didn't know that the couple Mike invited over was his best friend and his only friend. He didn't think to ask Mike about the couple he had invited over.

Mike and Pat went to the grocery store and Pat felt kind of relieved while driving. She felt free once again. She hadn't been outside since Bill locked her up in the house and had forgotten where the store was . For the first time in almost ten years she was outside. As they were approaching the store Pat began to warn Mike about his actions, reminding him about the last time they went into the store.

Mike said nothing;

She warned him that if his behavior can cause serious problems and her stick is still in her new closet waiting. "Mike, please don't embarrass me in the store." Pat continued to say;

Mike just sat thinking about what happened the last time they were out shopping and the horrible after affects. "I won't go into the store. I'll wait out here, but I need you to pay for everything." Mike went into the store and they arrived home without any problems.

When John and his wife Joan arrived they noticed that the house looked really strange. "Look at the bars on the windows and the door. They must really be scared". Joan said.

"But this isn't a bad neighborhood and this is the only house within the last mile with bars on the windows and doors."

As they walked up to the house Joan noticed the dead bolt on the door. "Wow! John, look at that. Either they're scared or they're having serious problems."

John rang the doorbell and when Bill opened it he looked in shocked. "What in the world are you doing here?"

"What are you doing here?" Bill,

"I live here!"

"Oh really? Well, Bill, I'm looking for Mike. Does he live here?"

Mike went to the door, "Oh! Hi, John. Come in, it's good to see you. We were all waiting."

John and Bill stood and looked at one another in shock, staring as if they had seen a ghost. Pat ran into the room, "Joan! Hi, what are you doing here?"

"Mike invited us over for dinner.",

"Well, come in and have a seat."

Mike then said, "I gather you know one another ."

"Yes," they answered at the same time.

"Mike is this the family you were telling me about?"

"Yes, and this should be easier since you guys know each other. Since you guys are not strangers it makes it a little better; it will make us feel a little more comfortable expressing our problems to one another. So, let's all go and have dinner, then we can have a healthy conversation."

Mike took them into the dining room and seated them. As he sat down no one said a word. Everyone was in shock. John and Joan had never been to Bill's house so they didn't know what expect of them. The last time they got together it turned out horribly and now they were sitting awkwardly at the English table for the first time, even though John and Bill had been friends for years. They hadn't realized that Bill and Pat were still having problems because Bill no longer discussed his problems with John.

Joan just sat quietly thinking and smiling to herself, "I knew that one day they were going to need help, that he was going to give in. He is so cruel I bet he has her locked up in the house and beats her all the time. I told her to call me, now I know why the bars are on the windows, it's so she wouldn't get out. I've seen this kind of problem before. Just look at her face, it's pushed all out of proportion. He's been beating her for a long time, I can't even look at her and eat because she looks so bad. Whoever thought of having dinner with her? This was definitely hard, she looks horrible. How could she let him do this to her?" Joan looked at Pat and smiled.

"Joan how are things going? I haven't seen you in a long time" Pat said.

"I've tried to call you several times while Bill was out of town but the phone just ranged and ranged. Why is that, Pat? Why don't you answer the phone? I thought you moved".

"Well the phone isn't working, Joan. Bill stopped all outgoing calls."

Bill dropped his fork loudly in his plate causing a crack in his thin china plate and looked at Pat with a stern look.

"Well, we have to get it out in the open." Pat said calmly. '

"That's right, Pat, we need to talk. Why do you have bars on the windows?" Joan asked. "And why do you need a dead bolt on the door? This is a very good neighborhood and there's not a single bit of crime. Are you scared, Pat?"

"No, why would I be scared? I've been living here for twenty-five years."

***"Then what is the problem?"***

Bill interrupted Joan by saying, "John, how are things going with you? You seem to be pretty happy. I haven't seen you in awhile, where have you been?"

"Well, Bill, I've been around and I also told you if you needed to talk to call me. How come it took this long? I've been waiting for you to come and talk to me about your problem. You agreed that if you needed someone you would call me."

"Yeah! John, you know how things get. Bill continued to ignore the heart of his situation. Actually John, I've been really busy working we picked up a new contract at the bank, John's conversation was no longer in existence. Mike wants to solve this problem and that's how this dinner occurred I'm doing just fine and couldn't be any better. It's Pat who has the problem." Bill said happily;

Everyone turned and looked at Bill but no one said a word and Bill kept talking, "Pat, she needs to go to a shelter and receive help. She's losing her mind maybe a mental hospital would be better. I can no longer deal with her, she has gotten out of hand and it's a good thing Mike came home because she was cracking up. I told her over and over again that she needs help and she won't listen to me. Maybe she'll listen to Joan and seek help."

"Well Pat, Joan said; I guess we've come to an end, it's time to settle this problem that you and Bill have been suffering from all these years. We really need to sit down and have a talk, just you and me."

The men got up and left the table and went into the other room where they began talking about the English family problems. John needed to understand why all this happened so he could figure out how he could help. As John began speaking Pat and Joan walked into the room where they were sitting and sat down next to their husbands. Joan began speaking, "We thought we might join in, that way we can talk about this without leaving anything out so we can definitely get to the bottom of this or at least get it out into the open."

When Joan said this, she interrupted Bill's conversation. He was telling John how he had abused Pat, that the very thought of what she had done to Mike provoked his drinking and caused the abuse.

"Let's try not to blame anyone," responded John, "because when we blame others it makes matters worse, and that's what we all need to avoid right now."

Bill and Mike agreed with what John was saying because Pat would have been blamed for everything. Rather than helping, she would be humiliated in front of Joan and she wouldn't feel very good when they got finished. Joan sensed that Pat didn't want her to have an even worse opinion of her.

Pat said; should we start by admitting to ourselves that all of us has a problem." Joan agreed.

Bill began by saying, "I have an alcoholic problem, and it has led me to abuse my wife, but I never abused my son."

Mike turn came up and he continued the story. "Suffering an abusive past is very devastating my thought are to help it vanish away and continue on with my life. Like most people to complete life most difficult talk the raise a family without brutally destroying my kids we all know for a fact that something as serious as abuse wont completely go away, setting here discussing the problem leaves relief and a clear conscious it helps me to go on."

Pat started saying, "Not to mention, I'm a beast of my worst kind. Abuse has a tendency to add control-that wasn't my problem abuse became a need a reason to accomplish a goal of raising a perfect child it was my only personality.. Sadness fell upon Joan staring at Pats face badly bruised) it happened Pat yelled out!

"Okay, that's enough. We heard everyone's problem. Joan said lightly; it all boils down to anger, manipulation, cruelty or hatred. That's what abuse is, it's not a way to solve problems particularly for people who don't like to talk their problems out. It's their way of solving problems or expressing themselves. But you people don't seem to have that problem, letting go is the most important theory that allowed coming to reality getting to the bottom of a situation is solving the problem. Exploiting your situation in open helps ease the tension in an abrupt environment. Facing your problem is expressing to others about the difficulties of the present problems and this is a wonderful start."

Mike began telling how he has nightmares of Pat coming after him with a stick and he slams his head into the wall this constantly continues to invade my dreams.

"How come I never knew about this? Bill shouted! How come you never told me? We would have gotten you help right away when it first started."

"I didn't want you to suffer, Dad, or worry about me, John and Joan are here to help us overcome the fears and destruction of one another Well, My anger would increase my anger lead me to hitting and fussing with everyone I came in contact with they became so frightened and afraid, fearing my vehement nature. It lead to emptiness and isolation, absolutely no one wanted to talk or get near me my problem continue to increase. So here I am searching out for help believing Pat would have some answers or help me understand more about my problems of anger. Mike continue to explain as sadness crept through his mind I'm suffering form anger and its driving me crazy. I don't want to go crazy. I want to be normal like the rest of the people my age or just be an adult but a good adult."

John then said, "Why didn't you seek help sooner, a teacher or your counselor at school. I know there was someone for you to talk to, like a social worker. There had to be someone in your school."

"I was confused thinking it would just go away or no one would have understood my temper of personality that's why I'm here to talk to my mother hoping that a solution would come out of it but only to find out she's worst off than before, our problem as a family continues to worsen (Bill dropped his head) counseling is our only way out, we're all suffering from some type of abuse. Mom still thinks I'm a child this has to change her approach is terrible I'm a man, trying to kill the very fundamentals of unwanted abuse at least my world.

"If I had known the criteria of seeking help it would have stopped a long time ago. But I thought my father was involved not knowing are realizing he was absent minded to our house hold feud, hiding abuse allows danger, every child should learn to speak out the truth about abuse because hiding makes the situation worse you cant change a brutally minded person. Mike continues to say; so it's better to tell someone right away and suffer later. Its better to be embarrassed than live in hell, because abuse doesn't just go away, it needs help and coaching."

***Joan asked, "Who's going to tell their story next?"***

"I guess I'm next," Pat began to say, (Every one stared widely at Pat) barely seeing through her swollen eyes. "I really feel bad about what Mike is going through and I know it's all my fault. It was so hard for me to give him love, His suffering maybe my fault he's a strong man and elude it form his mind, but at least he will be free and clear. He will be able to seek help, knowing that others are suffering just like him."

"Bill was a loving husband. He wasn't always home his comfort of a loving husband left the house in perfect condition its my fault he's a beast, he got real angry and that's how he got caught up in the middle of this. He cant handle himself. He's drinks, Bills madness is understandable and its because of me that my husband drinks a lot, he closed off the house because he felt sorry for me and needed to get back at me and its all my fault. We had a bad fishing trip and I'm the blame for all this. I just have to admit that I was wrong. I've never admitted to it my husband, my lies went on continuously he caught me in the act, I was afraid he would leave me and go away. But maybe I should of left and went on my own way but I love Bill and these last years has been horrible for me. Joan said; Pat stop blaming yourself, you're not responsible for Bill's actions. I brought misery along with me. I drove him to drinking and it hurts both of us. Every time he takes a look at me he feels pain and a need for revenge.

"My fears of Mike taking over gaining control of hour household fearing he wouldn't listen. I felt spanking him was taking care of everything. But the spankings turned into beatings. Then it got much worse and if he hadn't been hospitalized it could of gone further trying to explain my problems to Bill was a waste because he was always so loving besides he would not have understood. I just could not have spoken with him about this. I was too embarrassed and full of shame. Although I tried it would not come out."

Pat started crying and ran out the room. Joan followed behind to comfort her, telling her, "No one's blaming you, it will be all right, Pat, I will help you. Don't worry; you won't have to put up with this anymore. Why don't you come and stay with us until things gets better it might be good to escape from this horrible JAIL, Pat now come back into the room and finish telling us about how it all happened and you'll feel much better once you've finished. This is just lifting a load off your mind so please come tell us more, to lift off that heavy burden, so your life can change."

Pat and Joan went back into the room and sat down. Pat continued her story, "Well, I didn't tell anyone about the abuse assuming it was smart, ignoring the teachers and lying to them. They knew that something was going on, but I told them that everything was all right and that Mike was getting into fights with the boys in the neighborhood. We could have gotten help. While they were reaching out to us my fears were strong hoping Bill wouldn't find out. It's really my fault.

"I tried apologizing to my husband but he was too drunk and too angry to even listen. He was mad as hell and there was no way of getting inside of him. Bill didn't want to hear anything my mouth released not anything at all. He began to ignore me in every way, insinuating with a vituperate temper its a good thing Mike was seeking help, not to mention he has more to face and its the whole family that needs help, because when he left the abuse didn't stop, it continued on. Well Joan you're quite familiar with our situation per our fishing trip was quite a nightmare for every one whom took notice and I owe you and John an apology we have to learn to forgive and forget Pat turned to look at Mike searching for a sign of relief its important for us to forgive one another that's the only way we'll continue on with out any repugnance. "Tears streamed down Pat's face, (she cried out) " I'm tired of being abused and locked behind bars in my own home. When does freedom settle in how long will it take? Sorrow fell upon Pats face staring at Bill, it feels like I'm a in jail or a mental hospital. Not being able to function properly. Help me, help me get out of here. It felt really good to just be outside to see other people, Pat explained; speaking to everyone felt human again. Not being able to go outside in almost ten years. I felt relieved, I felt like a flower blooming for the first time. Knowing that it can be worked out and we can be a normal family again. I know that we can be a family."

Finally it was Bill's turn to admit to this shameful abusive problem. He put his head down, not able to look at anyone because of his guilt. He had the most dramatic story of them all to tell. He began to break down and cry like he never cried before, hearing his wife and son and how he played right into this cycle. He became more of an abuser than anyone, he was paying her back for what she had done to his son. He began by terrorizing his wife for his son's sake. He stopped caring about her and couldn't find love in his heart, only hatred. He began hating her, not wanting to be around her, so he put her out of the room several times.

"But I'm sorry, Pat, for everything I've done to you but you deserved it, I was teaching you a lesson that got out of control, it was wrong but at the time it was needed to show you how it feels to be brutal, how pain actually feels. My apology may not be enough."

He turned to look at Pat but she didn't say a word because she had said enough and she wanted to hear everything he had to say and much more.

"I wanted to love you so bad, but my heart wasn't in it. You destroyed all my feelings but animosity controlled my feelings. You made me angry and the only way to get back at you was to beat you, so that's what happened, Pat."

Bill had a strong memory; he seemed to never forget anything and that was really bad for Pat. Ever time he had a drink he would remember the things that she had done. He was strongly driven to drinking and the flash backs would appear of the way Pat abused his son. He was explaining this to them and as he was talking John blurted out, "I can witness to the drinking. I've never seen you drink like that. It's like you completely lost control of yourself it came to mind that something was wrong but you seemed too disturbed to talk about it. That's why I plainly told you if you needed to talk, to feel free and call me and I left you alone. I knew that exhaustion would bring your situation to an end, then perhaps Bill my phone would be ringing with your voice on the other end.

"I know you were just trying to help, John, but the drinking is so powerful I couldn't stop and it became uncontrollable. I'm addicted to it. Help was probably my next step, not realizing the alcohol was causing a serious problem. Assuring myself about what I was doing, was getting back at my wife. Both of us have the same problem not to mention it will stop right away. I'm not certain that the abuse will stop because the alcohol takes over my mind.

Were planning to  seek help meaning putting forth every effort to try therapy, We need all the help we can get. As for me I will give it a try and leave the alcohol alone as much as possible. She is free to go, and if she wants to leave  she can it hurts me just as much as its hurting her, she had to be taught a  lesson. There are a lot of things that went on here, like when I chained her to the table for several days without any food or water. It was all part of letting her see what abuse was about. I felt pretty bad, but the guilt of abuse tore holes in my mind. but those feelings had to be overlooked. She  needed to see that pain is a serious game.

"Abuse is something no one wants to live with and it's not fun at all, hurting someone else. When you abuse someone you are also hurting yourself. the hurt cursed my mind also on several occasions I made sure she understood what was going on just by letting her know that it can come much worse than the first time. What you give out you shall receive. If Pat doesn't understand that by now then she will later, because it won't go away. The abuse and the controlling will continue to teach her a lesson. Of course my feelings are mutual but abuse isn't nice and that's a known fact."

Bill continued talking about his problem, "I'm not able to control myself and I can't blame the alcohol for what's going on. It is apart of losing self control, alcohol is just an excuse for my vehement behavior I'd planned to beat her anyway. Beating Pat can very well be done without alcohol, it was used to exclude the feeling of pain and shame about me beating Pat, this problem drove me into drunkenness. I know I have another problem to face and that's my addiction to alcohol. I'm now suffering from a real serious problem. The need to have a drink comes across my mind and it won't go away, so what am I to do now?"

Bill looked at John with confusion waiting for an answer. It came as a shock to John and his wife Joan, how Bill abused Pat. "I can't believe you would do such a thing. I didn't know you had that type of evil in you Bill to take it that far? Some things were uncoiled, you've done enough to her."

Joan was speechless, unable to speak or respond to Bill's actions. She was in total shock and wouldn't know where to start if she had responded to Bill.

No one said a word, so Bill continued to speak.

"I don't know where start or how to stop. The anguish would-n't go away and it turned into pure bitterness. I'm not denying what happened the important thing is to overlook corruption by excluding the past from our lives and its not something that happen overnight but its worth a try.

"John openly responded."

"Well, you can start by taking the bars off the windows and doors and turning back on the telephone or would that be too a big step for you to handle? Or is it you don't trust your wife? It has to end somewhere Bill, unless your temperament feeling of authority thinks payback is still your only solution. Bill have to start by releasing some of the build up of hatred and vituperative. Pat needs freedom she's so badly bruised you can't tell what her real image looks like. She needs help Bill can't you see?

"Well, I can't answer anything at this point but as the situation comes across for seeking help she's free to go."

Pat spoke softly"

"Honey! I don't want to leave, this is just driving me crazy. The abuse is way out of control, it needs to stop! Murder would be your next step, I'm hurting Bill my love is stronger than enmity-but isolation is driving me mentally ill, "I NEED HELP!

"Well," Joan began to say," we need to set you up for some therapy sessions at the battered women program. They have a shelter and you can receive help while living there. It won't help for you to stay here because the abuse will never end Bill will continue to scold you the drinking will continue and the next time will meet it will definitely at your funeral. There's a big problem here the home made jail Bill's vituperative temper which continues to worsen. Bill has too much authority this has to be settled before someone gets seriously hurt. The police should be involved this has to stop Pat have you looked in the mirror? There's people reaching out to help. This problem can't be solved alone, it takes work and time talking without action is dad Bill I demand you to let her go or else you'll end up in jail and that's final. Pat stood up eyeing Bill, Joan continued to say; There no excuse in the world for this horrible vehement control. Please John we have to leave turning to Pat, I'll be in touch."

So John and Joan left. On the way home, Joan said, "Wow. I had no idea about the seriousness of their situation it seemed so suspicious because the telephone went unanswered. It seemed rather strange that Bill would do something like that, he doesn't seem like the type of person who would lock his wife up and beat her."

"Well, Joan, you can't judge for appearance. Bill keeps

drinking and drinking. Anger would often flare up if I'd mad a comment about his drinking, I sat speechless often wanting to respond. I just watched as he stumbled out of the bar having no idea it was leading to the abuse of his wife, (my eyes watered) although on the boat he beat her pretty bad and It felt bad watching, not being able to do anything. I really feel for her, she looks really bad. My constant advice soaked right through him. It's a good thing Mike showed up, knows what might have happened to Pat. Mike seems very concerned and it's a good thing he loves his mother in spite of her brutal past. Pay-back isn't such a good solution, Mike turned out to be caring, we know Bill's next step in hurting Pat Bill could of killed her the way he beat her. It's horrible. He claims he love her well he's misjudging himself or the definition of love.

It took two days for Bill to decide whether or not he was going to take the bars off the windows and locks off the doors. It took lots of pleading from Mike. Mike wouldn't stop until Bill finally said okay, and everything was changed back to normal. Pat was able to hear the telephone ring once again, Bill warned her it wasn't for her use. He wasn't sure about her yet. Bill felt very uneasy about this whole thing. Considering the option ( wiping his eyes) of her being free to leave if she wanted to the drinking might cause him to change his mind. It would take more than just someone talking to him, it would take a lot of convincing. Bill didn't trust Pat inside the house he felt uneasy unlocking the doors. He felt he needed to know where she was at all times. Making the situation more difficult, Pat was trying to seek helped!

Bill didn't want help, he wanted to continue in the same disruptive mind. He wanted control and vituperative. Allowing Pat her freedom would lead to problems, having Bill put in jail at the voice of Joan this constantly wore on Bill's mind the thought of him being locked up behind bars at the mouth of someone else. Pat strongly love Bill despite his horrible ways wanting to continue her life of disorderly conduct of abuse.

Pat was standing in the kitchen there was a knock on the

door. A mailman stood holding a package it seemed awfully strange its been almost ten years, Pat asked him, "Where have you been all these years? I mean how come you haven't delivered mail here?"

"There wasn't any mail to deliver here" he said.

"I can't believe that. No bills, no magazines, nothing?"

"Lady, I would love to talk to you but I have to go. I'll see you later. You should talk to your husband about this, it isn't my problem." And he walked off.

She stood staring at him. Until he disappeared Pat thought about the mailman and where was the mail going if it wasn't coming to our house.

"I wonder if Bill had the mail going to his job? At least he's trying to change, putting forth some effort. After talking with Mike, Bill realized this problem was serious at least he's trying to over come his disorderly authority.

The household was returning back to normal a little bit at a time. Bill was finally giving Pat her freedom back, her right to live without being locked up in a homemade jail . She was now able to come and go whenever she wanted to. She had the right to be free; free from this prison that he had created for her. He was learning to accept her being free from his abusive ways. As Bill let go, Pat began to feel at ease once again the happiness appeared to cure all Pat's fears.

As she was learning to smile again, her face and mind began to heal. She could admit that happiness was crossing her path once again. She felt a little relieved knowing that at least he was trying to face his portion of abuse, letting go of hatred, Bill finally accepted his wrong doing.

Bill made up in his mind that he was going to seek help. He was going to return to normal and start living again. He finally called John to tell him about what he was doing. John invited Bill to a men's meeting, at his church and Bill agreed. Bill called the Alcoholics Anonymous Association and he joined the group. He really wanted to change, he really wanted help. His son had convinced him to seek help. Mike lead Bill to believing that Payback isn't a good solution especially falling in the foot steps of wrong doing. His father decided to seek help he believed in Mike truthful ways.

Bill began going to church with John at his Seventh Day Adventist church. Bill had never attended church. He had his doubts but John assured him needed help and to forget his feelings about being in a church. Bill took it into consideration and went along with John. He felt uncomfortable, after awhile it began to settle in realizing that he wasn't the only one with a problem. He started to relax while talking his problems out. Discussing his horrible situation seemed to release some of the pressure as the church found ways to comfort Bill, assuring that God would help.

Bill needed some self esteem and motivation. Trying to overcome his most addictive problem -his drinking allowing himself to feel free once again from the build up of anger he lured himself into. This group of men help put a smile on Bill's face. He never liked music but after awhile it began to settle in. Bill became very familiar with his surrounding trying to ignore everything that had occurred. It helped him let loose of what he had done to his wife, and even the thought of having a drink. The people around Bill were so full of life and caring that he could not have resisted the treatment even if he had tried. When it came time to talk about his problems he had forgotten that it existed. This program was really working for Bill. He really loved it because some of the men were having the same problem or had been through something similar. They knew how to react to Bill, they knew what to say and answered every question he asked. This was a humorous group, they laughed at almost everything. Bill enjoyed it because it was a simple way of therapy and it appeared to have worked for most of the people who came in. There weren't any pressure or blaming. Bill had a good time and even learned to sing. They sang a song that said "there's nothing like a good wife." Bill loved this song, it made him appreciate having a wife. Everyday Bill would sing this song alone without his group session. It did something to him, this song was great.

It made him love his wife deep within his heart, He would be able to face her without thinking about abuse. His heart was coming to life once again.

Mike came back home still suffering, still sad and still trying to find answers to his problems. He couldn't seem to find the counseling needed and by being a man he couldn't find help anywhere. He was told that there was nothing wrong with him and he was perfectly healthy. But Mike was still lost and still confused. Bill saw that his son wasn't happy and that he still hadn't found help. Bill told him about the church that he was going to and offered to take him. Mike insisted that wasn't such a great idea because he had never been to church and he didn't know how the people would react about him coming.

"I insist that you go, Mike. It will do you some good because you are searching and you can't seem to find help, I want you to be happy. You are helping us so we have to help you. Come, they won't mind one bit. They are very understanding and a great group of people. It's been a whole year and look at me, don't I look happy? Isn't this what you want?"

"Yes, you look quite well, Dad, but it's not for me. I'll have to suffer until it goes away by itself."

"You don't have to suffer, Mike. Look at me, no more alcohol. I haven't had a drink since I've been into this program. It's working for me and I know it will work for you. Just come once, Mike. It's a place for abused minds and if you don't like it then you could leave. I won't force you to go, but you need help like me and this will definitely help you. You'll love this therapy. Remember, you are the one that inquired that we needed help. Now come on, give it a try!!

"Okay, Dad, I'll go and if I don't like it I will leave so please don't be upset."

"I won't," Bill answered," because you will see that it's great and needed."

Bill and Mike went to the meeting together and they began their session with music. The men began singing and introducing themselves to Mike and shaking his hand and welcoming him to the session. They made him feel very much at home and a part of the group. Mike began telling his story and why he thought he needed help. He said he was suffering from a mental abuse syndrome and no one really understood what was going on with him. He explained the nightmares and how he needed a clear conscience because he thought about the abuse all day long.

When he finished they all gave him another handshake and he felt well accepted by this group. He had never felt like this before. They seemed like people that cared and were easy to talk to. It wasn't like his father never cared for him, but the thought of having someone else to listen to his problems and not receiving a negative response gave Mike hope. Mike felt a loved, a love to help clear those abusive thoughts out of his mind and out of his heart. Before this he couldn't clear this problem out his life because he never felt loved. Although his parents loved him it was a strange love. The group began to sing songs. Mike thought how different this was. He had never seen a therapy session where they sang songs or even laughed.

"Most therapy sessions are quiet and people seem to get more depressed as they previously were, (before entering) refusing to follow through with their therapy. At times therapy sessions can be useless by talking and not reacting out your problems, the bruised minds escapes more angrier than when the entered. Angry that you have not accomplished anything and no one seems to care. It's all different here. You guys seem to be enjoying yourselves without a worry in the world."

The group continued to sing about a "good wife" and Mike joined in even though he wasn't married and didn't know the words. He tried to sing and began to feel really good about himself. The thought of his mother pierced his mind when they sang the part about loving your wife. The session ended, Mike wasn't finished. He wanted to stay to continue talking and singing he felt really good like his father. Releasing the pressure Mike suffered form would take more than one night to release those horrible nightmares means to substitute your daily mindly activity with new positive thinking Mike's patience was well worth it.

ˋ After the session was over they thanked Mike for coming and told him that he was welcome to return while in search for help. Mike was well pleased with this group. On the way home Bill asked Mike, "So son how did you like the session? Well, you didn't leave and you appeared to be very active in the session."

"Well, Dad, that's the best thing in the world. Where did you find this place? All the group sessions that I've been to my problems seems to worsen with more nightmares, but I feel different now. (Smiling) with his brown red hair neatly shaved to satisfy U.S. army, standing tall in his brown suit to match, feeling happy that someone wants to finally help him, so who told you about this place?"

"John, he came with me for about six months then I told him that he no longer needed to come. John goes to church here and they help lots of people with abusive problems. Now I come to church with John, but I haven't joined assuring myself that the demon is completely dissolved,of all my problems so that I may live in peace with my wife.

Mike felt happy for himself and for his father, they could now have a peace of mind and go on with their lives. Finally they had found real help for their problems. He could see a glow in his father's eyes, a sign of happiness and a need for real love. Mike thought how happy his mother would be seeing is father in a different state as the thoughts of abuse were now gone south.

Mike began attending these sessions three times a week with his father he felt that they belonged together and not wanting to leave Bill, this program was helping him and it seemed to be working for Mike. The problem was finally going away, Mike thought "Finally, my mind is at peace where moving on wouldn't be a problem."

It took five months for Mike to clear his mind of those horrible attributes and he didn't miss a meeting. He was there every day that the sessions went on. Mike started going to church, considering the amount of help he received he felt compelled to join hoping he would continue to keep a peace of mind by eluding his abusive past. John felt very happy for Mike and Bill, that he was able to be a benefit in their lives. He knew that Bill would like this program but he didn't know that Mike would also benefit from it. He was happy for Mike. It pleased John that Mike was able conquer whatever it was he was suffering from.

Pat and Joan were having sessions at the battered women's shelter with other women. For two years this has been going on, but it seemed as if something wasn't right. It wasn't working for Pat. They read books to define abuse, they explained their stories about their abusive lives, Pat felt she wasn't getting anywhere remaining in same frame of mind, cluttered with abuse, her thinking was very imperative. Bill visited Pat occasionally at the shelter making sure it was working as he continued to clean and clear his life. After viewing Pats condition Bill decided that his present was causing Pat to lose focus he informed John that it wasn't a good idea and he shouldn't see her until she got better or mentally stable and John agreed. Bill insisted that Pat to join the church when she came home, he wanted everything to be perfect like before.

# DEALING WITH AN ABUSIVE PERSON 5

When Joan and Pat began their sessions, Joan believed that since she and Pat were friends that it would be easy. Little did Joan know that Pat was hard to deal with, she was nothing but a problem and set in her own ways. Joan had dealt with complicated people before in her working life time, but never like this she never had to take the existing problem home with her Joan hadn't dealt with an abusive friend. Pat was her friend and she couldn't turn her down. Dealing with Pat made Joan frustrated, angry, and uncontrollable. Every time they would have a conversation Pat would get angry and run into another room. Joan would then run after her and say to her in a nice way, "Look Pat, we're trying to solve this problem that you have, now let's try to talk so we can get it out into the open. Running won't solve the problem, it makes matters worse, and that's all you need is for matters to get worse."

"Okay Joan, I will cooperate with you but you must understand that I'm emotional, especially when we talk about this."

"Pat just sit down so we can talk."

Pat would sit down and cry and Joan would always ask her, "Why are you crying? It isn't that bad Pat. Come on, straighten up."

Pat replied the same answer as guilt constantly took control over Pat. Hurting your love one portray a sense of mentally ignorance. The feeling of anxiety has taken its toll while Pat's behavior continued to stressed Joan, she began to feel pressured trying to exclude herself for Pat's problems but since she agreed to help, she tried to overlook her feelings and go along with the program. She really wanted to see Pat get better. The sessions began with Pat and the other battered women telling their stories of the reason their husbands abused them. While in session Pat began to tell her life story staring with her eyes wide open glancing at each lady. My baby, that sweet little infant kept crying and crying my shaking wasn't enough he would never shut up, the spanking got out of control and I began viciously hitting him, striking him every where trying to make him behave as my child grew older my vicious spankings turned into beating. The room fell quite as every one tuned into Pat horrible situation she became the center of attention, I  searched the woods for a prefect stick to keep in line swatting him in the head and everywhere with this stick, making sure I hadn't missed a spot covering his whole body with bruises, I constantly beat him until he passed out! Pat began to make her story more dramatic than it actually was, while the women were getting offended at what they were hearing.

Speaking out, "How could you, you terrible witch, one lady with jet black hair appearing out the darkness of her mental abuse, her  skin pale white tarnished in purple from the beating she'd suffered loudly expressing her self in anger,  You deserve to be beaten!"

"No one deserves to be beaten and that's why we're all here because everyone needs help, even you." said another.

One of the ladies asked Pat, "Is that why your husband beat you because you beat your son?"

"Yes, that's what I'm trying to explain to you ladies and that's why I'm so miserable because he felt he was paying me back."

"But I've never heard of such thing.  Are you sure that's why your husband beat you? Is that  an excuse, he probably had another woman?  Men have a tendency to get out of things " said a young blond haired woman.

Pat interrupted her by saying, "My husband would never cheat on me. I know the truth, I know what happened."

Pat began telling the rest of the story about what happened, "I know the truth and if you don't believe me then that's too bad."

After hearing each of the ladies' situation, the committee decided that everyone should be dealt with on their own emotional level.

Each one had a seriously abusive past which affected their state of mind in different ways. Although everyone was sensitive to abuse, some problems were more serious than others so the committee felt that everyone should be dealt with on their own level.

Joan spoke up about the coaching program. "Considering that Pat is my friend Pat, I'm familiar with the seriousness of her problem and her mental state."

The council didn't agree with this but Pat agreed, she was more than happy to have Joan help her with her mental state. Questions were raised, about the extent of their friendship and the extreme of Pat's abuse.

Joan replied, "Were starting from rock bottom, concentrating on getting her well."

Mrs. Harrison, the head of the committee, wasn't too happy with the agreement but she accepted this answer and moved on securing every one. As time went on Pat begin to grow angry about explaining her abusive past over and over again. Mrs. Harrison explained, speaking out! (yelling at Pat) "The only way to get it out of your system is to talk about it, put it out in the open, and it will clear from your mind."

Pat disagreed; this isn't helping me, explaining the same problem month after month. Maladjustment became a way of life for me, not wanting to talk of anything that reminded me of the past vehement mature of my husband. Wanting to excluded it from my mind and move on constantly repeating my self, left memories but Mrs. Harrison explained in order to live a normal life after leaving the shelter that there wouldn't be any more discussion on our past abusive problems, every one agreed day after day we discussed the same old ugly story until it was definitely out in the open.

This discussion wasn't relieving my problem, the need to be abused constantly crossed my mind wanting to feel the pain that had taken over my life an emptiness tremble my body while speaking, trying to explain this feeling, as the odd looks threaten my thoughts, Mrs. Harrison said, That's a normal feeling after being abused for several years, lots of women experience that same feeling. It never vanishes completely, but talking about it helps relieve some of the pressure this was a continuous explanation coming from Mrs. Harrison its meaningful for her to help the women move on with their lives.

Pat still didn't agree with this idea so she began crying at every meeting and not trying to help herself at all. Instead she spent her time looking for someone to lean on. Time after time Pat would do this until Joan was so fed up with her behavior that she decided she wasn't going to coach her anymore. Pat was really getting out of hand so Joan took her to the side and simply asked her, "Pat why are you acting like this? We are never going to get to the bottom of this."

She began shaking Pat. "Pat please! Stop acting like this, you're getting out of control and I can't handle it. I'm asking you Pat, please gain control of your self, stop acting out of control. You are making it worse for me and for yourself if you keep acting like this. They are going to put you out and then what will you do? How will you seek help then Pat?"

Pat agreed to cooperate in the meeting. She promised Joan that she wouldn't cry anymore and she didn't, instead she started complaining loudly, making sure everyone heard her. Pat started taking over the meetings, interrupting everyone. Mrs. Harrison could no longer handle Pat. She was furious with Pat's actions. She tried talking with Pat but Pat didn't want to listen. Pat felt that she had already explained everything and it hadn't worked. She thought it was all a lie and she felt this meeting wasn't going to help her at all and that no one wanted to listen to her. She thought that they felt she was losing her mind but she wasn't, the session just weren't working.

Mrs. Harrison politely asked her not to attend any more meetings until she resolved her problems. Pat felt that she had just as much rights as anyone to attend the meetings so they argued at length about this. Pat started complaining to Joan about Mrs. Harrison and her actions.

Joan told Pat, "You need to calm down and stop getting so

depressed. You are making matters worse for yourself and I'm warning you to shut up and listen to what they are saying because you're not the only one with a problem. Do you understand Pat? Your attitude stinks! Its doing more harm, so please cooperate with Mrs. Harrison and you'll be treated with respect. Pat continued to complain her unstable problem to Joan. You can't leave until you get help, so you might as well act right and be cooperative with Mrs. Harrison so she will treat you better. Pat, it isn't her, it's you."

Pat was very confused about the operation of the program growing angrier wondering why no one wanted to her problems. They were all trying to overcome the same type of abusive situation. After realizing that her problem was severe her anger flared even more, enraged by the sight of the women entering into the shelter with broken skin and bruised faces, Pat was till uncooperative.

Nine months had passed by and Pat was still living at the shelter with her problems. Women had come and gone, solving their problems and going on with their lives, but not Pat. Women had come and gone, solving their problems and continuing on, but not Pat helpless in her mental state became very vocal and a mess to deal with.

Thoughts ran through Joan's mind about Pat insanity her problems were real, "Bill beat her to long" her craziness settled in her strange behaviors but theirs still hope of her getting well. Joan resented telling Bill about his wife, about her abruptness and dissatisfaction, Pat was a serious problem and some way this had to be explained to Bill. Joan emotions began taking a course on her mind dealing with Pat was taking its toll and making Joan crazy, before long Joan would probably be sitting in the meetings as a client instead of a counselor nervous and as confused unsure about her mission of helping Pat overcome her problems-becoming attached wasn't healthy for Joan, refusing to leave Pat by herself, in her condition worsen from her complaining, Pat was soaking in misery. Devastated by her action Joan had no other choice, for depression settled in, angry and frustrated Joan cried for hours while leaving the shelter, it seemed to help Joan, she drove for hours trying to release the pressure of her unhappiness, before returning to her husband.

Joan needed to get away from Pat abiding by all rules the shelter required sticking to the plans of helping other women Joan had no other choice but to get away from Pat she could no longer handle her. Pat had been at he shelter for one year and six months and her behavior continued to worsen. Pat was getting worse and taking Joan with her in a downward spiral. Joan became uncomfortable finally grabbing enough nerves to discuss her problem with John.

While sitting in upward position staring at the television.

"John," I called out,

"Honey, what can I do?"

It's been one and a half years since Pat went in the shelter and it's not helping her. She's not getting better. She uses profanity when she can't get her way, and talks loudly her voice carries through out the room she's really obnoxious, out of control I can't stand it anymore, ( Joan anger increase the more she explained) it's putting me in a bad position. I've been helping women for so long but I just can't help her.

I'm really trying. What's next John?

If I never go back and she'll think I gave up on her then she will feel worse. All she does is cry and complain like she's not trying to help herself and I'm really tired, John. I just can't take anymore of this."

"Well, Joan, tell her that you'll call her from now on because your boss changed your working shift and you have to work at night and you won't get off until real late. Tell Mrs. Harrison that you won't be around for a while and ask her if she could get someone else to coach Pat. If things are as bad as you say they are I advise you not to go back there or you could be looking for help yourself."

The next meeting Joan did as John had advised her and she left Pat. Joan called Mrs. Harrison into the room for a private meeting to discuss Pat. She began saying to her, "I don't think it's a great idea if I coach Pat."

Mrs. Harrison interrupted, Oh! "I told you in the beginning that it wasn't a good idea but you insisted that you help her, since you two were friends. I can find someone else to coach her and maybe her attitude will change. Why don't you take some time off because it has been stressful for you. Dealing with Pat is like dealing with a lost lion! It's not an easy task."

Joan agreed! with what Mrs. Harrison was saying and did not go to the next meeting. Joan didn't bother to tell Pat about what she was doing. In fact, she didn't say anything to Pat, she just wanted to get away from her. Pat searched for Joan but she never came or called to say that she couldn't make it. Pat situation was known by everyone, refusing to tell Pat because of her emotional state. Worry settled in wondering where Joan had disappeared after never missing a meeting, sadden by own behavior of pushing Joan away, while considering only my self as my thoughts were erupting Joan didn't call, or notified me some friend (abandonment) disgruntled in my own thoughts staring looking through the doors while Mrs. Harrison appeared in the doorway with a brown hair green eyed woman smiling at me and explaining the situation of Joan to me assuring me she would take care of everything (frantic exploding) "Where is Joan? Viciously looking at Mrs. Harrison, is she okay? Did something happened to her? Is she sick? Maybe I'd better call her to check, what's going on Mr. Harrison!"

"That won't be necessary Pat. We'll take care of you, don't worry, Lisa replied.

"I'm not worried about you taking care of me, its Joan I'm worried about, she's my friend and... what are you implying, you'll take care of me?"

Emptiness crossed my mind , No longer wanting to be here the thought of relinquishment arouse, the shelter wasn't working! It probably didn't work for the other women, did they really leave problem free? pretending that they were healed. Staring at Lisa while thoughts rumbled through my mind of still suffering? Where did Joan go leaving me here alone with these crazy people?"

Everyone at the shelter seemed crazy to me, considering my self the only normal person that existed.  Pat sat at these meeting for six more months until her restless mind erupted hating her peers and coach staff. Desperately wanting to get away from here searching for a way out walking the halls trying to escape, but there was no way out!

Something wasn't quite right For Pat, her situation was getting worse day by day while missing her family,  The shelter became boring and uncomfortable my concentration was off as loneliness settled in trying to find a solution to my problem because this wasn't the answer the feeling of a waste grabbed my mind my conversation went unheard the food made my mind sicker the complaining took its toll on every one in the shelter.

"It just isn't working," relinquish ran across my mind daily wanting my husband my freedom looking for happiness comparing it to the abuse it was running nick to neck in my life the thoughts of returning back to my abusive life wore hard on my mind my husband not wanting to release his wicked ways (pacing the floor warping  my brain thin with cruel thoughts"

Bill had gone on with his life excluding his wicked ways letting the therapy cleanse him while seeking happiness. Speaking in abusive terms was dangerous for Bill refusing to deal with Pat unless she was better any manner that would bring abuse and alcohol back into his life. Still living in misery Pat called Joan to tell her about how she felt about the sessions with the women. How her problem was much too serious to handle in the open, around strangers.

Joan answered the phone  listening to Pat complain.  "Why do you think it's not working and what exactly do you expect to get out of this?  Therapy is a system to help you get over your abusive ways, maybe you should pay more attention it might help you! Joan spoke out strongly"

"I know that and it's not working, sitting and talking for months at a time and still  there's isn't a  solution, there's no way out."  Pat complained. "It's working for your family and they're not complaining so why are you?  tell me Pat why isn't it working for you? Why can't you get over this problem? At least give it one more try and if it doesn't work we'll try something else, okay Pat?"

"What else is there to try what will work? Joan, tell me is it another shelter?"

"You don't understand, Joan.

I need my husband. I need to go home and I've been here for two years my mental state continues to worsen, Joan. Please tell me something to release the anxiety of unwanted pressure while I'm in here these thoughts wont vanish away you must understand what I'm talking about, Joan how long will it take for my mind to be healed?"

Pat, "I don't know I'm a nurse and you need serious help, I'm trying help you so Please cooperate with me, okay, Pat?"

Pat and Joan had plenty of arguments at the shelter) Joan, "How do you face abuse? Have you ever been abused ? have you Joan? Just tell me, then I can see whether you can help me or if you really know what I'm going through."

"No, I have never been abused but I've been working with battered women for ten years and I do know what you are going through and you are not by yourself Pat."

"But how can you tell me what can and cannot work? Everyone is different."

"Well, I volunteer my time at people's homes and help them and you are no different. I'm trying to tell you that women come and go all the time but you have 75 percent chance to recover when you come in here. It isn't a grantee it doesn't happened right away some women recover and some don't, but you must admit to yourself that you went through a very long period of hard horrible abuse. Pat release your thoughts so you can continue on with your life, recover for yourself ! Your problem is more devastating, its stored deep into your brain, you created the problem and it takes time, You don't seem to understand the program, Pat.

Explaining your problem, constantly trying to help you, wasting my time when you don't appreciate it! Anger began to flair up in Joan's voice) that's all.  My husband is helping your husband, so let me help you, okay Pat?  Redirect your self, abuse is for the mental and the mental only, Pat, abuse isn't for you, listen to me! Love is what you want, not misery take the right road Pat stay away from the cycle of abuse!

"Well, Joan, where is my husband? I haven't seen him.  Don't you understand Pat,  Joan, did he give up on me?  My heart is hurting for him, please tell him to call me? Please, Joan."

Pat you need help! "I don't think you should see him,  get better before you see him and kill the negativity It isn't  good for you and Bill.  Constantly elucidating, Pat you need help! (agitated with lack of understanding)  running back will only make matters worse.  I've grown to love you like my own sister so let's get this over with, and stop thinking about your husband and get yourself together.  Please! Pat, do it for your family, change your attitude put some change in your life quit being selfish!

"Well, you're right, Joan.  I'll try give it another try then I'm excusing my self form here.

"It will work, just put forth some effort, consider not only your self but others. This problem can be resolved seeing you like this really hurts tormenting your self can be dreadful, abuse isn't fun, so please, let's give it another try at least a month while I search for something else,  I can't stand to see you like this and I don't want you to go through any more abuse.  So please, let's give it one more try, at least another month while I search for something else, okay? Does that sound good to you?

Pat felt bad for the way she had been treating Joan.  Joan was only trying to help her.  "I'll stay one more month.  I'll stay one more month. I'll see you later."

Pat and Joan hung up the phone.  Joan began looking searching  shelters to Pat satisfaction, to prove there's more to life than being abused.  However, Joan wasn't having any luck frustration took its tool as depression once again settled in,  Joan tried explaining to her husband about Pat and how she was feeling. The commitment she promised Pat. John nothing is working (as tears flowed)  Pat would rather go home and be abused than stay in a shelter. "She feels it isn't helping and that's because she's not listening to what going on. I'm afraid she's never going to get well. I really feel sorry for her, John, I really do."

"Well, Joan, why don't you try talking with someone at church to see if some of the women can help her. It seems to be working for Bill and Mike. They seem very happy and maybe it might work for her. Besides, how can you go wrong? At least you are trying to help and she must understand that or else she would be out on her own. She needs to understand a clean heart makes a clean mind."

"Yes, I agree with you, John. But sometimes it can be too clean and you get hurt in the process of purifying. I don't want to lose her friendship because she doesn't have anyone to lean on."

"But if she can't help herself then how can you help her? You can only do so much for her, don't worry so much, okay, honey?" Joan agreed to what John was saying. "If she doesn't get help Bill is not going to allow himself to be disruptive with abuse. He's trying to leave the problem behind him, the reason for receiving therapy is not to allow abuse to enter into your life ever again, he's serious! Pat's really messed up pretty bad and it takes time. Pat's has to understand the task to recovery isn't a joke and shouldn't be toiled with, make her understand what you are saying. Continue to coach her until you find someone else then give it a brake. Let the church help her before she completely loses it and blames you.

Joan thanked John for his words of wisdom. Joan began calling around to different ladies' houses, dialing and dialing for hours there has to be someone in the church could help. Finally reaching wife of the director of the men's abuse program. Joan left messages for almost a week when finally the woman called her back. "Hello! Is Joan in?"

"Hi, this is Joan. Who is this?"

"This is Cindy. You left a message about someone needing help."

"Oh, yes."

, Joan began telling Cindy about Pat and her situation and how Pat had been in a shelter for two years trying to get help but just wasn't working and she was getting very frustrated there.

"I was wondering if you can help her. We've tried everything but nothing seems to work. She cannot clear the word abuse out of her mind. It's so bad and I really feel for her. I've been trying to help her ever since but nothing is working." Joan continued to explain the problems that existed while the tears rolled down her deep brown face.

"Well, Joan, I'll have to call you back after I talk to my husband and see what he has to say about all this. Then maybe we can help her. If I can't help her then we'll find someone who can. I will let you know as soon as possible."

"Thanks, Cindy, I really appreciate this and thanks for returning my call."

"I will call back. He should be home within the next hour."

Joan hung up the phone. Three days later Cindy called Joan back and told her to bring Pat over to her house and she could stay with them until she got better.

"It shouldn't take long if Pat really wants to get well and everyone is willing to help her. I've talked to other women that had the same problem she has and they seem to be doing quite well using our program. I'm quite sure it will work for her too. I think she will be pleased afterward. So go pick her up and give me a call. I'll be here waiting for her and I'll set up a group of people that could come over and help or maybe talk to Pat about her problems. She can probably express herself a little more here than she could in the shelter because sometimes shelters can be too much when you are around people you don't know. We will give her a try and see how it works and go from there. It doesn't matter how long she stays. She can stay as long as she wants, until she feels she's ready to go back to her husband. No one is going to pressure her, it will be on her own terms. Is that okay with you, Joan?"

"Oh, yes, that's perfectly fine with me as long as she gets well and finds what she needs. I'm sure she'll be happy, she can't seem to stop complaining about the shelter and she'll be very, very happy. Thank you a lot, Cindy, it's greatly appreciated." .

"Well good bye Joan".

"I'll probably see you tomorrow."

"That's fine, Joan, whenever you're ready."

Joan was overwhelmed by Cindy's news. After she hung up the phone she started jumping around and singing, happy that Pat would finally have help. Maybe this time she would get a little better. What had Cindy said? She said that they would help Pat. Finally, finally help is on the way for Pat.

"You seem very happy, Joan." John said as he walked into the room.

"Cindy is going to help Pat and she can stay at their house and she found other women who will also talk to Pat and help her.".

That's great, honey! I knew you would find a solution.

The next day Joan called Pat. A month had passed and Pat wasn't there. Joan kept calling because she wanted to tell Pat the good news she had found a new place for her. But Pat wasn't there, she was nowhere to be found and there was no way Joan could find Pat. Joan kept calling. Finally the people at the shelter told her that Pat had left three days ago because she had not been happy there. She took all her stuff and left and didn't call or come back. Joan started feeling sad, wondering thinking letting her mind go into shock about where she went wrong. She told Pat that it would be a month and she agreed to wait, but she left.

"Oh Pat, where did you go and how come you didn't call me to say you were leaving? Pat, where are you? Maybe I failed you. I tried to help, I know you weren't happy but everything takes time. I tried, I tried so hard to help you all the way, where could you have gone? Didn't you believe me? Oh God!" Joan cried out, "I only tried to help."

John came into the room. "John, Pat needs help but she left the shelter and didn't say where she was going. I hope she didn't go home because Bill doesn't want her ,there."

"She didn't go home because Bill would have called me by

now. Who knows where she is? Maybe she went home to her mother. She probably needed her family, she was obviously feeling really bad from the way you described her conversation over the phone."

As John and Joan were discussing this horrible turn of events, there was a knock on the door. The knock got a louder and more insistent. Joan ran to the door and opened it right away not knowing who was there. She opened the door and there was Pat standing with her brown face cursed with a muddle look of confusion, tears rolled down her face. Joan grabbed her hugging her telling her how worried she was becoming at Pat disappearance, you should have left a note or told someone, I told you it would be a month, why did you leave?"

"Let her in, Joan." John said.

"Oh, please, come in here right now so we can talk. I have good news to tell you but first please tell us why you left ?"

"Can I sit down, Joan?"

"Oh, yes! Please, sit down. I'm sorry, would you like something to drink?"

"No, thank you."

"Are you okay, Pat? Where have you been, what happened, how come you didn't wait for me to call? How come you just left like that? What's the matter with you?"

Joan was so overly excited that she didn't give Pat time to answer her questions. Pat just looked at Joan unable to answer the questions Joan was asking her. Joan never gave her a chance to talk.

"So tell me, Pat, don't be afraid to tell me where you went. Well, start talking."

"Well, Joan, I got confused and felt that I let myself down. I knew that you were trying to help and I took it out on you, then I started feeling even worse. I didn't think you were going to call back after our conversation. You seemed to be upset at me. Joan looked at Pat surprised. Well, that's the impression that I received but it's not your problem and you shouldn't have to deal with me like that. So I came over to apologize to you and I'm really sorry about the way I acted. I went home to see my husband and when I got to the steps, I stopped. I just couldn't go in there. My conscience wouldn't allow me. I couldn't face my husband still feeling the way I feel. I'm depressed and harmful and I still lose my self control."

She began to cry. He got up and went into another room, he didn't want to see her break down anymore. Joan touched Pat.

"Oh! I'm glad you didn't go in and he didn't see you. It would have torn him apart to see you like this, he's a changed man. Oh! Thank God you came here, Pat. Everything's going to be all right, I told you Pat that I will help you and that's what I've done. I found someone who can help you, but you've got to try to help yourself."

Joan began telling Pat all about Cindy and how they were going to help her get through her crisis. "You can stay with Cindy and her husband and they will take care of the rest."

Pat was excited about this news, "Finally, real help has come along, finally. Joan, are you telling me the truth?"

"Yes, Pat, but I must tell you that they go to church and you will probably have to go with them and if you don't feel comfortable just tell them."

"Well, I've never been to church before so how will they act if they find out? Will they still help me?"

"Of course they will."

"But what if I don't want to go to their church, then what?"

"Don't worry about that right now. Let's get this demon out of you first and get you back to normal. Just think about the help that you need then you can always go to church or anywhere you want to go. But you can't go anywhere without functioning properly and it's important for you to act right. They are very nice people and don't mess it up or you will be sorry because there's nothing I can do after this. I'm really trying to help you, Pat."

"Joan, I really appreciate what you are doing for me. If it wasn't for you I would probably be at home still being abused. You and John have really stuck your necks out for us and we appreciate that, we really do. No matter what happens I will always be grateful for it."

Joan went to call Cindy.

"Hi, Cindy, I called to tell you that Pat is here. When would you like to come and pick her up?"

"How long has she been there?" Cindy asked.

"She just came. I've been looking for her for three days, can you please come and get her."

"I'll be right over to get her, Joan." Cindy responded as she hung up the phone. Pat was shocked at how fast they arrived at Joan's house, before she could take another sip of her coffee they were knocking.

"Hi, Pat. I'm Cindy

Cindy spoke loudly, as she stood with her long jet black hair and fair skin smiling at Pat and this is my husband Tom greeting as he reached out and grabbed my hand with his hair shaven like a military cut dressed in evening attire. My thoughts began to release with trembling in my voice at these strangers so eager to help.

"Before I go with you, will this really work?" Pat asked.

"Oh, yes this will work. It's worked for lots of others and I'm sure it will work for you. So let's go get started like right away, We have a lot to discuss."

The thought of talking about my past, continuing to explain my horrible past ran dangerously through my mind, staring wildly at Cindy and her husband Tom with the expression of talking wont help me at all.

Little did Pat know Cindy didn't want to hear about it either, and it was never brought up it wasn't what she had in mind the topic of abuse wasn't a very good subject to discuss.

When they arrived Cindy's house Pat was amazed at how beautiful the house was after spending time in the shelter where the walls were unpainted and every room had the same look, astonished that they let a stranger come into their house the snow white furniture was neatly in place, a smell of richness poured through the air , examining my surrounding it seems like a very pleasant and comfortable place to stay. Cindy and her husband were very nice to Pat they treated her like family, a beautiful couple.

Cindy invited Pat to extend her stay until she heals or get over her problems Pat agreed. Informing her not to speak on her damaging abusive situation, Cindy, wasn't to fond of the horrible subject. She constantly remind Pat of this rule every time it was brought up, and Pat agreed. At times Pat tended to go back on her promises, Cindy, speaking out, "How am I'm supposed to keep quite? We are supposed to talk about it, the only way to get over abuse is by putting it out in the open." Although Pat did not understand the reason for not discussing abuse she went along with it.

After Pat slept and rested for a couple days, Cindy felt it was time to start the sessions. Cindy briefly explained the condition of the meeting. Pat agreed to go along with this to see if it would work. Feeling uneasy, the shelter condition for hours and hours taking about every ones abusive problems only to make things worse. Oh boy, I thought, here I go again!

That evening several ladies came over to Cindy's house to meet Pat and welcome her to a new world. One without any problems, at least problems not as severe as Pat's.

these women were dressed in business attire set aside form Pat's every day attire hugging and speaking comforting words to make Pat feel at home as they sat around drinking tea and having cake in Cindy finest China then they began their session by singing songs it appeared as if they were having a very good time while my face showed anger of disappointment but sang loudly, staring at them wondering if they knew the problems at hand. Forgetting the agreement between me and Cindy about leaving my abusive problems in the gutter. I stood up in the middle of the floor yelling ladies, ladies, I have a problem and we are supposed to be solving it. What's going on here? Don't you women understand?"

The women stopped and looked at me and one woman said with her blonde hair matching her tan suite speaking over every one a s if to explode! "You are so right, Mrs. English, but what problem do you have?"

Someone else said, "You look fine to me." A woman dressed in a blue and purple flowered suite said, "Oh, I know what your problem is."

"Finally, "someone knows my problem."

"Ladies, we are so rude and we must apologize to Pat."

"But why? We didn't do any thing!" the ladies murmured.

"She doesn't know the songs!"

"We are so sorry, Mrs. English."

They began teaching her the songs that they were singing. Pat didn't know what was happening when Cindy explained it to her. She didn't quite get what Cindy was saying even though she was plainly telling her what was going on. But Pat wasn't listening, she was too busy thinking about her problem and not about what Cindy was saying. Pat decided to join in on the songs but she didn't know how to sing. The ladies never complained about the way she sounded so she went right along and sang "Oh how I love my husband and my child." She liked the way it sounded, it pleased her and it brought back memories of when her husband first loved her.

For months this laughing and singing went on evening after evening. They never once talked about abuse and Pat never brought it up. She felt like a new person all over again. Her life was beginning to change around, it was a new direction for her, one she was able to handle. She no longer complained, everything was great and she was happy for the first time in a long time. Being around other people made her even more happy, she was able to accept this way of life without any doubts or worries. Pat was finally able to contain herself and she thought about living like this for the rest of her life. These people made her really happy.

Pat had a chance to go shopping, something she had not done in a long time. She shopped for clothes and did other things that Pat had forgotten about. She was finally coming back to life, waking up out of the dark, able to see the light. Pat was comfortable where she was; it felt like home but a little better than home. Cindy and her husband Tom were very nice to Pat and treated her like they had known her for a long time. Their house was filled with so much love and their conversations were very sweet and warm. Their house was very peaceful and it didn't take Pat long to get used to living in a peaceful environment. It took away the thought of abuse. By not being in contact with it at all she became happy. She forgot why she was there and she also forgot she had a husband and a family to go home to. She was happy, something she hadn't felt in a long time. She forgot where she came from, she was so overwhelmed with happiness.

Pat thought to herself, "This is the ticket and the ticket is to not think about my problem. I must forget it ever existed and just go on. But this is impossible, how did they do this and who thought of this? Is there really a God? I wonder, all the time I have been praying for help, is this the help that God sent to me? After praying my heart out help finally came. It took a while but it is here and I'm glad I don't have to cry anymore. He heard my cry, someone did and it works, it's finally over and now I can go home happy again like once before."

Bill and Mike were back at home peacefully sharing their thoughts. They were having a good time for the first time in years. It had been a long time since they were happy, knowing that nothing could take their happiness away.

Bill then said to Mike, "I wonder how Pat is doing, if she is coming along? I hope she's okay. I've haven't spoken with her in a while just wanting her to get well so her mental health is important. We've been having such a good time we almost forgot about her. I'm often concern about her where presents, She was in the shelter the last time we checked and she wasn't doing too well. She was upset about the way things were turning out and I just couldn't talk to her because she was upsetting me. Trying to prevent drinking."

"Well, Dad, we have no way of knowing, but I hope she's as happy as we are. I hope she's feeling great and like a new person. She didn't get the same treatment that we received so she might come out differently but whatever way she comes out I hope she's OK and not crazy like the way she was when she went in. I'm sure whoever is taking care of her is making sure she's getting what she deserves. Joan will make sure that she gets the treatment that she needs. Joan seems to really care about her. I'm glad Joan decided to help because Pat was losing her mind, she'll be happy to hear from us. We'll call her later."

Bill was grateful for the way Joan took care of Pat and made sure she was getting the right treatment. When Pat wasn't happy then Joan found another way to help her without complaining. Her husband John took care of Bill and Mike, they promised to help them and they did. John and Joan did all they could to satisfy the English family. Bill decided to call Joan to find out where Pat was and to see if she was okay and if she needed anything.

"Hello?"

"Hi Joan, this is Bill."

"Hi Bill, you sound great. How are you and Mike doing?"

"We're both okay, thanks. I called to see how Pat was coming along. Where is she? I haven't seen or heard from her, I hope she's okay."

"Pat's fine and doing great. She's well taken care of but I think she needs a little more time just to make sure she won't go back into that destructive state of mind. I'll call you when she's ready to come home. Is that okay, Bill?"

"Sure thing, Joan. I'll be waiting for your call."

"So everything is all right?" Joan inquired.

"Everything is wonderful, just wonderful, and I'll give you a call. I know you want to see your wife and I know you miss her very much. I will tell her that you love her and you are waiting for her to get well soon."

"Great. Thanks Joan." Then they hung up.

Joan hadn't talked to Pat since she went to Cindy's house. Joan really didn't know how Pat was doing because she never called to even see if Pat was still there. As long as Joan didn't have to deal with her she left all the problems up to Cindy. She felt that Cindy could handle her better interfering would just add to the problem Cindy was doing with Pat. "I guess I'd better call Pat to see what's going on before Bill calls back and asks more questions."

"Hi, is Cindy there?"

"No, is this Pat, who is this?"

"Hi Pat, this is Joan."

"Oh, hi Joan. I haven't spoken with you for awhile. I forgot what you sounded like. So what's new, Joan? Why are you calling now?"

Joan felt like swallowing her tongue at the sound of Pat's voice, she could tell Pat was upset that she hadn't called to say hi. "So how have you been Pat?"

"Great. Coming along just fine."

"That's what I thought. Are you ready to go home now and see your family?"

"Oh, my family! You mean my husband Bill and my beautiful son Mike.

Where are they?"

"They're at home and they were wondering about you."

"Oh really? I thought Bill wasn't ready to talk to me, has he changed his

mind?"

"He was just wondering how you were coming along and if you were getting well."

"So when did he call?"

"He called today and I called you right after he hung up the phone. Maybe you can give him a call and at least say hi or let him know how you are doing."

"I would love to call my family and at least talk to them and tell them how happy I am."

"Okay, Pat, then you should call them. I'm quite sure that there wouldn't be any problem, he wants to talk to you anyway."

"Joan, thanks so much for everything you have done for me. I want you to know that no matter what happens I'll always appreciate what you have done for me."

"Okay, Pat, I understand. Well, I have to go now. John just

came in. You call your husband and let him know that everything's okay, all right Pat? I'll talk to you later. Good bye." They
hung up the phone.

Pat decided to wait until Cindy came home before she called
Bill, to make sure that it was okay with her. Confused-focusing
on the previous problem only Cindy had answers to Pats problems unable to sort them out for herself, so Pat thought. Cindy
arrived home a little late and Pat was getting worried pacing the
floor while glancing at the yellow house across the way maybe
Joan was unsure of Bill conversation. As Cindy walked in Pat
was sitting on the sofa and looking as if she saw a ghost.

"What's the matter Pat, are you okay?"

"Do you think I should call my husband?"

"Why? Where in the world did this come from? I haven't
heard you talk about your husband since you've been here, who
told you to call your husband?"

"Well, Joan called today and she said my husband was worried about me, so she thought it would be best if I called him to
let him know how I was doing. Then she asked me if I was ready
to go back."

"Well, I guess we need to talk. Are you happy? Do you feel
comfortable? What do you think about when you are by yourself?
What are your thoughts? The reason I ask, reassuring your self
of returning home, you have to be ready. Do you think that you
could handle talking to your husband?"

"I feel really great, as happy as I can be. I've never been this
happy before but I don't know, I'm not to sure about talking to
him. His reaction to me may be different and I don't want this
wonderful feeling to change. When I'm by myself all think about
is how wonderful life is and how I want it to remain this way."

"You are happy, do you think your ready to commit yourself
all over again and start a new life?"

*"What do you mean, what are you getting at Cindy?"*

"Just answer yes or no, do you think you are ready to commit
yourself to church? Because if you are then you are ready to see
your husband. If not I advise you not to call or even bother him

until you are sure you are ready and that's only my opinion. You have to decide for yourself, no one can tell you what you can and cannot do, so think about it. I personally don't think you're ready. It wouldn't be questioned about him take some time and think about it real hard the situation you left Bill viciously beating and beating-the secondary abuse being toiled locked in a shell think Pat, just think! Real hard then ask your self that question exam your life for what its worth. You were pretty messed up, so think about it real hard. I'll cancel the meeting for tonight so you can have plenty of time. I want you to be happy, very happy and if going back makes you happy then I'm with you all the way. I don't know why Joan called to talk to you about your husband without informing me first, She was supposed to call and talk to me and now you're confused about what to do. If you were ready to go back you wouldn't be confused, but you are really confused about what to do. I need to go over to Joan's house and have a talk with her."

Cindy called the ladies and canceled the meeting and explained to them about Pat's situation. The very next day Cindy went over to Joan's house to talk about Pat's situation. She was very upset at Joan and had to calm herself down before knocking on the door.

John opened the door. "Oh, Cindy, what are you doing here? Is every thing okay?" He spoke as if he knew why she was there.

"Is Joan here?"

"Yes come in."

"Hi Cindy," Joan called out, "how are you?

"Is everything all right? How's Pat?" John asked.

"She's great, at least she was when I left. Thanks, John, for asking,.

"What brings you here?" Joan asked as she entered the room.

"Well, we should talk about Pat."

"Is everything all right with her? Sit down, Cindy, you look pretty serious about this." They all sat down to hear what Cindy had to say.

"I came over here because you asked me to help you with Pat

and that's what I'm doing. But when you called you startled her and we have not gotten to the point of sending her back to her family. She's still going through therapy with us. What exactly are you trying to do? Do you want us to help her or not? You can't distract her like this and confuse her. Now she's sitting at home wondering what to do about all this. If you had any questions you should have called and talked to me before you said anything to her. I'm the director of this program and you know you weren't supposed to call, no matter how close you were to her. Now she is all mixed up. She's probably sitting at home crying. I'm angry at you, Joan, because now we have to start all over again. She's been through a lot and I guess you would know that because you are her friend. All I'm asking is that you don't do anything to mix her up. Call me first if you have any questions about whether or not she needs to talk to her husband. I'll let you know if the time is right or else we can't help her. She's pretty hard to deal with, Joan. We're doing the best we can for her and it has been working. In the meantime, please inform me of any questions and I will let you know what's going on with Pat."

"Okay Cindy, we had no clue it was this serious or I wouldn't have talked to her. Pat days were number as Joan express her thoughts to Cindy, she's been at your house for almost a year. Forgive me for interrupting her husband asked about her and that's the only reason why I called just checking to see if every thing was okay, maybe you should touch basis with me on her condition it would help. Cindy thanks for coming by and letting us know how you felt it helps us respond to Bill if he calls again."

"She's just not ready yet. I'll alert you when she's ready." Cindy explained.

"Okay, that's fine with us, right, John?"

"Sure, I don't have anything to say about it." John replied.

Cindy left their house feeling a little better. Knowing that Joan would not interfere again. When she returned home the ladies' had already started the meeting. As she approached they were talking about family.

"What about family? What's going on in here?" Cindy asked

worriedly.

One of the ladies said, "Well, we were getting to the point of discussing our family life. Pat wanted to know if we had a family, husbands and children. We were going to tell her how wonderful it is, how glorious it is to have a loving family. Pat seem to be confused about how to love her family and she wanted to know how we felt, so we told her all we knew."

"Yes, the focus of family must be love. It's has to be a gift from your heart, something you want to treasure and respect because once the family structure breaks up that's it. Putting forth effort keeps family value together when tow are involved, its more like working together like a job team work, relates more to a perfect family as Susan continued to express looking straight at Pat without an blink or smile getting straight to the point of family life other wise there wont be any special love to cherish keeping them close to your heart will allow happiness.

All the ladies agreed shaking their heads in response to Susan. They began to singing and laughing Pat loneliness settled in taking its course regretting every moment of the loss of love something that gradually dissolved away. The feeling of guilt cursed knowing that when these ladies left that they were going home to their loving families. Not wanting to return to her empty room where she would cry all alone pat wanted love.

Pat felt miserable wanting to sing or laugh anymore. One of the ladies noticed Pat wasn't singing or laughing and she asked, "Is every thing okay, Pat?"

"Yes, everything is fine, thank you."

"Then why the mournful look? You look so pale, are you really okay, Pat? We're here to talk if you need to."

Pat just looked around the room and noticed that all the women were staring at her. She jump up and ran to her room leaving an echo behind. She felt ashamed in front of her new friends. Cindy knew what was going on. Ever since Joan had called, Pat had been sad and confused about going back home.

"Maybe it's time for her to go back to her husband, but somehow I know she's not ready. Look at her, if she was ready she would be happy. He doesn't want her back until she has taken care of herself and is ready to commit herself to church like he did. Everyone knows this, even Joan. That's why I can't understand why she called and told Pat about her husband wanting to see her, she's just not ready." Cindy explained to the women.

"Have you talked to her about this, about her husband in church?" They asked.

"No, we haven't gotten to that point yet. Her husband really wants her to be ready to come home. He doesn't want the same lady, he wants her to be a new wife. I'm trying to teach her how to be that new wife."

While the ladies were talking, Pat was standing out in the hall listened to every word. She was shocked at what she heard. She couldn't believe what she was hearing.

"So they do know about my situation. How come they didn't say anything about it? If he knows where I am, how come he called Joan instead of me? Why would he join a church and say those things to people he didn't know? They know more about our relationship and what's going than I do."

Pat went back into the room where the ladies were and she apologized to them for the way she ran out and asked for their forgiveness. The ladies said nothing, they just hugged her and told her how much they loved her. She felt was like a sister to them. Even though she really didn't understand what was going on they forgave her and still wanted to help her so she could go back to her husband. One of the ladies suggested that she go to church with them and she agreed, thinking that if her husband was going to this church like they said then she would get a chance to see him. "But what if he doesn't want to see me? What will I do then? Will they still help me. . .is this just for him?"

Pat kept these doubts and questions to herself. "Why is Cindy teaching me how to love my husband? I know how. Did Bill tell her to teach me about that?"

Pat was tired, she was tired of talking and thinking. Cindy was also tired, it was a long hard day for her and she didn't want to continue this session so she said, "I'm going to bed."

Suddenly Pat was left with the ladies, "Well, Pat, we hope that you will be okay because we're kind of exhausted, too. It's been a long day for all of us." The ladies got up, gathered their things and left Pat sitting alone.

Pat sat in the room by herself thinking how had she messed everything up and how she had upset Cindy and the rest of the ladies. She could no longer contain herself. She started crying and blaming herself for everything that ever happened. "If only Joan had not called. I was doing just fine and now I'm getting depressed again, everything is coming back to reality and I just wish that Joan had not of called."

Pat started pacing the room and worrying about what Bill might think if he didn't like the way she looked. "I need some air. Maybe I'll go for a walk."

Pat left the house and went for a walk while Cindy and Tom slept. As she was walking, she saw a bar and decided uncharacteristically, to stop in and have a drink. Pat asked the bartender for something strong and he gave her scotch straight up. She spit it out, "Not that strong."

So he took it back and gave her some wine. She took two big swallows and it was all gone. "Boy! That went fast. Give me another one of those."

The more she drank, the more the pain of her life eased. Pat didn't know anyone in the bar but she kept looking around as if she was waiting for someone. The bartender began to feel sorry for her, she looked so lost so he introduced himself. "Hi, there my name is Jim. I've never seen you around here before. Are you new in town?"

"No." responding taking a long drink form my glass.

"Well, I've been working here for a long time and I know who comes in here.

You're not a normal customer what's your name?"

"Pat." Not answering looking up from my drink.

*"Well, Pat, you're drinking pretty heavily tonight. Is there a problem?"*

No, why would there be a problem?"

What are you doing tonight after you leave here? I'm free, would you like to do something?"

"Look Jim, I don't know you and I'm going back home if that's okay with you. I just came in for a drink."

"Are you going home to your husband or to sleep your life away by yourself? I know how to have fun and you should come along with me and have yourself a ball." Jim said having no idea that this was Bill's wife.

All Pat could do was drink and laugh. "I'm not interested in you, Jim, but thanks anyway. I'm married and I love my husband very much."

"If you ever get tired of your boring husband give me a call and we can make a night of it. You won't be sorry, I promise you, you will come back for more."

"I really don't know, Jim."

"We'll have to talk about it later. Would you like to go out for dinner with me? I want to get to know you before anyone else gets to you."

"Please! Jim, may I have my drink in peace please!" Pat cried.

"Okay but will you let me know when you are ready? I'm always here?"

"I will. Now leave me alone. Please!"

Jim walked off and went to serve other customers. Pat continued to drink until she fell off the bar stool. Embarrassed, she left the bar and stumbled back to Cindy's house.        The next day, a Saturday, Pat hung over slept until 2:00 p.m.. Cindy finally came into the room. "Pat, are you awake? Are you okay? It's time to go shopping. Did you forget what we were doing to day?

Tomorrow is your big day to meet some very nice people." Feeling terrible Pat didn't say a word, she just turned over. Cindy walked up to her bed, "Pat, are you okay? I've never seen you sleep like this. Did you stay up and worry about Bill? He's okay. He is doing just fine, you don't have to worry. We will get you back as soon as "possible, okay?"

"Cindy, I hear you but I'm really tired and I want to sleep. Can we cancel it until tomorrow?"

"Sure, if you don't want to go you don't have to, but I'm going. It will be a lot of fun."

"Maybe next time."

Cindy left and went to meet the other ladies at the mall while Pat slept. When Cindy returned, Pat's hangover was so bad she couldn't even turn her head and look to see what Cindy had bought. Every time she tried to lift her head it felt worse than when Bill would hit her. She could take that type of pain but not this kind.

"Pat, are you still sleeping?" Cindy asked. "It's 7:00 p.m. and I've been gone all day. Do you want some food? Are you okay, Pat?"

"Yes, I'm okay Cindy. What time did you say it was?"

"7:00 p.m." Cindy answered concerned.

Pat jumped up thinking about the bar and Jim. "Oh, I have to take a shower and fast!"

***"Why, are you going somewhere?"***

"Oh, no. It's just that it's almost dinnertime and I have a headache from yesterday's meeting." As Pat went to take a shower. she began to plan how she would get back to the bar. After her shower Pat felt slightly better and joined Cindy and Tom for dinner. Cindy gave Pat lots of Sprite and aspirin since she had a headache. Pat began feeling good all over again. "Well, dinner was good Cindy, but I have to go back into my room. I'm really tired".

As Pat walked back into her room Tom said to Cindy, "Is everything all right? She doesn't seem too well."

"I told you about what happened last night. She hasn't been the same since. Maybe she's trying to get over the fact that she'll eventually have to face her husband. She's probably thinking about how she's going to act. She's not ready to go to church yet so I won't push her. Whenever she's ready then we can go. I'm going anyway. Pat can stay here and get herself together so when she leaves us she won't have to come back and we can help someone else."

Cindy and Tom stayed up talking half the night. Pat sat by the door listening and waiting for them to go to sleep so she could sneak out to the bar. The house was finally quiet and Pat walked into the kitchen to make sure that Cindy and Tom were asleep. Pat turned on her radio in her room walked down the stairs and left.

Pat sat down at the bar and Jim asked, "What would you like today? It's on me. Was it wine you were drinking?"

"Yes, but it made me sick so I'll try something else."

"Okay Pat. Here, try this."

He gave her Margarita on the rocks and she liked it so he gave her another one and told her to drink it slow and she wouldn't get so sick. Pat stayed at the bar until it closed and Jim didn't bother her until it was time to go. "I guess you are coming home with me, Pat. Everyone else has gone home and you are still here. Are you waiting for me?"

***"No. Can I please have another drink?"***

"It's after 2:00 in the morning. What will your husband think about you staying out late like this?"

"Oh, he doesn't mind. He wants me to go out and have fun. That's what I'm doing having fun like I never had it before."

"Well, since you're having fun I'll give you another drink but this is your last one, then you have to go home before you get me into trouble."

"Okay Jim. I knew you would understand, that's why I came back."

"Well drink up so I can go home."

Pat drank her Margarita and stumbled out the door. Jim ran after her, "Do you want me to walk you home? It's dark out here."

"No, I'll be fine, thank you Jim."

Shaking his head, Jim watched her as she stumbled home . Pat  sang the songs that the women had taught her, laughing at herself.  Pat was having a good time and talking to herself, "Didn't know you could feel so good drinking. I should do this all the time. Bill drinks so why can't I? Why should he have all the fun and leave me out? There's nothing wrong with drinking, it makes you feel really good."

Pat didn't know that this could make people feel really evil and free to do things they wouldn't normally do, but this was something Pat had to experience for herself. Pat stumbled into the house, trying not to wake up anyone. If they found out that she had been out drinking they would not help her anymore. Pat went straight to bed and slept the whole day. Cindy tried waking her up before she and her husband went to church but it was no use. Later they went with some friends to dinner returning home very late. Pat never woke up until it was time to go back to the bar.

Week after week this went on without any questions. Pat pretended that nothing was going on. She continued to go to the meetings as if she was trying to get better. In reality she was getting worse and didn't know it. She thought the alcohol was making her feel better but it was making her forget what she was doing. The ladies planned another trip to the mall with Pat. They really wanted to take her to church to meet other people. Pat wasn't really ready to meet anyone, especially church members, but she agreed to go anyway. The session continued as usual. When it was over and Cindy went to bed, Pat once again went to the bar to have a drink.

Once again she got really drunk and she stumbled right into bed and slept as if there were no tomorrow. The next morning she couldn't get up. Cindy forced her out of bed, grabbing her and pulling her.

"Pat. get up. You're going with us. You are not getting out of this, Pat so get up."

Pat got up and took a long shower, not wanting to go anywhere. Cindy and the ladies patiently waited for her as she slowly got ready. As the hotness of the water ran over my body not considering the time at the bar my thoughts were in a glass of wind until Cindy finally knocked on the bathroom door.

***"Open the door Pat!"***

"I'm coming, I'll be out in a minute!" Cindy sat back down as Pat finally came out of the bathroom and rushed and got dressed. Finally they were ready to go but Pat wasn't feeling up to it. She had a hangover from the night before and her head spinning round and round, full of alcohol.

"What's going on with you, Pat?" one of the ladies asked, "You've change a whole lot since that talk we had not too long ago."

Pat didn't feel like answering any questions. She was very tired and didn't want to be bothered. She snapped and growled at everything the ladies said. When they got to the mall she was mean, cruel and couldn't find a dress although she tried on plenty. This wasn't a very good day for Pat. She shouted at the ladies, not wanting to buy anything. It became a real problem for Cindy and her friends. Cindy was getting very angry at Pat, but Pat didn't care anymore, all she wanted to do was go back to the bar and drink some more. When they arrived home Pat went straight to bed without saying a word to anyone.

Cindy and the ladies began talking about how Pat was doing. One of the ladies said, "I think we shouldn't brought up the fact she had to go to church."

"I don't think that's it, I think its her husband. She wants to see him".

"Well, she was going to see him on Sunday when she goes to church."

"I don't know! She's acting quite strange. I've never seen her get this way. I know it's not that bad, but if she doesn't straighten up she will never see her husband." Cindy said concerned.

*"Then what will you do with her, Cindy?"*

"I don't know. I'll have to ask Tom. He always has the answers, but we won't be stuck with her and we won't throw her out on the street. I guess I will have to give her back to Joan and let Joan deal with her."

"That's a great thought."

Cindy said, "Joan should be here. She should be here helping since she messed everything up. If it wasn't for her calling it wouldn't have gotten this way. If things don't get better Joan will have to come over and give Pat some advice on what she should do. Things were going great until Joan decided to talk to Pat. Now I don't know what to do. Pat was doing good, I hope she continues to do good because I want to see her back home with her family. Her husband seems to be doing great and very happy. I've really grown to like Pat a lot, but her attitude has changed dramatically and I can't deal with it anymore."

"Then may be you should have a talk with her and find out what's going on. But be careful because she'll want to pull that crying act on you and start looking very sad then make you feel really guilty about what you are saying to her." One woman responded.

"Well, I'm tired. It's been another one of those long days and I can't take anymore. I'm going to have some lemonade and then go to sleep. Maybe tomorrow will be a better day, a new day. I'll have to pray for her tonight like I've never prayed before."

The ladies gave Cindy a hug and told her goodnight. Everyone was tired. Pat had worn everyone out by the way she was acting. The ladies went home and Cindy went to bed concerned about Pat. Cindy's night was sleepless as she tossed and turned all night. She got up and went into Pat's room. Pat was sound asleep. Cindy wanted to talk. She couldn't sleep until she told Pat what was on her mind but she didn't want to wake up Pat. Worried Cindy stayed up all night drinking lemonade, hoping Pat would get up and go to the bathroom. But Pat didn't move, not for Cindy or anyone else.

Pat began at a new therapy session at Cindy's with a different group, something she hadn't expected but Joan had decided to stay completely away from Pat. Joan didn't want to be embarrassed so she stayed away, not even calling Pat to see how she was doing. Joan left it up to Cindy to deal with Pat; she had never told Cindy about Pat's attitude or her bad manners. Joan completely deserted Pat as if she had never known her. The ladies were so nice to Pat that she didn't even think about Joan. They treated her like she belonged on the earth and they gave Pat plenty of love.

Pat completely forgot about her problems she was happy until the day that Joan called. When she called Pat's behavior got much worse than it had been before. Pat was getting along with everyone but Joan's call startled Pat and she suddenly became something like a beast in front of the nice ladies. They didn't know what happened and why Pat was acting like she was, they didn't know what to do or how to handle this problem. They tried to calm her down but she would calm down only briefly. Then she would get way out of control and begin to cry all the time. Cindy didn't know how to handle Pat and became afraid of her. Pat was getting worse secretly drinking something Cindy had no knowledge of. Uncontrollable, Cindy tried to help by telling her that me husband would love me no matter what the abusive ways vanished away. Pat tried explaining to Cindy the problems were her own making, she was the cause of the abuse that arose in her family she was in control of the change. Cindy agreed.

Cindy (my lips openly spoke) your kindness was appreciated but it made the situation worse. Blaming Cindy for all faults, stating that she needed to recognize what happened and by her failing to do so, the situation had gotten much worse than they knew. If Bill had called Pat instead of Joan, maybe things would be different, the solution is still unknown of my problem.

Cindy constantly explained to Pat all she needed to do was forget about what happened and go on being happy. As long as she meditated and focused on good things she would forget all about the problems that she previously experienced. Pat cried out that she needed help really bad, but Cindy didn't know what to say. She tried to make Pat forget but she couldn't, she couldn't make Pat leave her sorrowful state of mind. Cindy was teaching Pat how to go on with her life and it had worked for a short period of time. It would have continued to work but Joan called and brought the memories of her old life right back. With those memories Pat regressed back to her old frame of mind. Cindy tried explaining this to Pat to make her understand that she was helping her and it was working.

Pat cried out, "That's it, it won't go away. Every time someone brings it up it comes right back to reality but much worse. What is it that I have to do to get over this horrible thing that keeps invading my mind? Why can't I just let go?"

"Pat, I don't have answers for your questions. I tried to do what I thought was best in helping you solve your problems and it didn't work. So now I really don't know what to do for you. I have to talk to my husband and see what we should do next."

Pat began to drink and drink a lot, thinking that drinking would help her get over her problems. But it didn't, she got worse and was soon unable to control herself. She thought of it as fun away of overlooking reality and then she began to get very sick because of the alcohol. She was drinking too much and her body wasn't used to this type of treatment. Pat began having terrible headaches and Cindy took her to the hospital but there was nothing they could do for her. Cindy didn't know what to do, she didn't know why Pat was acting so strange and getting sick all of the time, she couldn't understand or figure it out. But Pat knew, she knew why she was getting sick, she was no longer able to control what the alcohol was doing to her, she was becoming her own worst enemy, one that was stuck in a bottle of alcohol. Before she started drinking Pat knew almost nothing about alcohol, she didn't know that it could consume the mind and completely take over.

Cindy finally asked Pat to sit down so they could have a talk. She explained to Pat that things were getting out of hand, "We took you to a hospital and they said that there was nothing wrong with you."

"I'm not sick there's absolutely nothing wrong with me, I'm okay." Pat replied.

"Really, Pat?" Cindy looked at her then got up and went to

bed and left Pat sitting at the table.

"Oh, well! I guess I'll go back to the bar." Pat got up and went back to the bar to have another drink, her usual drink that had become her favorite and it wasn't apple juice, it was straight alcohol. She finished her drink and returned back home, this time drunker than before. As Pat was walking around the house she decided to call Cindy into the room to have a talk with her. Since it was really late Cindy was fast asleep but Pat kept calling until she answered.

"Do you know what time it is?" Cindy asked incredulously.

"Yes, sit down I would like to talk to you, it's important that we have this

conversation."

*"A conversation about what, Pat?"*

"About my problem." "Okay, Pat start talking. You don't seem right, have you been drinking? Where have you been, Pat? You are drunk, how long has this been going on? Is this why you've been so sick?"

"Sit down!" Pat yelled out, "I want to talk to you!"

Cindy knew there was a serious problem , Pat seemed more serious than before. Cindy asked, "What will the alcohol do to help you with your problem? How can we talk when you're drunk and you won't even remember what we talked about? What drove you to drinking? I thought you were happy here. Why, Pat, why? Do you think your husband wants you drunk?"

Pat got up from the table and grabbed Cindy like her husband used to grab her and pushed her up against the wall. She began hitting her like her husband would do to her and said, "This is why! Cindy, don't you understand what I'm trying to tell you?"

*"Yes, Pat I understand your problem, please let me go!"*

They began making so much noise fighting in the kitchen that Tom woke up and came running telling them to stop. He pulled them apart like they were kids and shouted at them, "Go to our room, Cindy."

Cindy walked away crying, not looking back at Pat because she felt so ashamed of what had just happened. She had told her husband so many good things about Pat that for him to experience this last scene humiliated Cindy. She walked with her head down to their room. Tom started yelling at Pat telling her, "My wife is really trying to help you and I can't understand why you've been acting so ugly to her. She went away sad, sad about the way you've been acting when she reached out to help you. She took you into her home and treated you like a sister and look what she gets in return. Your problem is not her problem and all she wants to do is see you happy! Why are you treating her like this and why are you going out drinking? We can't handle this, Pat, we are doing all we can for you but if you can't help yourself, then we can't help you. Look at yourself! Look what you are doing to yourself. If this continues then we can no longer help you, you will have to go somewhere else for help. This doesn't make any sense at all, Pat. I know my wife has tried to talk to you, she really likes you. You will apologize to her for your ridiculous actions. Mrs. English you have to straighten up because we can no longer handle you, let me know what the problem is. So far I've been letting my wife handle you but it looks like I have to step in and take over. It seems as if things have gotten way out of hand. I want you to go to bed and not another word out of you. If you need to go back to the bar don't come back, stay there and we will discuss this with your husband. I will deal with you tomorrow."

Pat got up feeling horrible about what she had done. She went to her room and cried until she fell asleep. The next day Cindy decided that they would no longer help Pat. While she was at work she called Joan and told her about Pat, what happened last night and how Pat was uncontrollable. Joan listened to Cindy without saying a word then asked her if she could call her back when she got home.

After Joan hung up she called her husband and told him all about Pat and her actions at Cindy's house. He wasn't surprised since he'd heard that she could do just about anything. She told John that Pat would have to go back home because she could no longer help her and that she done all that she could for her; let her husband deal with her since she has gotten that bad.

"We really tried hard to get her out of her situation, and Cindy is fed up with her because she's drinking a lot."

"But where would Pat get alcohol?" John wondered.

"I don't know, I guess she's been going out to the bar."

"I'll have to check with Jim to see if she been going there. This just doesn't make any sense, I can't understand why she would drink. Wasn't she happy there? What happened all of a sudden?" John pondered.

"I don't know John. I know that they don't keep alcohol in the house, but where would she get so much to drink that she could be getting that drunk?

Are you sure she's drinking, Joan?" John asked.

"That's what Cindy said, that Pat was drinking."

"Okay honey, I'll call Bill and tell him that she will be back home but I won't tell him that she started drinking, let him deal with this problem the best way he can." John said.

John called Bill, "Hi Bill, this is John. Are you ready for your wife to come home?"

"Sure, where is she?"

"We will bring her home in the morning,"

"Is there a problem John?"

"Well she just needs to come home. Is that okay?"

"Sure no problem." Bill answered.

"Then we will see you later." John replied.

They hung up and John paced the floor until Joan arrived home. John worried about what Bill might think when he found out that Pat had started drinking. He thought Bill might do something much worse than before. When Joan walked into the house he told her to call Pat and make sure she had all her things together and that she should be ready to go home when we pick her up. Joan called Pat but Cindy had forgotten to tell her that they couldn't help her anymore and that she would be going home to her husband. Pat didn't know what to say to Joan except, "I'll be ready when you come to pick me up."

Pat was nervous about going back home knowing that instead

of getting better she was even worse than before. Pat's thinking was more confused than usual; maybe Joan will let me live with her, I can't go back I just can't. As she began to put her things together and took them to the door Cindy walked in and looked a little surprised. Pat asked, "Cindy, why didn't you tell me that I had to leave. I thought we were going to give it one more try. I'm really sorry! Cindy I know I got out of hand."

"Pat you got way out of hand and all we were trying to do was help you with your problem, but we can't take that chance again. Cindy was apathy while speaking about What happened last night really hurt me and my husband. You disappointed me Pat and I can't live with you anymore. Who knows if you will sneak out and drink again, and when you drink you become uncontrollable. You do not know what you are doing and that's a chance we can't take any more. You were trying to fight me. I'm not like that and you know that Pat. We can no longer help you. Whatever happened last night will be forgotten about. Your husband will never know so don't worry about it, all you have to do is go home and be nice. I have to go on with my life I can't keep baby sitting you. Maybe Joan can help you but I can't, I just can't help you anymore."

As Cindy was talking the door bell rang and it was John and Joan.. "Hi! Come in. We were just discussing Pat's departure and she's glad to be going back to her husband."

As they were getting ready to sit down Pat stopped them by saying, "I'll be right out!"

She had made such a mess of herself and her life that she really didn't want to face them. She was ashamed of her image. John grabbed Pat's bags and Joan apologized to Cindy and thanked her for all that she had done.

As Pat walked into the room Cindy looked at her sadly and said, "Well, Pat, it's been nice having you the times that you were okay and I'm sorry that we have to part on unhappy terms. I hope you can see through all of this and maybe some day we can be friends after you seek real help."

Pat looked at Cindy, turned and left knowing that she would never see Cindy again. As she walked out she never looked back or thanked Cindy for letting her stay. She was really upset not only at Cindy but also herself. Cindy had tried so hard to help and Pat had let her down. Pat silently thought about her actions all the way home. Joan and John were silent too, knowing that Pat was probably thinking about what she had done and what Bill would do to her when he found out that she was drinking. When they arrived at Bill's house Pat said out loud, "I can't, I just cannot go in there. I can't let Bill see me like this; I've started drinking and he just can't find out about this! Did you tell him John? Did you tell Bill that I was drinking, John?"

"No, Pat, that's for you to do. We tried to help you but now we're finished with you we can no longer help."

They got out of the car and went into the house. Bill was waiting for them and for his wife whom he hadn't seen in a long time. He was very glad to see her. He took her into his arms and started kissing her and holding her really tight, telling her that he loved her. All Pat could do was cry knowing that she was wrong, knowing that she still needed help because she didn't want to be hurt by her husband anymore especially after she pleaded for freedom and the right not to be abused.

As she was hugging her husband back she began to cry knowing that her problem still existed but as she began thinking that as long as he didn't know about her drinking it would be all right. But how long could she live without alcohol? How long would it be before she sneaked out for a drink and he discovered what she was doing? And what would he do if he found out about her addiction? How would she get out of the house without him knowing? Pat's problems revolved around in head like a Ferris wheel that could not stop. She simply did not realize how much her husband really loved her, all she had to do was give in to him but that became the hardest thing for her.

"Would anyone like something to drink in celebration that were finally together and that the system worked for me and Pat?" Bill said happily ignorant of the turmoil going on around him.

"No," John said, "I wouldn't like anything to drink. We have to get home. Maybe you and Pat should have this celebration alone, I'm sure you guys have a lot to talk about. Joan and I have to go."

"Are you sure John?" Bill asked.

"I'm very sure Bill. You need to talk with your wife and get to know her all over again. my wife and I would just be in the way. Call us if you need help or if you need to talk."

On their way home Joan said to John, "Do you think he will start abusing her again if he finds out that she started drinking?"

"I really don't know and I don't want to find out so let's not talk about it. Let's go on with our lives, let's get back to the way it was before we got involved with them and their problems." John replied quickly.

"Pat might be calling us tomorrow." Joan suggested.

"Then we will tell to her that she should move out and never go back." John responded.

"She's never worked before, how will she support herself?" Joan worried.

"Joan I'm sure she will figure out something or some way to survive, so let's not talk about it anymore, please." John answered shortly.

Bill and Pat sat down to talk and find out how each other had been getting along. Bill began telling Pat about his life without her and how great he felt and how wonderful everything has been from the start. He told her he was very happy. He began asking her about what was going on with her but she could not answer. She claimed to be tired and wanted to go to bed. "It's been a long day." She said.

Bill insisted that she tell him because he wanted to know where she had been. "Pat it's been almost three years since I've seen you, honey. I don't want to wait to talk. Where have you been staying and who have you been with?"

"Some friends of Joan's and they were helping me with my problems, they were really nice people but I wanted to be with you, I wanted to see my husband. I really missed you honey and I'm still suffering and I would like to go to bed if that's okay with you!"

Bill was shocked at her tone, she spoke as if she was demanding to get away or if he was going to do something to her. "Fine, Pat, go to bed and go to sleep and we will talk about it later. I know that you are probably tired from moving and I won't push you into doing anything you don't want to do."

Pat went upstairs and as she approached Bill's room she stopped stared, thinking about the time he had sexually abused her. All the memories started coming back. She felt as if there was a line here and wondered what would it cost her if she was to cross it? Just as she was standing and staring into the room Bill grabbed her. "Are you okay? Pat, is there something wrong? I thought you were tired. Go on into the room and go to bed!"

Fear ran across her face; she was afraid of him and of what he might do to her. Bill tried explaining to her that he was a changed man, but she didn't want to listen. She wanted to go to bed. He really wanted to tell her about how much he had changed and it broke his heart when she didn't want to listen to what he had to say. Pat spoke up and said, "I'll be all right. I came upstairs to go to sleep."

"Well go on into the room. Maybe you need a shower to help relax you!" Bill suggested.

Pat finally got into the bed and he followed her, wanting to be next to her. "What are you doing, Bill?"

"I'm going to sleep next to you, I'm your husband, remember? Pat have you forgotten about me, have you been gone that long?"

"No, it's just that we haven't slept together in a long time. I'm sorry, Bill, it's been a long time for me." Pat said nervously.

"I understand, Pat. You're a little nervous and that's okay with me but I'm going to sleep right here with you so get used to it, and fast."

Bill fell fast to sleep. Pat stayed awake for hours and hours thinking about how bad she needed a drink. She contemplated how she was going to slip out without Bill finding out. If she got up to go to the bathroom would he wake up? She took the chance and got up. Bill didn't move, he just turned over. He was so used to sleeping by himself that he forgot she was even in the bed. Pat went into the bathroom, got dressed and left, not caring if Bill woke up. Bill never even moved.

Pat was at the bar having her usual drink when Jim walked up and said, "I'm getting off in one hour, would you care to join me?"

"No I will not join you. I've told you over and over again I can't go with you!" Pat told him.

***"Why? Are you married?"***

"Yes I am. Have you forgotten our previous conversations? Stop asking me to go out with you. Leave me alone and serve me another drink please!" Pat cried.

"Where's your husband?" Jim asked curiously.

"He's in bed, where else would he be?" Pat replied.

"Well I don't know unless you tell me!" Jim answered as he smiled in spite of her bad humor.

Pat began to get angry about not being able to have her drink in peace.

"Here's my phone number. If you ever need someone to talk to give me a call, because you are drinking much too fast. I don't know where you came from but you seem like you are having a lot of problems. I've been watching you for a very long time and it doesn't look good for a lady to be drinking like that." Jim said as her looked at her with understanding.

"Thanks for your concern, Jim, but can you please leave me alone?" Pat said.

"Sure!" Jim said as he turned to serve another customer.

As Pat was finishing off her third drink, John walked in and sat down in his usual seat. He didn't see Pat but when she saw him she swallowed down her drink, got up and ran out of the bar quickly. Jim watched Pat's reaction and the way she left then asked John, "Do you know that lady that was sitting over there at the end of the bar?"

"What lady, I didn't see anyone." John said as he turned to look where Jim was pointing.

"When she saw you she ran out," Jim said "it looked like she sure knew you."

"I don't know what you're talking about, what lady?" John asked again.

"Oh forget it, something was probably on her mind. She always seems confused when she comes in here. I've been trying to get this lady to go out with me but she won't go, she claims she's married but I've never seen her with a man. I think she just putting me on John." Jim murmured.

"Well that could be, but if she says she's married then I think she is married. Maybe she's having problems and doesn't want to get you involved, it could be serious you know." John told Jim.

"You could be right John, but I will keep trying until she brings her husband in, then I will leave her alone. But I won't be satisfied until I see her with a man and she comes in here all the time." Jim countered.

"Well, Jim, maybe she will give in one day if you keep trying. Sometimes it takes a whole lot to get some people to understand where you're coming from, so keep trying that might be your wife one day." John said as he finished his drink.

Pat ran home as fast as she could to answer the phone in case John decided to call. She sat by the phone and didn't move, but John never called. Pat was relieved, hoping that he wouldn't tell Bill. After waiting for a long time she finally went upstairs, took a shower then went to bed trying not to wake Bill up. Bill never moved or knew she had left. He was used to sleeping by himself so whenever she got up to leave he never knew. Once he went to sleep he was out for the night. Bill slept so deeply that he didn't hear anything that went on. After a while Pat figured out Bill's pattern and began to go out all the time. She was having a good time hanging out at the bar and drinking until she was drunk. This went on for a whole month until one night Bill woke up to use the bathroom. This night was the last night that Pat went out to the bar. When Bill woke up the bed was empty and Pat was not there, the house was completely quiet that he called out Pat's name. When there was no answer he called again, and still no answer. He went downstairs and Pat had disappeared. Where in the world had she gone?

Bill called John, "Hi, John, this is Bill. Is Pat there?"

"No." John answered sleepily.

"Is Joan there?"

"Yes she's asleep. Is there something wrong Bill?"

"Yes! Pat's gone. I woke up and she's not here, does Joan know where she could be?" Bill asked worriedly.

"Joan hasn't spoken to Pat since she brought her home," John said, "and

besides that she's been asleep for hours."

"Well thanks, John, sorry to have bothered you at this late hour."

"Well let me know if she comes in and if I can be of any help." John replied as he turned over and hung up the phone.

***"Sure John, I will. Good bye!"***

Bill started getting furious while he was waiting for Pat. He began pacing the floor, not knowing how to act if she came in. He was trying to gain control of himself so he wouldn't do something he would regret the rest of his life. He began saying to himself, "I won't hurt her no matter what the situation is. I'm a changed man now and I won't hurt my wife. But if she doesn't come in here soon it will be all over for her."

The longer Bill waited the madder he got, he was consumed with rage as he waited for his wife. Just as Bill picked up the phone to call John again Pat sneaked in drunk as usual and walked into the kitchen. Bill stood there waiting, wondering, and mad as hell. "Where have you been?" he said.

He said this in such a horrible voice that it scared Pat half to death. She just stood and stared at him.

***"Look at you, you're drunk! Who have you been with?"***

Bill worked on controlling himself so long but his control was gradually fading away and he was getting angry at Pat. He didn't want to hit her or hurt his wife, he still loved her very much, so he tried to gain control. He wondered how he could keep from hitting his wife, how could he walk away from this and away from her? As he was thinking about self-control the phone rang and it was John, breaking the cycle of increasing rage. Pat took a deep sigh and put her head down.

**"Bill, this is John. Has Pat come home yet?"**

"Yes she's here. So help me, John, I'm getting ready knock her right out on the floor. She's drunk, can you believe this? She's been drinking. Pat has been out with someone and she's been gone a long time. Do you know any thing about this?" Bill asked John.

"No, how long has this been going on with her?" John lied.

"I don't know." Bill answered.

"Why don't you ask her? I just called to see if she was okay. Don't do anything to her. Just go to bed and remember all the things you worked on for a long time and don't let it go to waste. Don't let her spoil your happiness."

As John was talking Bill didn't say a word. He just stared at Pat with anger, wondering what he was going to do to her next.

"Bill!" John called out, "Are you still there? Don't let that demon come out of you, do you hear me Bill?"

"Yes, John, but I have to go. I'll call you tomorrow."

Bill hung up the phone and walked by Pat, pushed her and stared at her, then he went up to bed. Pat didn't know what to do. She was surprised that all he did was fuss at her, she was expecting a whole lot more to go on but he went on about his way not doing what she expected him to do.

"What am I going to say if he starts questioning me about my drinking and where am I going at night? How long has he known and just waited to catch me? I wonder if John told him where the bar was, maybe he will start hitting on me again." Pat thought nervously.

Pat stood for hours thinking about what was to come or if he had really changed. "I can't see that he's changed. They said he was a changed man but he seems like the same old Bill to me, he's still a demon. If he ever hits me again I'm leaving and I'm going to stay with Jim. He wants me, I don't have to take this anymore now. I have somewhere to go, he hasn't changed one bit."

Pat sat for hours analyzing Bill and what he would do to her. When she finally got tired of trying to figure him out Pat went upstairs to go to bed. She took off her clothes and got in, trying not to wake him up. But he wasn't sleep, he just laid there awake wondering why she started drinking. When Pat settled down next to him and she put her hands on him and he pushed them off. "I'm sorry, honey." Pat said.

"Just how sorry are you? Tell me Pat how sorry are you?"

"I'm real sorry Bill." she started rubbing him.

"Get your hands off me right now before I break your arm!"

Pat continued rubbing him trying to comfort him but he got angrier and got up out of bed pulling her with him. He threw her up against the wall twisted her arm and saying, "I told you that I was going to break your arm if you didn't get your hands off me!" he yelled at her.

He twisted her arm until he heard it pop, pushing her into the other room he told her to stay away from him. Bill went back to bed, he didn't care what happened to Pat, he left her in the other room with a broken arm. Pat was in tears, she started screaming, "Why, Bill, why can't we get along!'

Bill never answered as he listened to Pat get up off the floor and walk out of the house. She walked until reached the hospital. Her arm was very swollen. Pat explained to the doctor that her husband had beaten her. As the doctor put the cast on Pat's arm she asked her, if Pat would like to press charges against her husband for beating her. Pat looked bewildered the hospital staff began asking so many questions at one time that Pat didn't know what to say. She screamed, ran out of the emergency room and stumbled back home with her broken arm.

The next day Bill got up and went to work without saying a word to Pat. He hoped that he wouldn't have to do this to her again. He really didn't want to beat her but, he rationalized, if she hadn't learned her lesson she would get it worse than she ever had it before. Bill thought by breaking her arm Pat would quit drinking.

While Pat's arm was healing she didn't go out to the bar because she didn't want Jim to see her like that, but she never stopped drinking. She waited until Bill went to work then she went drinking. No one was at the bar but her, not even Jim. Pat spent her all her mornings drinking at the bar making sure she was sober when Bill came home. She acted as if she never had a drink and he felt good about the "fact" that she had finally she learned her lesson and he wouldn't have beat her anymore. Bill didn't want to abuse Pat, he loved her so much he never mentioned anything about her drinking. Bill thought Pat had completely stopped. For six months Pat did not leave the house and he had not seen her drunk. He explained to John that she stopped drinking and John believed Bill.

Bill began to bring Pat flowers and gifts showing her that he really appreciated her, something he had never done before. He began to show her a lot of love but Pat didn't pay any attention to him, she kept her growing sorrows to herself. Pat was getting really addicted to alcohol and she began drinking heavily every day. She thought that drinking was solving her problems, and thought that as long as Bill didn't find out, she was okay and free to drink. One day Bill decided to surprise Pat and take her shopping and out to lunch so he only worked a couple of hours.

He really wanted to spend time with her so he left and went home. Pat had gotten an early start on her drinking that day, she wanted to get so drunk that she could fool herself into thinking that all her problems were solved. Instead she only created more problems. Pat was really drunk when Bill came home. She was passed out on the floor by Bill's favorite sofa with a bottle of some strong alcohol, something that was so strong that Bill wouldn't even think about drinking it. Bill walked in and saw Pat on the floor, he thought something was wrong so he ran over to her and grabbed her and picked her up. She looked up in surprise and was so shocked that she threw up on him. He grabbed her and started shaking her saying, "Look at you, Pat, you're drunk."

Bill began viciously shaking her but she was so drunk she couldn't gain control of herself. He took her upstairs and threw her in the shower so hard she hit her head and passed out. "Pat!" He called. "Pat wake up right now!"

She didn't wake up so he turned on the water cold enough to shock her into consciousness. Pat woke up coughing, soaking wet and screaming, "Where am I? Help! Get me out of here, I'm drowning. Help me! Please, Bill, I'm drowning!"

Bill politely said, " You Witch! You're drunk, that's what's wrong. You're not drowning."

***"Bill, what are you doing here?"***

He took her out of the shower and threw her on the bed and began taking off his belt saying, "I'll teach you to play with me you little witch! I'll beat you until you bleed. You'll regret this little game you're playing!"

"Bill, please. I'm not playing a game. I needed a drink, don't you understand?" Pat pleaded.

"I'll show you how much I understand. You'll know just how much when I'm finished beating you." Bill began striking her with his belt, "I'll teach you to lie to me and treat me bad."

"Bill I never did anything to you. Please don't hit me anymore!" Pat cried hysterically.

He continued hitting her with his belt, bruising her badly not caring where he hit her. Bill then went into the bathroom once again and filled the tub with very, very hot water. He put baking soda into the water so that when she sat in the water she would feel every bit of the pain he wanted her to feel. Bill tried to make Pat get into the water but she refused this time, remembering what it felt like and how badly it had hurt her before. He started dragging her but she wouldn't go, she wouldn't get in to the water. She held onto the bed and as he pried her hands open Pat started screaming, "No! Bill, No!"

But Bill didn't care how much she cried it was like he didn't even hear her, all he could think about was teaching her a lesson, making sure this time she would understand. But this time it was hard for Bill, because she was much stronger than before and he had a hard time pulling her into the bathroom. He finally just he picked her up and threw her into the tub of hot water but she jumped back out and ran. He ran after her, grabbing her and choking her and he threw her in again daring her to get out this time. She stayed in as her heart was crying out with pain. Helpless tears streamed down her face as the baking soda dissolved into her skin where the belt made deep cuts.

Pat started screaming for help and Bill started brutally beating her face and head, striking her with his fist. He couldn't stop this time, this time he was sober and cold rage filled him he was worse than ever before. All Pat could do was scream for help and he still would not stop, he took her out of the bath tub and threw her down the steps, trying to break every bone in her body. Bill raced down the stairs like a mad man and started beating her again until she passed out. He didn't even bother to touch her to see if she was still alive, he just left her there on the floor all by herself, unconscious. He stepped over her as if he didn't care, as if she were a piece of rug.

Bill had brutalized his wife in once again without any feelings of humanity. Bill walked out of the house not looking back to see if she was dead from the fall that she had took when he threw her down the stairs. He went on his way without calling for help and without feeling guilty about what he had just done to his wife. Poor Pat was left all alone with no one to care for her or to help her off the floor when she regained consciousness. Bill had thought he was a changed man, but how changed was he when he couldn't even walk away from his anger? He sensed that he had gone too far this time, that he could never make this up to Pat, especially because he left her all alone on the floor.

Bill went to the bar hoping to see John. He had to talk to someone and not just anyone about what he had just done to his wife, how he had really hurt her this time. This time was different for Bill, this time he felt the pain that he put his wife through and knew she would never understand how much pain he felt this time. Bill had to talk to John and fast, but he didn't know where John was. As Bill sat at the bar Jim asked, "Are you okay? You look like you've seen a ghost! You're in kind of early."

"Give me a coke." Bill replied, holding his head in his hands.

"You act like you need a drink." Jim remarked.

"I want a coke!" Bill said.

"Okay, I'll give you a coke if that's what you want." Jim replied shaking his head as he poured the coke.

Bill sat drinking coke for three hours until John finally came in and sat next to him. "What's going on, Bill? I haven't seen you in here in awhile."

"Well there's a lot going on." Bill answered.

"A lot of what?" John said, noticing the troubled look on Bill's face.

"A whole lot of problems." Bill put his head down, ashamed of what he had to tell John. "I couldn't control myself I went to take Pat to lunch and she was out on the floor drunk with a bottle of liquor next to her. I thought something was wrong with her but when I went to pick her up she threw up on me and I got very angry and then it started all over again. I got uncontrollably mad and I started beating her, and I beat her so badly she passed out."

"WHAT! You did what? She passed out? Oh Bill! Why didn't you just leave instead of getting yourself into trouble like that?" John responded, looking at Bill with a mixture of pity and disgust.

"I tried to get away from her but she kept coming at me and I got so out of control. I thought she'd stopped drinking and all the time she had me fooled. I told her that I would teach her to play games with me, she was drinking while I was at work and sobered up by the time I got home. What am I'm going to do, John? I think I really hurt her this time. I had to get away and she's probably still out on the floor. I thought I was over beating her, but I'm not. It's beginning all over again I can feel it."

"Where is she Bill?" John asked concerned that Pat might be seriously hurt.

"At home passed out on the floor." Bill answered.

"Bill you left her on the floor?" John could not believe what he was hearing.

"I had to leave or else I would have continued to beat her. I broke her arm six

months ago." Bill tried to explain.

***"You broke her arm?"***

"Yes, remember that night she came in drunk? She started bothering me and I warned her that I was going to break her arm but she didn't believe me and she wouldn't stop, so I twisted her arm until I broke it then I went to bed. She took her self to the hospital." Bill explained.

"She went to the hospital by herself ,Bill?" Bill shook his head.

"I don't believe this. She wore a cast for a period of six months and I thought she had learned her lesson, but she didn't. As soon as she got the cast off she started drinking again." Bill cried.

"Bill, are you hitting her because she's drinking? Is it doing you any harm?" John couldn't believe what he was hearing.

"No, I told her I didn't want her drinking but she's not listening to me, she's doing what she wants to do and I can't have that in my house. If I don't drink then she's not going to drink." Bill said trying to justify his actions.

John listened to Bill without saying a word, just thinking that Bill was the one that had the problem and not Pat. He thought to himself, "She's not doing him any harm but he continues to harm her. I wonder if he really loves her like he says he does."

Then John turned away from Bill as Bill went on saying, "I don't want her drunk. Wherever she went for help they weren't keeping a close eye on her. I know she's not a baby but they were supposed to help her. Pat is worse off than before, I've never seen her like this and if I have to beat her to show her that I don't like her then that's what I'll do. She doesn't need alcohol, and she doesn't understand when I talk to her about this."

John didn't have an answer for Bill. "Maybe I should call Joan and have her go over to your house and check on Pat."

"That will be okay, John, because I don't know if I can face her after what just happened. Joan will see if she's okay and if she isn't then Joan will take care of her." Bill answered, grateful for John's help.

"So let's go to my house and talk to Joan." John suggested.

Jim was listening to their conversation and he was shocked at what he heard. He wondered what Bill's wife looked like and how come he'd never met her not realizing Pat was Bill's wife.

John and Bill arrived at his house and Joan was in the kitchen preparing a meal when they walked in. "You're home early, John. Hi Bill, how are things going? How's Pat? I bet you guys are getting along great."

"Sit down, Joan. I have something for you to do." John said.

"Okay, what?" Joan began to worry as she noticed the seriously looks on each man's face. "Why don't you go over to Bill's house and see how Pat is doing and spend a little time with her." Bill suggested. "But I'm preparing dinner!" Joan protested."Don't worry about dinner, we'll eat later. Besides, I'm not hungry right now." John explained. "Are you sure John?" Joan asked. "Yes Joan." John said seriously.

Joan worried to herself, "This is strange. Why is John acting like this? I've never seen him act this strange before and he never misses dinner. I wonder if he's getting like Bill, then we will have real problems because I don't know how I would handle him. I would have to leave because I couldn't take it like Pat, she can handle abuse but not me."

Joan reluctantly left and drove over to Bill's house. He gave her a key and told her to go right in and she should see Pat. Joan knocked on the door anyway although she had a key. There was no answer so she went in. She softly called Pat's name and when there was no answer she called again. She went upstairs calling Pat's name loudly. When there was still no answer, Joan thought, "Boy this is strange. Where is Pat? Maybe she's not here. Is this some kind of joke?" She checked the first room and it was empty. "That's funny! They said that she was here."

She went into another room and there was Pat sitting in the corner crying and all bruised up. "Pat, it's Joan, your friend. Is everything okay?"

When Pat turned Joan screamed, "Oh my God Pat! What happened to you? Who did this to you?"

"Bill!" Pat whispered.

"Bill did this to you? Oh Pat." Joan could not believe this was happening again.

Pat slowly got up and showed Joan the rest of her body where the baking soda had gone into her skin. "He beat me, then he made me take a baking soda bath in very hot water. I tried to get away but I couldn't. He came after me. I'm scared, Joan."

"Don't be scared, he won't hurt you anymore. He let your body peel like that and the hot water really burned you Pat." Joan said angrily, hardly believing the horror she was seeing.

All Pat could do was cry.

"Look at you, Pat you are all bruised up and your face is disfigured. When did he do this to you?" Joan asked.

"Today. He came home from work early." Pat replied still looking at the floor.

"No wonder he told me to come over and check on you. He didn't want to see what he had done. Let's go!" Joan bent down to help Pat stand.

"No, I can't leave. He will be back!" Pat shook off Joan's hand.

"Come on, I'm taking you to the hospital." Joan insisted.

"What about Bill?" Pat looked at Joan pleadingly.

"Don't worry about Bill, he knows." Joan answered as once again she gently tried to coax Pat off the floor.

*"Really, Joan, he knows you are here? And how does he know, and how did you get in anyway?"*

"Bill gave me a key. He's at my house with John, so let's leave right now!" Joan said as Pat finally stood up.

Joan helped Pat with her clothes and took her to the hospital, she needed treatment right away for her first degree burns. When they got there Joan took Pat to the emergency department and they admitted her right away. The nurse exclaimed, "Oh my God what happened to you?" Pat didn't say a word, she just cried. "You look like a burn victim. Was she in a fire?" the nurse inquired of Joan.

"No, her husband did this to her he made her sit in a bath tub of baking soda and hot water." Joan whispered to the nurse not wanting to upset Pat again.

"Well she is going to have to stay her until we find a place for her. She can't go back there." the nurse explained.

Joan went to call John and Bill and told them that they were keeping Pat at the hospital and told them that she'd be home later to report the rest of the story. When John told him the news Bill said, "I didn't try to hurt her but I lost control of myself and that's why I didn't go back home. Do you understand, John?"

"Yeah, Bill I understand are you feeling guilty and ashamed that you beat your wife and now she's in the hospital. Are you happy Bill? Will this satisfy you?"

"John, I didn't mean to hurt her. Besides, it's over now."

Do you really think it's over Bill? Think about your wife and the situation you put her in, then ask yourself if it's over. Keep the answer to yourself because I don't want to hear it. At least she's still alive, at least you didn't kill her. I'll bet she's in so much pain that she wishes she were dead."

Bill got up, saddened.

"Where are you going?" John inquired.

"To the hospital to see my wife!"

"You can't go there, they will put you in jail!" Bill could not believe what he was hearing.

"Well, then, I'm going home and going to bed. I've done enough damage for the day, I feel kind of bad." Bill admitted.

"Bill, I know that you tried but you didn't try hard enough. You flunked your own test, something you worked so hard on to accomplish, and you flunked it. So what now Bill? What are you going to do now?" John gazed at Bill and wondered not for the first time who this guy really was.

"I don't know John I'll just go home and wait for Pat to call and apologize to her. If she wants to drink then she can." Bill said knowing he a made a huge mistake.

"The reason we didn't alert you about her drinking is because we didn't want you to worry, we wanted you to be happy and being with your wife makes you happy. I didn't think she was going to drink when she came home. The reason Pat started drinking was because she couldn't come home to you. Bill, I'm feeling really bad that I didn't tell you, if I had of told you it probably would not have gotten this far. I guess I'm just as much a part of this and just as guilty as you are. Things probably would have turned out differently. We should have taken her somewhere else instead of bringing her home." Bill shook his head sadly.

"So when did all this start?" Bill asked John, not understanding why he hadn't been told.

"When she was staying at Cindy's. She was sneaking out to a bar, it was going on for a while until she started a fight with Cindy. That's when they decided to let her go and we had no other choice but to bring her home. We thought if she was with you she wouldn't drink anymore." John felt guilty that they had not been open with Bill form the start.

"So what am I suppose to do now John? I can't handle her drinking, I just got over being an alcoholic myself and I can't promise you I won't beat her when she comes home, especially if she's drinking. What am I to do John?" Bill cried desperate for answers.

"Just go home and think about it. I'll talk to my wife to see if we can help. Abuse is really serious Bill and it can kill the person you love. You don't want to kill your wife, you would never forgive yourself. Bill, you need more help. You should continue to go to therapy and if that doesn't work then you need to get a divorce from your wife. This is not a game, you are playing with someone's life, you need to go home or take a vacation away from everyone and think about what your next step is, its very important that you stop abusing your wife before it's too late. Look where she's at now and this could have been much worse. We'll find someone to help her, someone that's more experienced and that's not her friend because friends can only go so far in helping one another."

Bill agreed with everything John was telling him. He knew

that John was right. He decided to let John handle everything that had to do with his wife. Bill knew if he took care of her that she would end up more hurt than she'd ever been before. Bill was lost in his own sorrows. For the first time he felt bad about what he had done to his wife. He couldn't think straight, he couldn't function properly and his conscience began to really eat him up. Even though Bill was isolating himself from the outside world he still managed to refrain from drinking. Bill paced the floor day and night while Pat lay battered in the hospital with broken bones from being thrown down the stairs. Not once did Bill bother to call or attempt to go see her. He was too ashamed and lost in his own thoughts.

Pat spent five days in the hospital wounded and deeply scared. She kept searching for away to clear this anguish out of her life; she was trying to escape this horrible terror that had come upon her, that had entered into her life like some inexplicable force. She stayed in the hospital until most of the bruises cleared up , but her skin was so scarred that no medicine could make them disappear. Emotional scars were also deeply imprinted in her mind.

Help finally came for Pat. Ladies from the domestic violence group they came to help her, but she explained to them that she'd been there already. One of the ladies said, "But we have no record of you ever coming to us for help."

"What? I was in a shelter for two years."

"It wasn't our group that was helping you, it was someone else, so let us help you. Pat, you don't have to go through this alone."

"I need help because things are not going well but I need to call my husband and let him know where I am so he won't worry about me." Pat explained.

"You don't have to worry Pat. I've taken care of your husband, he knows already."

"Bill knows who are you and that I'm leaving with you?" Pat was amazed.

"My name is Karen and I'll be helping you for awhile. I help abused women and I have a place for you to stay, so don't worry about clothes or food. Everything is taken care of, so just get yourself together and I'll be waiting to take you to your new home where you will be happy."

"Okay, I'll be ready in a moment." Pat continued thinking to herself, "Here I go back to another shelter all over again. I wonder if there is another way to get help. I'm tired of living in shelters. This will never go away, my life is now built around other people, strangers, now my problems are known by the world because I have nowhere to go and no one to turn to for help except people that are unknown to me. At least these people feel for someone they've never met or seen before, someone whose past they do not know but still they reach out to a stranger. This is something I have to accept until I'm completely over my problem. I have a problem which I might never overcome because it's been in my life along time and part of it will always remain with me."

Pat left the hospital for her new home hoping that this time it would work, hoping that she would find some relief for her misery and pain, pain that she once brought upon herself then blamed everyone but herself. Pat went on to receive help, and for her it was on its way.

Bill, in the isolated world of his misery, he was not able to love his wife and was hurting her. He packed his clothes went away to find answers to his problems, to find a way to love his wife all over again and to have forgiveness in his heart no matter what situation occurred. He just wanted to fall in love all over again, he wanted a third chance.

# WORDS
# FOR
# THE
# ABUSER
6

In the event that you find yourself in a world of animosity with love ones, applying anger creates strong adversity which leads to strong vehement nature. Abuse repeatedly spoken of is not human. Any type of vehement nature is an expressive part of antipathy not caring or being able to fully lavish out pleasurable love, there are meaningful ways to exclude anger, an aversion of the conscious which is simply a way of proving your self, vehement is unconditional for an passionate person abuse is closing a person in a shell malevolence where it becomes a silent world, one where existence isn't allowed. Repugnance keeps a person hiding from the real world.

To the abuser, as you are hitting, punching, viciously working to hurt the one you claim you really love, think about how you would feel if you were suffering the same afflictions. Think about the anguish that your loved one has to suffer from; think about the feelings that turn into pain the moment that the abuse started. To the abuser, if you watch and pay close attention to the act your are committing, then you will see just how horrible abuse is. Put a mirror to your face view the dislike of your violence, how your disgusting conscious created the face of an abuser and its no beauty, its ugly anger. After you finish abusing, then take a look at your work and see if it's profitable or if it really worked. To those who abuse, hit yourself as hard as you can, burn yourself with hot water and then ask yourself if it hurts, see if tears that come flowing from your eyes. Look and see who is crying. Don't abuse, love your family.

In moments of abuse you lose focus and forget about loving. You tend to put your focus on something that's not important, like hurting the ones you love. You lose contact with what love is about and began hitting and hitting until it becomes normal to you. You feel that abuse is something you have to do or else you will probably lose contact with yourself. You no longer care about what you are doing to your loved ones. Abuse falls into all types of categories like verbal abuse, physical abuse, and mental abuse. When a person is being abused it goes directly into their minds, it affects everyone that's involved. The reason the abuser has to abuse is often unclear, even to the abuser. He or she doesn't know why this occurs and they can't share their secret with others. It's something that's kept deep inside their minds and is too complicated for them to express. There's no way out of the mental shell that they are in. The way to help abusers is to help them clear their minds, and mentally eliminate their problems. If the abuser thinks abusive thoughts then these thoughts create a serious problem, because he will no longer have a conscience to stop him from abusing another. He will abuse while he suffers from something that might be considered an unknown, a problem that cannot be fully analyzed or solved.

To the abuser, before you abuse find out why this need or desire to hurt your loved ones is even in your mind. Ask yourself how can you get rid of this horrible thinking before it's too late, before you harm someone that you truly love more than anything in this world. If you harm this person, where would you be and what excuse would you have after you have finished abusing them? When you're finished you will probably be in a world by yourself, with no one to love and no one to love you or even care for you. Just imagine what that will be like, living in a lonely world of your own creation searching for someone to love, but who? Who will want to love you, an abuser with no self respect whatsoever. All it takes is time to think before acting, and thinking doesn't cost anything. It's free but it takes a lot of time to sit down and think about something before you react, before you begin to abuse. Abusers usually don't think about what they're doing, instead they find ways to avoid punishment by rationalizing the crime that they are going to commit. They find excuses for their behavior, blaming alcohol, drugs or their past for their faults, so that their conscience will give them a little time to start over again. But it's not really the alcohol, drugs or their past, it's their mental state of mind that's causing them to behave in such an uncontrollable manner. It's as though a sickness has overcome their minds and if they don't seek help it becomes contagious to everyone in the abuser's environment. Abusers don't find time to think because thinking is more difficult than actually performing the abuse.

Such self reflection harms the abuser, making them unable to function as they normally do. Then what's left to fill the void? If the abuser would think before he acted then this world be a whole lot different.

To the abused and the non-abused and for the abuser and the non-abuser, problems arise when we think about searching for help, it seems as though abuse with all of its unknown causes cannot be treated or solved once it has began. There is a fear of humiliation that friends and family might become involved. Abuse can't be solved if you don't seek help. It can be solved however, you can be helped if you just reach out to the sources that are available. There's always someone who cares and who is waiting to help. Abusers feel too embarrassed to reach out, they feel like someone is judging them; but the only way to receive help is to reach out and overcome embarrassment and guilt. You can get rid of the guilt, pride, anger, and misplaced self honor so that you can stop hurting the people you love and mainly yourself.

Abusers don't realize how much they are hurting themselves when they abuse: when you hit, you hurt your hand; when you say things, you unknowingly hurt your heart; and when you think of such things, you hurt your mind. Both the abuser and the abused are suffering and hurting in different ways.

This section, "Words For the Abuser" is designed to help you stop hurting the people you claim you love and respect. Abusers, you can be helped before it's too late, before you harm yourself. If you're the one on the verge of being abused get help before it gets started, before you become like that other person you know that abuses. You don't want to be like that other person, you want to be better, do better and act better in order to help the one that's abusing. Don't add to it and be like him. Help him, make him feel and see what abuse is like. Abuse is serious, it's a dangerous and unwanted problem in families and in our lives. But what can be done about it? If thinking helps us solve our problems before it's too late, then thinking is what should be done about abuse in our society.

To the abuser, think before you act abusively and it won't cost you your life or your love ones;  you will be much happier with the one you love and care for forever.

## TO THE ABUSER

WHEN CAN IT STOP
HOW CAN IT STOP,
AND WHEN, THE ONE WE LOVE THE MOST
ENDS UP IN JAIL, THE GRAVE, A MENTAL HOSPI-
TAL
OR EVEN HANDICAPPED
IS THAT WHEN IT STOPS
WHEN ALL THESE THINGS HAPPENED
THEN YOU SIT AROUND THINKING, THINKING
ABOUT
OH! I SHOULD NOT HAVE DONE THAT
I FEEL BAD REALLY BAD
I NEED HELP, HOW CAN I EXPRESS MYSELF TO
OTHERS
OTHERS DON'T WANT TO LISTEN
OTHERS DON'T WANT TO TALK
OTHERS DON'T WANT TO BE AROUND YOU
BECAUSE, BECAUSE
OTHERS TRIED TO WARN YOU
TRIED TO TELL YOU
THAT WHAT YOU WERE DOING WAS WRONG
BUT YOU, YOU DIDN'T LISTEN
YOU DIDN'T WANT TO LISTEN
YOU THOUGHT YOU KNEW IT ALL
SO NOW WHAT? WHAT CAN YOU DO NOW
FIRST YOU WERE GREAT AND EVERYBODY LOVED
YOU
COULDN'T LIVE WITHOUT YOU
WANTED YOU BY THEIR SIDE
BUT NOW THEY'RE GONE AND THERE'S NOWHERE
TO TURN
NOWHERE TO HIDE, OR EVEN LOOK FOR A PLACE
TO HIDE
BUT TELL ME WHO CAN FORGIVE YOU

WHO CAN LOVE YOU FEARING FOR THEIR LIFE
FEARING THAT YOU MIGHT HURT THEM
FEARING THAT YOU WILL NEVER CHANGE
WHO! TELL ME WHO WILL BE BY YOUR SIDE
THEN AT LAST IT CAME TO YOU
THEN YOU DECIDED YOU NEEDED HELP
AT FIRST NOT WANTING TO BE HELPED
AND NOW IT'S TOO LATE FOR YOU
BEING PROUD AND BOASTING ABOUT WHAT YOU
WERE DOING
TO THE ONES YOU CLAIMED YOU LOVED THE
MOST
TO THE ABUSER; WHO WOULD BELIEVE YOU NOW
THINKING ABOUT THE SORROW AND THE PAIN
YOU     CAUSED
TO OTHERS THE HURTING AND THE EVIL YOU
BROUGHT
THINK ABOUT THE TOUCH, THE FEELING AND THE
MOURNING
THINK ABOUT HOW IT WASN'T WANTED
TO THE ABUSER THINK, PLEASE THINK BEFORE
YOU ABUSE

To the abuser, even if you have already started to abuse stop: the red light is on. Express yourself, it's never too late. You still have time before anyone finds out what you are thinking or even doing to your loved ones. Some abusers feel a misplaced sense of justice or honor when abusing their spouse or even their friends. Maybe you need to prove a point or let them know that you are bigger than abuse you have loving pride. You use physical force to "give them the right impression," or in your need for respect you show them who is the boss of your environment. You become the boss of abuse, the boss of your society, putting everyone in fear you while you're proclaiming to be the boss. This is a myth. Rather than making you a big person, abusing others makes you look smaller. People look at you as "the little person needing serious help, the one who is unable to cope with life." This uncontrollable frame of mind allows for no one else's suggestions or guidance, because the "boss" thinks he or she is absolutely right and has absolute control. The "boss" of abuse has all the answers.

In reality abuse doesn't make that person what you want them to be. Verbal abuse doesn't change that person into something you want him or her to become. Change comes through love, and abuse doesn't explore another  feelings, pain or thoughts. The only thing abuse does is hurt, it hurts you and it definitely hurts the one you love. The pain that you cause is more than physical bruises, you're also wounding someone emotionally and mentally. You're hurting them more than you can imagine, you're damaging someone for life. We should think about the people being abused and how they feel, it's a situation they cannot escape. Even if they try to make it disappear it will stay with them until death.

Here's a story of a little girl named Mary, that I once knew. She couldn't seem to get away from a horrible, unimaginable way of life. Mary was a child about 13 or 14 years of age and her mother was a single parent with two kids. Her mother would go out and party all the time, going from nightclub to nightclub. There was nothing really wrong with that, partying is a way to escape life's problems, for a moment then it no longer exist. But Mary's mother couldn't control her drinking, and she would come home sloppy, a falling down drunk with no one to help her out of her miseries. She was "kind of crazy like" with her drunkenness. she would call this Mary into the room and ask her strange questions like, "Who have you been with?"

Mary would look at her confused and answer, "No one mom."

Mary's mom would constantly ask her daughter this same question every time she was drunk, even though she knew that her daughter hadn't been with anyone. "Who have you been with?"

"No one."

"You been with someone!"

Mary didn't understand what was going on, all she knew was that her mother would verbally abuse her for hours and then physically abuse Mary. Her mom would grab her and began choking her, raking her nails across Mary's arm digging them in as deeply as she could. She would dig so hard that Mary would scream.

Mary's mom would continue to ask her where she'd been and who had she been with, and Mary continued to be confused, she didn't know what her mother was talking about. When Mary would try to answer her mother, her mother would begin to hit her hard in her head, constantly beating her. Her poisoned fingernails marked her daughter's skin so deeply that nothing would clear her skin of this terrible abuse. Mary's mom continued to do this until she felt that she was tired, tired of abusing her child. She would then make Mary sit for hours in a corner until she gave her the run down on what life was about or what she considered life was about.

Even though she was badly bruised Mary had to go to school and face other kids. She would try to hide what had happened the night before by not letting anyone see what her mother had done to her. Mary's mom did not realizing that her daughter had feelings deep inside. Mary's mom didn't care how her daughter felt, she was going to teach her daughter a lesson once and for all. As the beating got worse Mary began screaming loudly, trying to alert the neighbors. Some of the  would neighbors knocked on the door telling Mary  mom to stop to quite it down.  "What's going on in there?"  There were no answers.

Mary's mom would attack her young daughter from late at night until the early morning.  The screams would upset the whole neighborhood.  This lady would beat her child for reasons unknown even to herself.  She couldn't explain to Mary why she thought Mary was with someone else when her child was only sleeping as innocently as a bird.  Mary had to suffer from the abusiveness of her  mother and there was no way of stopping this painful thing.  This abuse that Mary was experiencing from her favorite person in the whole world, her mother.  No one came to help Mary, everyone attended to their own business, going their own way and ignoring the problem of the mother and her daughter.

When Mary turned sixteen she started going out to parties with her friends and having a good time.  She would stay at her friends' homes so her mother wouldn't find out what was going on.  Anytime her friends asked to stay at her house she felt uneasy, knowing her mother's situation.  Mary once thought that if someone stayed with her that her mother wouldn't come home drunk and abuse her, but Mary was wrong.  Her mother didn't stop because she had company.  She came home past midnight, drunk and called Mary into the room.  She began telling Mary how she didn't like her friends and how they were causing Mary to do bad things.  She told Mary that her friends weren't any good and she needed to get rid of them.  Mary didn't respond, so her mother started hitting her and calling her foul names.  She called Mary names you wouldn't call your dog.  In the middle of this verbal assault she called Mary's friends into the room and started on them, telling them how she didn't like them.  Her friends just stood and stared at her.  They couldn't believe what they were hearing and how she treated Mary.  They began talking back to her, treating her like she was treating Mary and talking to her like she was talking to Mary.  This enraged Mary's mom.  She started hitting the girls, grabbing them and choking them just like she always did to Mary. She couldn't stop. She was abusing someone else's kids. The girls finally got away and never look backed. They left Mary all by herself to deal with her drunken mother. Poor Mary had no one to run to, she was left all alone to get more abuse from her mother.

Things were getting out of hand and this abused girl had nowhere to turn to for help. There was never anyone around, everyone was frightened of her drunken mother. The neighbors kept quiet and never even called the police to find out what was happening. No one bothered this disturbed household and Mary was left hurting. Mary was lost in a world all by herself. When people asked her about the scars on her neck she would say, "I got into a fight with my sister."

Mary was badly bruised and she lied about the reason because she didn't want to tell the kids at school that her mother was abusing her every night. It was embarrassing for Mary, she couldn't face her friends anymore because they would laugh at her and talk about her mother. It was a situation that Mary was stuck with and couldn't do anything about. She had to learn to deal with the reactions at school and those of her neighbors. Mary blamed everything on her sister for she was too humiliated to say it was her mother who was doing those horrible things to her.

Mary's mom didn't feel guilty. How could she do this? Why didn't her conscious bother her? Maybe she didn't have a conscience, maybe the alcohol took it all away. This lady had a serious problem that no one knew about and she thought she could take it out on others, thinking that it would go away. Well it didn't go away. She began telling her daughter how she hated her and she wished she would go far away. She was so rude to her daughter, she hated her for no reason at all and she made sure Mary knew just how she felt. She would always tell her to get away from her. Mary finally moved out, as far away as possible from her mother just as her mother told her to do. Then her mother felt a need for her daughter. Her mom felt lonely but she didn't have any guilt about being wrong for what she had done to

Mary. She felt justified about how she abused Mary, unaware that she was creating a serious, lasting problem for Mary.

Mary couldn't trust people and didn't want to be around others. She feared that everyone knew what her mom had done to her even if they didn't know her. Mary was mentally troubled by a demon that her mother had created. A demon that should never have existed.

Why couldn't Mary's mom seek help? What was stopping her from talking to someone about her problems or from seeking advise or the help she needed? She could have received counseling before she started abusing her daughter or before she began abusing someone else. Mary's mom also had no one to turn to, not even her daughter. Mary didn't want anything to do with her, she didn't want to see her mother. Although once she loved her mother more than anything in the world, she no longer liked her mother.

Mary's mother grew crazier than ever, and created more problems for herself by baby sitting other kids. She knew she had a problem but the kids' parents weren't aware of her problem. She began drinking while she was watching the kids. While she was drunk she would verbally and physically abuse the kids, just like she had abused her daughter. She continued to do this until someone called the police and she spent the night in jail. She really hurt one of the kids, a little girl had a big knot on her head from being hit on the head with a jar.

This lady had a serious problem, the cause of which was unknown to her. She couldn't handle herself much less let someone else help her. After spending the night in jail she still didn't realize that she had a problem nor did she seek help of any kind. They told her where to find help but she didn't listen to what they said even though she knew deep in her heart that she did have a real problem. This lady was so abusive that when she saw her daughter she would attack her and start hitting her for no reason at all. Finally her daughter got a restraining order against her. Mary no longer wanted to speak to her. This lady went overboard with abuse took it for granted that she could abuse everyone in sight. Everyone began to tell her how she had a problem and how she needed help but she didn't understand. It could have been the alcohol but people recover from that. She just couldn't seem to recover and she just got worst.

Child abuse is just as serious as any other type abuse and it can become uncontrollable as well. It took a long time for this lady to seek help and when she finally got it she felt relieved of all her problems. It wasn't long before she returned back to normal again.

Help is important. If you think that you have a problem, whether it's abusing your spouse or your child, then you need to seek help or it will get worse and become uncontrollable. Pretty soon no one will be able to deal with you and your condition. People will no longer trust you. There's all kinds of help out there for you, help you can pay for and free help. There is no excuse for abuse. If you decide that you don't need help then your problem could get worse, just like Mary's mom. She didn't really know what her problem was or how to seek help. Her problem got worse so that the circle of her abuse included not only her daughter but also other people who didn't know of her problem. You, too, could end up like Mary's mom if you don't seek help for your abusiveness. There isn't any other way for the cycle of abuse to be eliminated; you need to get some kind of therapy or seek some advice before it's too late. At some point in your life you will suffer. It may seem great in the beginning but in the end any pleasure received from abuse runs out. When it goes it won't be a pretty sight for you. The people you need the most will not be there for you.

Abused kids grow up abusing, doing what they learned or what they have seen others do in an abusive situation they think that it's the thing to do. Kids are more easily damaged by abuse than adults. They have no way to cope with abuse and can't or won't express themselves because they fear that the abuse will become much worse. They never seem to forget what has been done to them, they carry it with them their whole lives. Even if they don't hate the one that abused them they learn unhealthy ways of dealing with people. Some kids grow up and put their families into the same situation they came from, it may not be something they understand but that's the cycle of abuse.

If nothing else, kids understand one thing about abuse: it's painful, it hurts, it's something that won't go away and the person responsible for this pain is the one they love. It's not supposed to be this way, they're not supposed to be doing this to them. When abuse comes into a child's life they have nowhere to run or hide. They have to accept whatever comes their way and the fear of telling someone becomes much worse as time goes on. They live in constant fear that the situation will get worse. At the beginning of child abuse the parent needs to think about what he or she is doing before committing this crime. It's easier to hurt a child because they're small. Remember however, kids have a long way to go and they have the right to grow into adulthood in an atmosphere of peace and love; in a home filled with joy and laughter.

Why do they have to experience abuse? Why should you put your child through such a horrible nightmare? If you think you have a problem with abuse, get help before it's too late, before you ruin your children's lives. No one wants to suffer from an abusive life, life is already too complicated.

Life is suppose to be beautiful, it is suppose to be bright and full of blooming love. For the abused it's dark and hollow, very dark with emptiness on both sides and very unpleasant to see. Abuse turns what could be beautiful into something that's mildewed and molded. There is an unseen smell so strong that the nose can't handle it, the sight of abuse turns away the faces of many that are near. Abuse is something that others don't like to solve or even discuss. People tend to move away from an abusive situation, trying not to involve themselves in such a horrible act. Abusing the one you love is not a form of consideration.

Put yourself in their place, try to experience the hurt and the suffering. Feel the burden of trying to hide the bruises and blaming it on someone else; someone innocent, someone that doesn't know what's going on. Try to pretend as though a major part of your life doesn't exist just so that your abuser won't look bad but can get away with the crime of hurting you. Feel the humiliation of knowing the one who hurt you isn't sorry for what was done, but rather he or she is a proud and allows someone else to take the blame for their abusiveness.

There are many stories of abuse. I'm writing this in the hopes that it may help someone and steer them in the right direction. The direction toward love and away from abuse. I want to let you see that abuse is wrong and it shouldn't be accepted in any type of relationship. Abuse is not the way to show love or to teach someone about the way you think. Being in an abusive relationship is a sorry way of living or wanting to live.

The thing about people who have been abused is that they make up excuses for the way things are, they offer to tell you their story and the way it happened but each time it varies. They start by telling you lies hoping that you won't find out the truth. Understand that the reason they do this is because they're ashamed of telling the truth, ashamed of what you might think or say. Scared that you or someone else might tell the one who hurts them and that they will suffer the consequences.

To the ones that are being abused, why do you feel ashamed? Open up that unknown world shame and expose the person who's harming you? Why? Bring him out into the open, let everyone know who he really is and what he's about so it can stop, so he can stop abusing you like he does. It's only fair. I know you're scared, scared of what might come next, scared that it will hurt all over again when it hasn't stop hurting yet. Even if you don't tell, you know it will happened anyway, so why not tell the truth. Don't be ashamed, don't let shame stop you from getting what you need. Don't let shame drive you into fear of surviving. Just tell the truth and all the shame and the fear will disappear. Face the truth of what's going on. How are you going to receive help if you don't tell the truth?

Maybe you're afraid to leave, thinking that your abuser will come looking for you, searching the earth until he find you. Your abuser might come looking for you but only if you called him and tell him where you are. If he finds you, he'll assure you that everything is going to be all right, that he is going to love you instead of beating you. You might believe him and you might return his love and think that he's going to change. You might believe that everything is going to be better. You believe him when he tells you he's seeking help and that he wants to overcome abuse. In his heart, maybe he does want help, maybe he really wants to be helped and can't express it out loud where it can be heard, where someone can hear his cry. Maybe he's just as ashamed as you are but since it's considered cowardly to cry out for help he has too much pride to admit he has a problem. He might rather live with the problem instead of solving what's damaging your lives, too proud and too stuck in his ways to change. It takes a man with self respect to admit that there's no shame in seeking help. The great men of the world seek out help, and this very act could clean abuse out of your lives.

To the abuser, do not be embarrassed to call for help, to look in unknown places for answers. No one will put you down, no one will hate you for looking for help. The one you claim that you love will love you more than ever because you show strength by coming forward and expresses your problem. The man who admits that he's doing something wrong and avoids getting help because of embarrassment can guarantee to himself that the problem will never go away.

Women that have been abused become addicted to abuse, it's like they have to be hit. They begin to experience a pattern of abuses. Every partner they choose abuses them because they do things to irritate them into abusing them. In doing this they make their situation worse until they get what they feel they deserve. This isn't the way it supposed to be. Abused women have a saying and it's, "Every time I meet a man he wants to abuse me or beat me." I didn't quite understand why battered women always run to men that abuse them, it didn't make any sense. How can someone continue to be battered by different men? Aggravation has a lot to do with it because it takes a lot for some men to hit the one they claim to love. Aggravation creates a nasty kind of unknown beast. Sometimes it goes away and sometimes it gets worse. It takes a lot to satisfy a previously abused person, it's a difficult situation and it can be addictive, as anything that goes on for a long periods of time tends to be. Like any other addiction, those who are abused and those who are abusive need to be treated.

Abuse isn't love and neither is aggravation, it promotes a far worse problem. Abuse is a form of hating someone, of not caring about another person. Abused people leave a relationship thinking that things are going to get better if they could just find a different partner. They don't realize that they, too, have a problem and it can continue on into the next relationship. The problem will get worse, because people fool themselves that abuse and all of the damage will go away by itself. This type of addiction needs more work and is time consuming. Abuse isn't what life is suppose to be about. It seems to be contagious, spreading all over the place from one household to another.

An abused man never admits to anyone about what his wife is doing to him because he's embarrassed of what others might think or say. He feels that people might even laugh at him thinking he's weak in the mind for letting a woman beat him. He thinks that people will believe he is not man enough to stand up to his wife. It strikes at his pride and manhood.

People expect men to be tough and able to handle every situation that comes a long. But some men can't handle it, they break down just like women and aren't "tough" at all when being abused. Most women use verbal abuse, it's easier for them to get away with it. In this type of situation people tend to laugh it off or laugh at the man not realizing that he, too, has feelings. Abusers seem to think that no one is human or vulnerable but themselves. They cannot allow another human to express their feelings, and they are afraid of what their abused partners might do or say next. Some men are very afraid of verbal abuse. Rather than lash out at the abuser in an effort to prevent the tragic accidents that such abuse could cause if they react to it. They become a victim of their environment. Much like abused women, they do not feel that they're able to escape or overcome such a horrible situation.

Most men that accept verbal abuse come from either an abusive marriage or childhood. They try to keep from going into the same darkness that they came out of, but they're mentally caught in a dismal cycle of isolation. They lose contact with others who might find out that they're being hurt. They just accept their situation as if nothing ever happened and they continue to allow themselves to be embarrassed in front of friends and family. Verbally abusing a man makes some women feel like they're the head of the household, and that he's just a bystander. They let everyone know that their husbands have no say in the household, and sometimes this turns the man into an abuser. He gets tired of the way he's being treated, of having private and humiliating matters discussed in a way that is painful.

Women that beat their men feel as if their man needs spanking for not carrying out all the duties that she assigned to him. Women who beat men have no feelings or a realistic outlook on life. They want their man to jump every time he looks up and some men do. Some women are more manly than their husbands and they tend to let their husbands know exactly how they feel about them through abuse. But how can that be? How can a woman overpower a man with abuse and then make it seem like he's the reason for the problem? People never believe it when a man is being abused. In our society we think that a man should be much stronger than a woman, but some men aren't stronger and some men refuse to strike back. These men live with the same type fear that abused women experience. They have nowhere to go and have a hard time finding anyone who will believe that their wife is the one damaging their ability to live in peace. If this person ever snaps, they go plain crazy for no reason at all.

Abuse is damaging to everyone, no matter what the situation might be or who's involved in it. It's a type of life where one person cruelly dominates another and ignores the other person's anguish because it is not his own. He himself is locked into a need to feel superior or powerful as he puts another person "in

his/her place." The abuser often feels proud about his circum-
stances, it makes him "bigger" than the person he's abusing and
controlling. Verbal abuse is as bad as physical abuse, and tears
apart the bond between two people. It ignores what's needed to
find ways of loving one another.

Abusers need serious help. They need to seek for help and
they will find that it's out there for both men and women. There's
plenty of help out there and there's always someone who will talk
to you about solving your problem. But if you go on thinking
there's not a problem it could be damaging to you. You might feel
embarrassed while seeking help but you have to reach out to
someone in order to solve your problem. Who cares what others
think or even what they might say about your search for help? It's
a good thing finding help, someone that can help you get better.
People might say things thinking they're making your situation
better, only to make matters worse for you and for the ones you
love. If your worried about what people might think, then your
problem is worse than you actually think because your using
excuses to keep you from conquering this sickness called abuse.

Why? Abusers, why can't you cry out for help to get rid of
that demon that has been created through sickness when you
abuse in the dark? One day it will come out to into the light so
hiding it won't help. Abuse is not love, it's a shameful desire that
produces no joy or laughter and it destroys lives; abuse should
never occur.

Abuse is a little word that may not seem worth a dime to the
abuser and the people that have never heard of abuse. We know
that life is not perfect and that man is not presumed to be perfect
in a relationship. But if you hurt the one you love you will hurt
yourself and it may never go away. It seems that abuse never goes
away, once it's in your mind it stays and there's no way of getting
rid of it. No matter how hard you try you will have to deal with
this unwanted problem. Even if you seek help there's absolutely
nothing in this world that can fully wipe your abusive situation
clean. That's why you need help so you can realize that what your
are doing is not right at all. You need to realize that you need to

get rid of the tension and anger you're feeling inside and over-come the anxiety that's a result of abuse. You need to clear your mind. If for nothing else to give yourself time to seek help.

Abuse is not a nice thing, you really shouldn't hurt your loved ones, especially your children because they grow up thinking that abuse is the way to cope with life and then they harm their chil-dren. Abusers often leave children with the idea that abuse is a form of love, but it's hate. Kids should be taught that abuse is a sick and ugly thing and that it can become a serious problem. Abuse affects the whole family, not just kids. Everyone in the family suffers from this horrible sickness, an illness that passes down from one generation to another. Each generation learns that abuse is normal so everyone suffers until finally the problem is taken care of. In an abusive home children don't understand about abuse, they're as innocent as life allows, and they make plenty of mistakes. This is a natural part of growing up to be an adult. How will they learn if they don't make mistakes? It's up to an adult to correct them and make them see what's right, but if the adult is wrong, who can the correct the problem that exists? How will they learn? How will they know the difference between right and wrong if mistakes are not made?

Don't beat them, teach them to understand the difference without the fear of pain. When teaching a child things can easi-ly be discussed. Ways can be found to work out the problems. Abuse is unnecessary. Think before you hurt. Children know that hurting is not fun and it doesn't feel good at all, at least not to them. Hurting someone is not the way to show a child that you love them. Giving them a kiss or a frequent hug to say I love you stops a child from learning all things that promotes abuse and it creates friendship between parents and the child. It creates a love that will never go away. Abuse creates hatred and unhealthy love. Children never forget the pain that they've gone through. The pain mixes with fear and this becomes deeply rooted in their minds. They lose the ability to communicate with their parents and with others. They live in a state of fear that any type of com-munication will be punished with abuse.

Parents should think really hard before they begin to commit such acts on their children. Children follow their parent's examples; they grow up doing what is done to them. No matter where you live there's someone who can help you, someone to advise you on how not to abuse your family. There are classes to calm you down. In case you are feeling uncontrollable anger towards a child there are emergency agencies which can temporarily help you. You need to get help before it's too late and your child is seriously harmed. Once abuse happens there's no way out. Child abuse is serious. It's not a form of caring discipline. People shouldn't have children if they don't have control over themselves. If you have children and abuse begins to occur, find someone to take care of them. Love is very beautiful when you love your children. Child abuse is serious. Pat abused her son Mike for many years even though she knew what she was doing was wrong. Instead of seeking help she continued to beat him, not realizing how badly he was hurting. She didn't care about his pain, she felt she had to raise him the right way and abuse was her way of being right. She put her son in a situation where he had to lie to others to protect himself from more abuse. But a lie can only last so long before the truth actually comes out. Pat refused to talk to anyone about her problem and she lived a lie, making others believe the illusion that everything was all right. Abuse is nothing to play with, and a child abuser is not thinking correctly. Abusers need help. Pat needed help. Although she suspected that what she was doing was wrong, she needed someone to reinforce this belief. Once you start abusing it becomes the thing to do. Pat felt that she was punishing her son the right way until that horrible day she went too far and knocked out Mike as she hit him with a board.

Child abuse goes beyond just spanking a child. Abusers will pick up anything to hit their children with no matter where they are or who's watching their minds are fixed on abuse. Child abuse comes in many forms, and no child should experience any of them. Some children are neglected for such long periods of time, abandoned in strange areas, or left home for months by themselves. Refusing to feed children is a type of abuse. Kids starve faster than adults and when they're left by themselves they tend to eat out of garbage cans as a means of survival. Kids are innocent and the innocent ones come out on the bad end of the stick. Children have a right to a decent life.

People that have children and don't want them should send them away to a safe place. Abuse doesn't give you a clear conscience, it brings on mental turmoil. Prevent this by getting help before it's too late. Get help before you go too far in abusing your child, before you leave him out on the street at everyone's mercy and starving to death. Before you permanently hurt them or even kill them. Don't let this happen to you and your loved ones because you refuse to get help. Get help before you get caught performing such a horrible acts creating a life from which there is no real escape. Don't abuse your children and you won't have to suffer.

For the abuser, get help before it's too late. In the beginning it may seem as though you're doing a good thing, you may feel justified and like it's your privilege. In the end there's no greatness in abuse: someone will suffer, someone will be hurt, someone will cry out for help. Where does that leave you, the abuser? Absolutely nowhere, nowhere at all because abusers suffer along with the ones they're abusing. You will suffer as much, if not more, than the one your abusing.

# FALLING IN
## LOVE
## AGAIN
# 7

Once abuse has begun in a family, everything starts falling apart. The family forgets the reason they were together and what made them one complete couple. When abuse begins, the desire of love fades away; each person becomes invisible. The love that brings two people together cannot overpower hate. Hatred is a very strong feeling. When there's hate, there is separation, no form of trust. That basis of marriage - trust is destroyed. Hate turns into abuse and you lose all trust that was ever formed. In an abusive situation, fear is formed in complete silence. Yet each person lives in hell together, suffering from what one has to distribute. No one ever wonders what went wrong or what happened to that family. Where did their love go that they once shared, and how can they come together and love again once abuse has taken over?

It takes more than love to bring a marriage back the way it was. It would be similar to starting over again, but abuse can never be forgotten. How can they start loving one another with abuse ever present. How can he say once again "Honey I Love You," without anger, or how can she accept, shivering in fear that one day he might snap on her? What can she say to him so that he believes in her, so he can confide in her without her lying or being sneaky, things he can't stand. What can he do to overcome a feeling of hurting his wife. After abuse, can they really start over again? Can it be love like it was when they first met? Can they trust one another again? Will the walls that went up in the beginning fall down? These are the walls of abuse that were once built, something that was created in their family that continued on for years and wouldn't go away. Where can love begin in their hearts? How can they find love in their minds and be honest with one another?

In our lifetime abuse runs away in the family. No one is interested in abusers. People never go back to the one that performs abuse, fearing for their life. But if they go back, matters are worse, especially when they're thinking negative, expecting things to go wrong. If you change your attitude to something more positive when you return, sometimes things change for the better. Almost everyone that has been through abuse never ends up with the same partner. They tend to leave, hoping that they forget about what happened. They hope that the next partner will be better, but only find out that he's worse. They need a great deal of help thinking that this time they will forget, and maybe someday forgive, the one they feared the most. Abuse sticks with you, wherever you go. Everyone you meet becomes abusive to your environment.

The English family tried to heal after both of them received some kind of therapy. They forgave one another. Somewhere in their hearts they still had passionate love for one another, which they promised until death parted them. Pat leaving Bill just didn't solve things, because once she was battered the problem never went away. People carry the problem along with them even into the next marriage, if there is one. So why leave, thought Bill. Why not work things out? Why not love again the one you loved at first, the one you agreed to be with forever and ever, the one you fell in love with at first sight. The English family didn't want to be split up. Bill loved his wife. He really wanted to be with her, but he knew he had a problem, a serious problem. He wanted help. He wanted to love her once again the way it was in the beginning. He felt he deserved to be loved, excluding the desire of loving other women. No other woman would do, no one could take the place of Pat. He felt bad for the way he treated her, but it had to be done, it had to be settled in his mind.

While Pat was away in a shelter seeking help, Bill thought he would date other woman. He was trying to find a love like his wife, in case she didn't return. His feeling were in depth fearing she would never return dampened by anger of past vehement attitude Bill would be the last person she wanted to see. Fearing brutal abuse of his previous actions. Bill tried loving other women, but it didn't work. His thoughts were passionate, loving her in his mind while arousing other women, in the mist of Bill's arousing he'd call Pat's name bringing adversary, as the women offensively stormed away. Being left all alone deep in thought the attachment she left on him guilty of his horrible acts of how he destroyed his wife. Bill was under the perception of starting over again having regrets, of reminiscence of loving his wife, if only the clocks could be returned.

Bill started feeling really sorry for himself and guilt fell over him. He was dysfunctional in his world, even his work suffered. He became a poor example for others. No one could understand him because guilt had taken over his life. His days and nights were sleepless. He wanted to be with his wife and as time went on he wanted her more and more, Her presents were unknown. Often wondered why she never called him to at least say hi. Bill was lost in his own world all alone, (deserted) As Mike continued on to find a better life, one without abuse without leaving contact of his whereabouts. Bill had no -one to turn to deserted by John after viewing Bill's situation of abuse fearing for his marriage.

Bill was in a no win position when it came to his wife. His thoughts were constantly erupting his mind of Pat's life, maybe she was living another life, or maybe she found someone else and married again. No one knew where she was, and if they did it was kept silent from Bill, fearing violently attack her. Pat's disappeared out of his sight, worried settled in about the whereabouts of his wife. Bill would continue to wonder where she was. He wished he could talk to her, "if she would just call, to say Hi, to say, I'm okay." he thought. It would make me feel much better. As Bill continued to wonder, Pat didn't call, nor did she have any intentions on calling. Pat needed all the help she could get while it was available.

While Pat was seeking serious therapy, no doubt, she thought about her husband Bill, the only man in her life. He was the only man she had ever known and loved, in her whole lifetime. Pat could no longer stand being away from her husband. She always wanted to be with him no matter what the situation turned out to be. While she was away, however, she couldn't stand to call him, it would make her more sensitive to her situation. She wanted to go home. But not knowing his state of mind, she had to be careful about how she approached her husband. She considered him crazy. Day by day she would wonder about him, her affection grew while in moments of silence Pat would pick up the phone to call, but she would hang up because she knew it wasn't time to talk to him.

The ladies would constantly remind her of horrible things he had done to her of his horrible actions that she was rescued she would likely be dead if Joan hadn't saved her. Pat would think about how right they were and how much they were telling the truth. Every time she called to talk to him these thoughts would run across her mind and she would hang up the telephone. She also thought about how much she really loved him and that was something that would never go away. It stuck in her mind forever. No matter how bad things got, she still loved Bill.

Pat's attachment was strong manifesting how love can once again conquer their hearts while forgetting the past. But can the past be easily forgotten? Can it be wiped out of her mind? Could she face Bill again after all he did to her. Could it be easy this time around? Could love really enter their hearts again?

Pat was doing some serious thinking about going back to her husband, not knowing if he wanted her back. She hadn't called him to let him know how much she really loved him, but her thoughts were as clear as speaking to him and her dreams were fixed on loving him the way he used to love her. Unfortunately dreams weren't good enough because it wasn't reality. Her dreams were like a fantasy that would never go away. Pat asked one of the ladies if there was such thing of going back to the one you really love?

"Well, there is, but you have to ask yourself will he contain himself, will he love you like you love him.' It takes a lot of thinking, Pat, before you go back. You can't just pack up and go back." the woman said hoping Pat was really hearing her message.

It was hard for Pat, not wanting to be hurt again, she just wanting to be loved which was something she hasn't felt in a long time. Pat was told that she couldn't call her husband or have any contact with Bill because of his vehement nature. Bill was a man of aversion, Pat knew it would be different. She knew that he wouldn't abuse her in front of others. Abuse never crossed her mind she thought more about how much she loved him and leaving him all alone, without knowledge of her whereabouts. It was up to Pat to make contact with Bill.

My thoughts constantly worried my mind of why my husband never called, he had to know something, this shelter wasn't a complete secret. Everyone came to the same shelter these perceptions ran through my mind as I began calling and hanging up the phone making it a habit.

Pat calling and hanging up went on for a while. At moments his voice caressed my mind listening to him call out speechless trying to figure out if a change had taken place, listening to his tone, wondering if he had started drinking. Insanity increased when it came to Bill more like am obsession, calling viciously hanging up because he never said a word until he finally figured out it was me, so the next time he called my name, "Pat is that you," still my voice went unheard. Fear pierced as my nerve curled up in knots wondering how Bill figured out that it was me "who was calling." Finally, calling ready to convey a nervous conversation with Bill. "Hello! Hi, Bill this is Pat, your wife." (My voice trembled and shook) afraid of what he might say, he might hang up on me. But he didn't, he didn't hang up he began pouring his heart out to expressing the ardent of his internal pause, the eagerness of heart, sweet heart, I want your lovely touch manifest me with your love, he continued to express how much he missed me and how much he really loved me. Please come home, because you're needed badly. Listening to him pleading it was unbelievable. Just couldn't believe the words his emotions the things he was saying. He hadn't expressed his feelings to her since the better days of our marriage.

He must really be lonely, twinkling my nerves. Does he really mean what he's saying, maybe its the abuse he missed? Afraid to ask any questions, not knowing his state of mind, so she hung up the phone while Bill continue to express his love. Pat could no longer take being away. She wanted to go home and test her husband. The last test almost cost Pat her life and she ended up half dead in the hospital. In spite of it all, she wanted to start all over again, start loving her husband again. It became really hard for Pat, hearing what she heard coming from her husband. Her heart was saying that she loved him too and she wanted to go back home, but her mind reminded her of the things he had done. Her mind was telling her to stay away but Pat wanted to follow her heart and not her mind. She didn't want to get any more confused than she was already. She just wanted to hear his voice and she wanted to tell him how much she loved him, but she couldn't after hearing him break down. She didn't have to, and that was enough to secure her heart if she went back.

Now she could call without any fear of what he might say. Everything was all right now. She felt relieved of her insecure feelings. She knew he still loved her no matter what anyone said. She didn't believe the others. She knew her husband and knew him well. Pat began to call every time she got a chance. She had to talk to him or her day wouldn't be complete without hearing her husband's voice. He wanted her to come home right away but she felt it wasn't time, although she wanted to. Bill and Pat began carrying on conversations as if they had just met and the liking became even more stronger. It had been a long time since Pat had even had a conversation with Bill.

It was strange at first, then it mellowed out. He told her things she never knew. She didn't think he had this type of love in him. This time he really let it out, he really opened up to her and she didn't have much to tell him except one day she would be home to accommodate him. He was pleased with that because he knew she had a conversation for him. His sweet talking made him a new Bill, something Pat learned to love. She never had anyone sweet talk her, but it felt good and it made her day. Pat never got a chance to say anything by the time he finished telling her how lovely she was and what a wonderful smile she had. It overwhelmed her so much all she could do was giggle like a little girl on the phone. When she giggled everyone got quiet that was in the presence of the phone. Pat began to believe everything Bill was saying without any doubt or questions and not saying anything. She became even more flattered as time went on.

Bill hadn't seen Pat for a long time. The disfigurement of her face that he had inflicted on her had cleared up. All the bruises had gone away and she was back to normal. He could not have possibly remembered her beauty for she was all bruised up for years. He never looked at her to see if she had beauty. Could he be telling the truth about her smile? She hadn't smiled in years. What was he really talking about? Did he realize who he was talking to? Was he serious about what he was saying?

Pat decided to call back to make sure he knew who he was talking to. As he started again she began telling him how sweet she thought his voice sounded. Then she began pouring her heart out to him letting him know that she felt the same way. She told him how much she loved him and how she wished she could kiss him.

He took over the conversation as usual, "I think about you day and night and you're in my dreams. I can't stop thinking about your warm sensitive ways, your beautiful skin."

Then he told her how lovely he thought she was. Pat was wondered at his reaction over the phone, wondering if all these things he was saying were true and whether he knew to whom he was talking. Did he really mean these things he's saying? Maybe he wanted her to come home. Pat had never heard him talk like this before, he was acting like he's falling in love for the first time. It sounded so good to her and she liked it and she didn't want him to stop saying what he was saying. This new Bill was like someone she just met. Pat kept asking herself if this was really the same Bill. It sounded like him, so Pat started calling even more than before. She would sneak to the phone when everyone was sleeping, calling more than three times a day to hear what Bill had to say to her. When Bill was working she would call to listen to his voice on the voice mail. She was possessed with his voice.

Pat was falling in love all over again and this time with her husband. She was in serious love, the right love, something she hadn't felt before. She was possessed with her husband's voice, wanting to be with him, having a feeling of not wanting to live without him. Her feelings were deep inside her mind, clearing out all other thinking. Her feelings were taking over her, she could no longer live without the love of her husband. She wanted to be with him. Then fear would come , fear of what he might do when he got tired of loving her. What would be the trade he would make? He couldn't possibly go on loving her like he said he does. What might happen when the love is tired and fades out? What will he do then.

Bill was happy just talking to her on the phone. It satisfied him. He was more than happy. They would talk for six and seven hours, not caring if someone else wanted to use the phone. Pat was in her own world when talking to him. If anyone said anything, she would just ignore them. Bill decided that when Pat came home it would be different. He wanted a new life with his wife. He wanted her to feel safe and not fear him. He wanted her to feel loved. Most of all he wanted her to be comfortable and happy, not jumping every time he raised his hand. He wanted to take care of her in all ways possible, not wanting for anything because he loved her dearly in his heart. He planned to take care of her for as long as they were together.

Bill went out to buy new furniture, changing the color from dark to light. He got rid of his favorite sofa, the one she hated the most. He was trying to get rid of all memories of where he abused her. He brought a new bedroom set. He changed all the furniture and had the walls painted on the inside of the house to match the furniture he had purchased. He was really making a change, like he found a new love. Pat really meant a lot to Bill.

He was going for a new start with his wife. He changed everything, even the paint on the outside, to her favorite colors. He felt
if she saw this then she would feel like she was at home. It would
also show that he really cares about her. Bill had the yard land-
scaped in the front and back of the house. He bought patio furniture to match. He did all of this so he could begin living his
new life with his wife, his loved one.

Bill had everything so beautiful and it seemed really wonderful to him. He felt good about what he had just done, he felt it
couldn't get any better. Bill took all of Pat's old clothes and put
them in the attic, thinking to buy her new clothes. He even
bought himself new clothes. Bill spent a lot of time preparing for
his new love, which was of old. He spent time picking new
friends, which didn't last very long, but he still looked forward to
a new life when Pat returned home. Through all this change there
was something missing, though, something he couldn't buy with
money. It was something he couldn't change and something he
had to wait patiently for. That something was his wife, who he
waited on, wondering if she would come back. She sounded like
she wanted to come back. After all that he had done we was not
sure if she was going to return where he wanted her the most,
with him.

Pat had not thought of coming so soon. She wasn't in a rush,
no matter how sweet he sounded on the phone. She was going to
make sure that everything was safe and he was what she wanted
this time. Pat wanted it to be right. She didn't want to waste her
time after all the therapy she went through to get her back to normal. She wanted to make sure she really loved him and couldn't
live without him. She didn't want to have any doubts about
returning home. She wanted to be sure when she walked up to
the door her thoughts about abuse would be cleared away. She
didn't want to have any fears of him. She wanted to be able to
stand anything he put out. Most of all she wanted to be happy this
time around, and that's what Bill had planned for her. This was
something she didn't know about Bill, how he was planning a
changed life where she would be more than happy with his

actions. He wanted to love her, and make sure she enjoyed life to the fullest when she returned home.

Pat wanted to clear all doubts. As she was discussing her problem, she was told that once a woman leaves an abusive situation she should never return home. Once you leave there is no going back. Pat thought about what was being said, and it went through her mind over and over again. She had no idea Bill was making a complete change for the better. It was a more exciting change, something different, unknown to Pat. Pat could not get over her fearful feeling. She explained how she felt insecure about being with her husband. She thought that all the things he saying weren't true. She was advised to stop calling him until she was confident about her feelings. As she thought about not going after her man until she was clear and free, it made sense. So she stopped calling Bill, turning her love completely away, ignoring the wonderful way he was acting and his sweet talking.

Pat stayed completely away from Bill refusing to pick up the phone. Pat didn't call Bill for a period of six months. Craziness settled into Bill's mind waiting for the phone to ring. Everyone he knew called, but there was never a call from Pat, nor did she have any intention of calling. Bill started getting worried, wondering if something happened to her or if he said something she didn't like. Bill began to worry and worry a lot. He really loved Pat. She was his first and only love and he didn't want to lose her. He felt really bad about abusing her. He realized with her gone how much he really loved her. Bill's hair began falling out. He was not functioning, sitting around, waiting for Pat to call. She never called, so he began calling around, trying to find her. He felt he couldn't live without her. He had to hear her voice. He had to find out something about her, about how she felt, whether she really loved him like she said.

So he called shelter after shelter, and still no Pat. She was nowhere in sight. He tried even harder to find her but he couldn't because she was listed under a different name, one unheard of, one Bill would not have figured out. He became possessed with looking for Pat. He drove around trying to find where the shelters were, but still no luck and no information about his wife. He even followed Joan around, hoping she would lead him to his wife, but she didn't. She went her own way because she had no idea where Pat was. Bill didn't believe Joan, he figured she had something to do with Pat's disappearance and the changing of her name. Bill started getting more and more lonely, it was so bad that you could tell on his face that he had a serious problem, worrying about his wife.

Bill began talking to himself while pacing the floor in his house. He missed his wife so much. If only he could hear her voice, if only he could kiss her soft lips. He began singing a song he once sang when he was in therapy about "oh how I love my wife." Bill got carried away with his singing, hoping that it would bring Pat back, hoping she would feel his vibes. Bill's loneliness was getting worse. He started walking in parks, looking at other couples and shedding tears. He walked all day and night until he could not walk anymore. He walked until he wore holes in his shoes. He was in love, a sad love, a love that was far away. This was a love he had to find, which was nowhere in sight. Bill's lonely heart was so bad he stopped eating, hoping that love would take the place of food. An emptiness grew inside of Bill. Loneliness fell all over him and affected him in all ways.

Bill would cry out day and night, "I need my lost love." Bill got pictures of Pat and began taking them around to different social services trying to find his sweet wife. He went from shelter to shelter, but he had no luck, none at all. No one seemed to help. He was left unguided. Bill finally gave up looking and waiting for her. He figured she went with someone else and forgot all about him. He thought she left him to suffer the love he lost forever. After long nights of looking for Pat he finally decided to sleep. As he dozed off, the phone rang. He was so frustrated that he didn't answer the phone. He was tired of talking to people who didn't know where his wife was. He was really fed up and as the person began speaking on the voice mail he heard her voice but it was too late.

Pat was finally calling him. She told him how much she

loved him then she hung up. After hearing her voice he felt sad because he refused to pick up the phone. She was finally calling. So he just listened to her voice several times until he couldn't listen anymore. He began talking back to the phone saying "I love you too honey." Bill felt relieved, knowing that she still loved him and wanted to be with him. But did she want to come home? This one thought ran through Bill's mind, does she really love me dearly? He questioned himself about her heart, his mind wandering thinking of Pat and their past that they had before he started abusing her. He hoped it would change him completely. He began thinking about how beautiful she was to him and if he could just hold her hand it would make him feel better. Just as Bill was sitting around thinking, the phone rang. It was Pat again. He was finally able to talk to her about coming home. He felt really happy and very much relived about her at least calling him.

"Hello! how are you Bill?"

"Great."

"I have something to tell you Bill!"

"OK, what is it?"

"I'll be home tomorrow for good. It will probably be in the morning, Bill. Honey I really miss you a lot, I can't go on without you. My nights are sleepless, I really need to see you, is it OK if I come home to you? I stopped drinking and I love you very much. I just want to hold you next to me at all times. My heart is saddened without you and I have no one else to turn to and nowhere to go but to you Bill. You are all I have and all I ever wanted. I want to love you more than I ever had in this world."

She hung up before he could say anything else or let her know whether or not he wanted her to come home. Pat hung up so fast it left him wordless, listening to the dial tone. He had no one to talk to. She's gone again, he thought, not knowing if she was really coming home. All she said was I'll be home in the morning, but what morning would she be there, would she be at home tomorrow morning? Would she arrive next week, next month? She didn't say what morning she was coming. Bill stayed up half the night, unable to sleep, wondering what morning his wife was coming home. He sat up drinking coffee, not able to eat. His stomach was getting very nervous from not seeing his wife for a long time. He had no idea of what his reaction would be. It had been two years since he had seen Pat, and in those years he was very much alone, seeing his son only once in a while.

Bill was growing very nervous, anxious and impatient while he was waiting for his wife to return home. The morning finally arrived. After being up all night, Bill began looking out the windows, up and down the streets. He was looking for his wife, pacing the floor, not caring about what she looked like as long as she returned home. Bill felt that he could deal with her in all manners without getting angry, even if she was still drinking. He didn't care as long as he was with her, as long as he had her in his arms day and night. Bill would accept her personality, he just wanted to be with her and to love forever. He wanted to apologize to her, to hold her and never ever let her go again. He had to have her more than anything in this world because no one else mattered to him. Nothing else existed. Life was meaningless without his wife.

He continued to look out the windows as hours and hours passed by. He could no longer contain himself. He walked outside and started looking down each street, waiting on corners for his wife, but she was nowhere in sight, nor was she on her way home to him. As Pat was at the shelter discussing her trip back home, they informed her that she should wait another week before returning home. Pat was saddened about what she heard, for she wanted to go home right away, but all the paperwork had to be taken care of before she could be released from the shelter.

Bill sat around waiting when the phone rang. "Hello, ...Pat is that you?" he called out.

But it wasn't her. It wasn't Pat, it was his old friend John whom he hadn't spoken with for a long time. He had decided to have new friends in his life in order to get rid of all the old memories.

"Hey, Bill this is John, how are you?"

"Great."

"Were you waiting for Pat to call?"

"Yes, I thought she would at least call."

"She hasn't called you yet?"

"Well no, she's supposed to be coming home today, I think, I hope. Well John, I have to go. I would talk to you a little longer but I'm waiting for Pat to call. She called me last night and I really don't want to miss her call."

"Well Bill if you need anything, I'll be here. Or if you need to talk, just call me and I'll meet you somewhere."

"Thanks John, and I will keep you in mind if I need help." Bill hung up the phone and went back to the window and continued his waiting. Bill waited and waited, well into the afternoon but there was no Pat in sight. He started getting angry because he figured he waited long enough for his wife. Still she was nowhere in sight. Pat was too angry and she didn't want to call Bill because she couldn't go home. She only wanted to be next to him and she didn't want to talk to him on the phone. She didn't want to hear his voice unless she could see him, touch him and feel his presence. Sooner or later she would have to call him and let him know that she wasn't coming home until five mornings later.

Day after day Bill sat by the window waiting for his Pat, hoping that she would show up, waiting to see if she was telling the truth about coming home. Every time the phone rang he ran to answered it but still it wasn't Pat. She never called to tell him why she didn't show up. All Bill could do was wait. He figured what was the use of getting angry, it just causes more problems because he wouldn't have anyone to take his anger out on. It was getting real hard to control his temper so he wouldn't get out of hand when he saw her.

When the time came for Pat to go home, the shelter counseled her all day making sure she understood what would happen when she returned home. They warned her how situations could get much worse when battered women returned to their abusive husbands. Pat didn't want to believe what they were saying to her. She really felt in her heart that Bill really loved her and if he said it was over, then it was over. She believed that she just wanted to go home no matter what anyone said or how they felt about her returning to her husband.

Pat packed her things and they watched her, feeling sorry for Pat because of what might happen next. He really did her a job the last time. She was really bad when she came into the shelter for help, they thought. But no one said anything as they watched her haul her things into the car. No one helped. Pat drove by the house four times, not knowing which house it was because of the new paint. It was different colors, a new house. Pat was so confused. She forgot the numbers on the house. So they kept driving around in circles, Bill was standing on the porch stretching, preparing to leave for work. As he was stretching, he looked up and down the street hoping to see his wife. He was hoping she would someday drive up into his presence. He still had a few hours before going to work and he took that time to stand on the porch and let his mind go crazy waiting for Pat.

Finally Pat looked up and saw Bill. She began yelling, "There he is! There's Bill on the porch of that green and white house. He's right there. Pull over there right now!"

"OK! OK!" said the lady that was driving Pat around. "You seem pretty anxious to get to your husband. I've never seen an abused woman return to her husband the way you are. You're acting like he's a new man. Most women don't want to be anywhere near their husband, but you, you're different Pat. I wish you all the luck in the world and I want you to know that you're are more than welcome to come back to the shelter if you need help. Please Pat, call us immediately if you need help."

Pat agreed to what the lady was saying and gave her a hug before she jumped out of the car. She acted as if she was a child running to an amusement park as she walked up the walkway to meet her husband. As she drew closer to him she stopped and they just stared at one another. They just stood and stared. No one made a move and no one said a word. They just stared, they were in shock from not seeing one another for quiet a while. Pat realized that the fear she had no longer existed. The doubt that

Bill had was cleared out of his mind, too.

Something was in the air and it wasn't hatred. It wasn't anxiety. It was nervous love, love was in the air for Pat and Bill all over again. Finally they were coming together. This time it was for love and not hate. What a good feeling Pat felt. It was a sign of relief, a sign of being wanted once again. Bill finally grabbed Pat and gave her tight hugs and soft kisses. Pat returned what Bill was giving her, hugging him back and they were holding one another in love. Bill loving Pat and Pat loving Bill. She began kissing him all over his face, telling him she loved him, she really missed him and she would never, ever leave him as long as she lived.

Bill stood there, not responding, in shock. Finally his wife had returned home. She was finally in his arms. Bill was in shock like he had never been before. He hugged her holding her tighter and tighter with all he had to offer, all his love. Bill was loving Pat for whom he waited for so long. He planned to love and to keep her forever, promising to never harm her again. He kissed her back and kissing her everywhere. He picked her up and carried her into the house where he could love her in private. Bill was happy about his love returning home, he wanted to share his love with everyone. He planned to have a party so all his new friends could meet his wife for whom he waited so long for.

The lady that brought Pat home had to take Pat's bags to the door. Pat forgot all about her bags when she saw her husband standing on the porch. The lady finally drove off. As she was driving she started thinking to herself, I have never seen anything like this before. A man and a woman falling in love after abuse. Women almost never return home and when they do they all ways end up leaving. Things get much worse and they always end up either back in the shelter or dead. Some are so badly beaten that no one can help them. I wondered how long this is going to last. Pat would probably be calling the shelter by the end of next week for help. And we'll probably end up going to the hospital to get her. These type of situations never last. There's always something that comes out later. I really feel sorry for her. It was sad to see her be suckered into something like this, like he really loves her and she fell for it. How can she do this to herself? Everyone at the shelter tried to stop her, but no one could. He was probably needing sex and thought maybe he would sucker his wife into coming home. It worked and he played his cards really good, whatever he told her to get her back must of been some really good words. Those smooth talkers really have their way of getting what they want. Bill really had nerve, hugging her and kissing her and picking her up and carrying her into the house. He really put on a real show.

I bet he took her straight to the bedroom. When he finished with her it would probably be a different story, something very different, one that everyone at the shelter expected to happened. He'll probably show her he loves her all right when he starts beating on her again and throwing her down the stairs like she's some kind of animal. He'll show her how he loves her when he tries to brake every bone in her body. He'll do it until all control is lost and he cant stop. I really felt bad for her. There is nothing worse than going back to an abuser, one who claims he loves you and promises to never do you any wrong. Those are the kind you watch out for. Once a man abuses, he will always abuse the one he claims to do right to. He will always abuse his wife one way or another. He'll find some type of way to go after her. I know for a fact that Pat would be right back in the same condition she was before, all bruised up, battered and in the wrong frame of mind.

Pat would be right back in the shelter before anyone could blink an eye. Poor Pat, the poor lady spent 10 years being abused, why couldn't she find another man, someone who will give her real love, not just infatuation. Silently, I really wished her good luck, all the luck in the world, because he really beat her bad. He beat her really bad she should not have gone back, not for anything in this world. She wouldn't want to live in misery. She thought, may "God Bless Pat" for what she's doing, although she knows once an abuser, always an abuser. She hated to think of her suffering the way she would suffer, going back to him, her so called love. But this time this well meaning woman was wrong, not everyone that comes out of an abusive situation and returns back is once again abused.

Bill really loved Pat and he really wanted to be with her. He really couldn't live without her and he promised himself that he would not abuse her ever again. He would not abuse her, not in his world and not in his lifetime. He was sure of the love that he had for his wife. This woman whom he had waited so patiently for. Bill carried Pat into the house, not saying a word about the changes.

As he put her down Pat looked around the room. "Wow! Everything is different. The house smells great, it looks great. The furniture is different, where did you get it?" Pat said marveling at how new and fresh everything looked.

He just smiled, knowing that she would like it when she came home. She had never seen him smile before. She couldn't remember the last time she had seen him smile. "Oh boy!" Pat continued to looking at the room and Bill in shock.

"The sofa, where is it? It's gone, your favorite sofa, you got rid of it?" Pat asked as she gazed at the brightly colored coach that sat in front of her.

"Yes, sit down Pat,"

Pat couldn't sit down. She had to see more of the house, how everything was different and new. It was all for her.

"It's for you Pat. I did all this for your homecoming. So I want you to enjoy it."

"For me Bill? All this is for me, really?"

Pat couldn't believe her husband changed the whole house for her. She went upstairs to look around, then she began to feel really happy, thinking maybe he did change. Maybe he really loved her. She had no more doubts and no more fear at all. She didn't have to worry about abuse ever again. Those ladies were wrong about returning to an abusive situation, it could work. All his ways have changed, he's a new man, she thought. Then she asked him if it was okay to take a shower, not knowing how to ask this question.

"Sure you may take a shower, it's your house as well as mine." Bill answered lovingly.

Pat ran into Mike's old room, to get some clothes and found they were gone. Her clothes were not there. She looked everywhere and still no clothes in sight.

"Bill," she screamed frightened, "where are my clothes?"

"In the attic." he replied innocently.

"In the attic!" Pat said wondering if perhaps she had made a mistake coming home. Was the abuse beginning to start again?

"We are going to buy you new clothes." Bill said quickly hoping that Pat would understand that they both needed to make a new start.

"But why?" Pat sat on the edge of the bed, looking at the beautifully flowered bed cover, hoping that Bill's reasons for putting her clothes away were from love not hate.

"Because you deserve new clothes, you deserve the world. I'm going to make sure that you have it. I want you to know that I love you," he said with a quiet passion. He looked at Pat, touched her gently and turned walking downstairs leaving her before she could answer. He went to make them coffee to go along with the homecoming cake he had bought a week ago for her.

As he was preparing these things, Pat walked into the bathroom to take a shower. She stood a moment in the middle of the room gazing at the lush green towels hanging on the rack, the multi-colored soaps in the new shell shaped soap dish and began to understand that indeed this was a new Bill she was seeing. After her shower she slowly put back on the same clothes still a little unsure of herself. She looked down at her wrinkled clothing, at least I smell good she thought to herself.

Pat walked downstairs drawn by the smell of the freshly brewed coffee. Bill waited for her before beginning to drink. He called her into the living room so he could talk a little more. As she approached the room, he told her to sit on the sofa where he had everything set up.

As she sat on the sofa, Bill gently held her hand and said, "Pat you know now that I love you very much, so much that I could barely contain myself. I changed my whole life around for you. Living without you was really hard. I want you to love me forever and ever, and I promise Pat to treat you good, better than I have ever treated you in our lifetime. I don't want you to ever have a need or a want for anything in any way possible. I want to show you that I love you dearly in my heart."

Pat just stared at Bill with tears in her eyes, listening to his precious words. He couldn't stop telling her how much he loved her. She really appreciated him for that. After all he put her through, she deserved to hear this from him.

"Bill, I love you too, and I want everything to be right with us. I'm willing to make it as right as possible. I want to be with you forever until death does us part. Leaving or being forced to leave really hurts me. Bill this is my home and this is where I want to be. If I can't be here, I would rather be nowhere at all. But most of all, I want to be happy. You are the person I want to be with and no one else. Bill you mean a whole lot to me, and without you I can't make it. I really can't make it Bill. I want you more than anything in this world and I can't express it enough. I just have to show you how much I really love you." She began to cry and cry loudly. Bill hugged her and told her he understood how she felt because he felt the same way about her.

"Pat," Bill called softly.

"Yes,"

"Will you marry me one more time all over again?"

"But we are married Bill."

"Pat, will you marry me again?"

"Yes! If that's what you want, sure we can marry one more time," she agreed, although she didn't really know what to think. She didn't know how to react to what Bill was asking her. She said OK because she didn't want in any way to make him mad or upset. So she agreed to marry him again and love him forever.

Pat and Bill sat drinking their coffee and eating red velvet love cake. They were in love with one another. He was happy that finally his wife had returned home to him. He promised that no matter what came up, he was going to keep his promise to love her and not ever beating her again. It was going to be a hard trip for him, but he would learn to control himself when situations came up. He would do as John once said, walk away and leave the house. He didn't want to ever again put his wife through that horrible nightmare. He missed her love and now he planned to keep it. He would go to whatever extent it would take him, he was happy and he planned to stay that way and with Pat.

As the days passed on, Bill and Pat planned their wedding. They planned to invite people they hadn't seen in years. They invited relatives who forgot that they even existed, friends they hadn't seen or spoken to since they got married the first time. Everyone was going to be invited to Pat and Bill's wedding. They invited people from the shelter where Pat had stayed. She wanted to show them you can love again the same person that was there before the abuse and you don't have to find a new love. Some men will change. She wanted to prove the ladies wrong. Who said that your man will never change? She wanted to show them he did change because he loved her and loved her right. All the things he said to her were true and very much full of love. Her husband was good to the heart and Pat knew that whatever he said, he meant. She knew that, and that is the reason she gave it another try. She wanted to show the ladies how true her husband was. Finally, to the ladies who said that he would never change, she wanted to show them that he did change because he loved her and he loved her right. He loves her more than anything that exists on earth, or anywhere else in the universe. She felt good about the way her man felt about her.

They planned their wedding and it came together wonderfully, like no other wedding they had ever seen. This was different for Pat, she felt like a new bride, one that has never been married before. She felt special, she felt wanted, she felt like expressing herself to others in a very happy way, a way she never had a chance to express herself before. She felt loved and loved for real. She was wanted once again by her husband. Pat felt her life brighten up. She could actually see a light shining bright, as if she was in a well lighted room where the lights will never be dimmed again. Her life had changed after so much darkness that came about, darkness that entered into her world without notice at all. She felt great all over and nothing could take this great feeling away.

Pat and Bill began to have friends, lots of friends, friends like they never had since they were married. They had parties and barb-b-Q at their house. Since Pat could remember, they had never had parties, and this was definitely a new life for her, sharing their love with others. Bill never hit Pat. He never thought about hurting his wife again, no matter how mad she made him. As time went on, Bill learned how to hide his anger fearing her loss. He would tell her how much he loved her and it took a whole lot to replace anger for love. He didn't want her to ever leave again. It was something he had to do in order to keep what he had. He knew if he showed anger that it would be over and over for good. He couldn't take the chance of losing the one he loved.

Bill and Pat began to really enjoy themselves, taking walks in parks for long hours at a time, spending lots of time with each other kissing and hugging and holding hands. They were really making a difference in their lives and feeling really loved. It was wonderful because they had been missing out on that love for quite a long time. They felt great being together. As Bill and his wife Pat continued to spend lots of time outside, he would pack lunches for them to have in the early afternoon. As they went for long rides in the mountains, where there was absolutely no one around, he would make wonderful love to her for hours and hours. Pat had no arguments about the way Bill was acting, in fact she liked it more than he did. She had nothing to say. She was wordless at his actions and was just enjoying whatever he had in mind, even the late night walks and swims at the beach where they made more love than ever before. The only words that came out of Pat's mouth was how much she adored him and that she would never leave him again as long as she lived. She would tell him how she felt that their love was one of pure magic, once broken up and now mended back together.

Their lovemaking on the beach water became obsessive for Bill, and they always made love outside. Pat didn't have any problem with this, she just enjoyed every moment of it. Her nights were joyous. Bill also became full of joy as he was forgetting the past and everything that went along with it. Bill started taking Pat out to dinners and dancing. He never had taken her out since they had been married, so this was something new. It was a great experience for Pat. Bill felt he owed it to her. After all she had been through, she sure deserved it. Bill took Pat to the finest restaurants San Francisco had to offer.

He spent a lot of time buying her new clothes so that when he took her on ferry rides she would be well dressed, enjoying the early evening breeze from the ferry as it moved swiftly across the water. The ocean breeze would capture their hearts like something they had never felt before and the music would send them dancing along the deck. There was no one to question them as to why they were dancing on the deck. They were off to a good time as if they had just met. They felt love, and it was a new meeting for them, a new meeting of love.

Bill gave Pat all he had to offer and more. He would give her everything he could think of or take any suggestion that someone else made. He do anything to make his wife happy and comfortable with his presence so that all fear would fade away and nothing would ever come between them again. Bill made sure she forgot the past by giving her the love she could not resist, and it worked. Bill and Pat had a wonderful time being all alone. When they would arrive at a restaurant they would dance all through dinner, sharing their love with one another. They were such a happy couple once again and no one would ever believe the horrible nightmare that they experienced as a family through the years of anger and hatred.

Friday nights became very special to them. Friday was a night of love for Pat and Bill "This is something I've never experience before, something I would not have thought of, something out of this world: a ride on the ferry to the most beautiful restaurant in the country, on an island all alone where people can enjoy themselves without anyone bothering them..."

She felt very loved and wanted by her husband. He went out of his way to make her happy, something he didn't have to do, but it was in his heart. She was more than honored to have him treat her in this manner of love. He had a new heart and now she believed all the things he said over the phone because he showed her that he was true to his heart. She believed that when he made a promise he would keep it. This made life so wonderful and she enjoyed every minute.

As time went on Bill never changed he just got better and better. He would bring her flowers, something she learned to enjoy. He would take her shopping for silk and chiffon, something he loved the most. Bill figured nothing could be better than loving his wife. He made sure he kept Pat on his mind all day while he was working. He would call her three times a day to make sure she was happy. He bought her gifts and he also tried to make sure that she would never leave him again or even have the thought of leaving. When you love someone you will do almost any thing to keep them around in your life.

While sitting at home one afternoon the phone rang. Pat answered it, "Hello!"

"Hi is this Pat?"

"Yes, who is this?" Pat answered not recognizing the voice at the other end of the phone.

"This is Jim, remember me, the bartender where you used to come for a drink when things weren't going so good? I tried to get you to go out with me and you wouldn't;"

"How did you get my number?" Pat asked wondering why Jim would call her now.

"John." Jim replied hoping Pat was not angry with him for calling.

"I didn't know you knew John."

"He was telling me all about how you and Bill weren't getting along, so I thought maybe I should give you a friendly call to tell you my offer still stands. You never called me Pat and I've been waiting for your call. I really miss you around here, you don't come in any more. Is it that bad there? You shouldn't have to take that. No one should be treated like an animal." Jim said thinking how beautiful and vulnerable Pat had been the last time he saw her.

"What are you talking about Jim?" Pat said as she gripped the phone tightly.

"Why don't you come to the bar and see. Have a drink with me. We'll have lunch and you can let me wine and of course dine you for once in your lifetime. You deserve the best of what a man has to offer, and I should be the one to make sure you are well taken care of. You didn't tell me it was Bill that was abusing you. I could of saved you a long time ago. I used to see him all the time drunk. He was one of my favorite customers when it came to buying alcohol and that is no joke. So come and let me take real good care of you Pat." Jim waited for Pat to reply. He knew she had been vulnerable in the past and he hoped that her state of mind was still shaky.

"I'm married! And were getting married again in a couple of months." Pat could not believe what she was hearing, how dare this man try to destroy her new found happiness.

"Why would you want to marry him? He'll probably beat you to death. Why would you want to go through hell again? What's the matter with you? Can't you see I'm trying to pull you out of hell?" Jim did not understand the transformation Pat had been through. He could not and did want to believe that she was really happy with Bill.

"Jim, it was nice of you to call and your concern is greatly appreciated. I'll inform Bill that you called to wish us a great marriage. I'll forget this conversation we had today or maybe I'll tell Bill to stop in and see you and John to let you guys know that everything is OK and were getting along just fine. I'm quite sure Bill will be glad to discuss any problems that you and John have about us being together and our lifestyle. Is that OK with you Jim?"

"Sure Pat and I'm sorry for bothering you, but if you ever

need a friend I'm available for you always. You know where you can find me if you need to talk and just remember there's always someone who cares." Jim stared at the phone still not quite sure who this new Pat was.

"OK Jim, good-bye. I think we've talked enough for now." Pat's grip relaxed as she hung up the phone while Jim was still trying to talk to her and comfort her.

A few minutes later Bill called as usual and asked, "Why was the phone busy so long? Who were you talking to?"

"It was Jim the bartender."

"The bartender. What was he calling about?" Bill said wondering how Pat knew Jim and why he would call her.

"He was wondering how you were doing. They haven't heard from you in a while and they really miss you down at the bar, John and Jim." Pat answered, hoping Bill would not ask too many questions about the call from Jim.

"OK Pat, but what is Jim doing calling and how did he get my number?" his suspicions growing, Jim calling did not make sense

"John, honey. John gave him your number. I told him that you would come down and visit them later then I hung up the phone." Pat knew Bill did not completely believe her but she was not going to let anything disturb their happiness.

Bill hung up the phone not believing Pat. He was having second thoughts, thinking that Pat hadn't got over her sneaky ways. She never told him about Jim. Jim had never called the house before as long as Bill had known him. Or maybe he had, and Bill didn't know about it. Bill knew he had been good to Pat and they were getting married again. Why would she be talking to Jim and why would he be concerned about Bill all of a sudden. Bill felt that there was something else going on that Pat didn't tell him about. By this time Bill was getting very angry and uncontrollable. As he sat at his desk he started feeling very insecure about this situation with Jim, wondering what he was getting at and why all of sudden he was coming into their lives. Maybe that's who she had been sneaking out with when she was coming in drunk. Jim hasn't seen her in a long time, so how would he remember her? John must have reminded Jim of who she was. Maybe John was telling Jim about their problems. Pat was not the type of person to go around telling her business, especially to people she didn't know, so it must have been John.

Bill decided to get to the bottom of this. What did Jim want with Pat? He had never called his house before as long as Bill had known him. Bill was getting very angry and was losing control of himself. He was not capable of handling this, so he left work early and went to the bar to see Jim. Jim was talking to John.

"Hey Jim," Bill walked angrily into the bar.

John turned around, "Hey, Bill. We were just talking about you."

"Well, what were you talking about? Is the conversation about my wife? You better sit down Jim and let me tell you a little something about my wife who you seem so interested in."

"OK, Bill, since there are no customers, I guess I could hear a little about your wife, since you know so much and there's a lot you have to tell me," Jim sat down next to John and Bill.

Bill shifted in chair barely able to control himself, "Is there a problem here! I want to know what are you trying to get going with my wife. Don't you have other women to pick on besides someone else's love?"

"No! Bill, I don't think so. She's a pretty lady and she shouldn't be abused. I happen to like her very much." Jim looked straight into Bill's eyes not willing to back down from him.

"Why are you calling my house? If you like her that much then you should wait for her on the outside."

Jim swallowed very hard, so hard you could hear it, "Your wife and I happen to be friends."

Bill grabbed Jim by the throat and said, "If I ever catch you talking about, or getting anywhere near my wife, I will kill you myself. Do you understand that Jim? Don't you ever in life call my house again or you will definitely pay. I will promise you that Jim, you will pay for what you're doing. It won't come on a platter, at least not from me."

"Let go of me Bill. I'm really sorry. What would I do with a battered woman anyway?" Jim backed down realizing Bill was close to hysteria.

Bill got even angrier and began punching Jim and throwing him around the bar until John pulled Bill away from Jim. John, "that's enough! It was my fault, because I gave Jim your telephone number. I'm really sorry about that,".

Bill looked at John, pushed him away and left the bar feeling angry and uneasy. He drove around and he realized he was really mad. He had to cool off before going home. He didn't want Pat to see him like this, nor did he want to go home showing that he was angry. He feared that he would say something to Pat, and he didn't want to make her angry because she would leave. He didn't want her to ever leave him again. He just couldn't take living by himself, so he drove around for several hours until he finally cooled down. His temper finally went away and he was back to normal, back to smiling again. He was able to handle his wife without letting her know what went on at the bar. She must not find out how he got out of control with his old friends. He was supposed to walk away from that type of environment, but he had to stop them before things got carried away.

Bill stopped at the mall to pick up a nice gift for Pat in order to show her his appreciation. He wanted to show her that she never had to worry about him abusing her ever again. Then he picked up flowers and went home to Pat, trying to forget what went on earlier that day with Jim and John. He decided it was over and well settled. He would never have to worry about Jim coming on to his wife again. Bill decided that he wasn't going to let anyone destroy his love for his wife, or come between them. He promised himself he was going to love his wife forever and that was a promise he made to both of them. As he walked in the door, Pat had dinner on the table waiting for him. He took longer than usual, so she had to put dinner into the microwave to heat it up. He didn't mind, whatever she did, he was going to be pleased with her actions.

When she heard him come in, she ran to him to greet him at

the door. She wanted to prove to him that the phone call had no effect on their new love. She hugged him and gave him a real nice kiss, one he enjoyed so much. He gave her the flowers and the really nice gift he had purchased at the mall.

"Wow! Bill, what is this? You didn't have to do this. I love you with my heart."

"I know Pat, just open it."

When she opened it she couldn't believe her eyes. It was a beautiful glittery chiffon dress. Tears began to fall down from her eyes at the way things had been going. He was making her so happy. It was unbelievable, it was like a fairy tale. He was marvelous and he pleased her. She had never been so happy in her life.

"Honey, I really love you and nothing or nobody will ever take your love away from me again. I can promise you that I'm not going anywhere, nowhere at all."

So they sat down to have dinner, then went for a long walk in the darkness of the night. They held hands and stopped at every block to kiss. He loved his wife so much, much more than anyone could ever imagine. Jim and John had things all wrong. John had not seen Bill in a long time. He thought Bill was abusing Pat again, he also thought Bill was probably locking Pat up in the house again. Pat never called Joan to tell her that everything was all right and that she was OK. She never had time to even say hi to Joan because Bill took up all of Pat's time. He made sure she was always busy with something when he wasn't around. He also made sure she kept busy around the house.

Pat stayed happy while she was getting ready for her wedding. She was checking everything and making last minute adjustments. She sent out her invitations and made sure everything was grand and right on time. She had a lot to do, preparing her wedding all by herself.

The next day Joan called Pat. Pat answered the phone as if it was Bill, "Hi honey, are you having a great day? Excuse me, oh... who is this?"

"It's Joan, were you expecting a call from Bill?"

"Yes, how are you Joan?"

"Great,"

"How are things going with you and John?"

"I should be asking you that question."

"Well Bill and I are doing great. It couldn't be better. Is there something wrong? First Jim calls, then you call, is every thing OK?"

"Yes, everything is all right. Would you like to have lunch with me Pat?"

"Sure, why don't you come over here. I cant leave the house, Bill is going to call."

"OK Pat, I'll be right over." They hung up and Pat went back to preparing things for her wedding. She was enjoying this. As she sat down, the doorbell rang. It was Joan.

"Wow! That was fast. Did you drive a hundred miles an hour?"

"No, I was in the neighborhood visiting someone when I called you. That's why I asked you if you would like to go out and have lunch with me. We can have lunch here if you like. So what are we having for lunch?" Joan asked. As she was talking she looked around. "Wow!"

"What Joan? You look like you've seen a ghost."

"Is everything different or is it my imagination?"

"Everything is different. Bill bought new furniture and had the whole house painted for my return home. Everything is my favorite color. He has been so wonderful to me, I can't begin to tell you how great things that have been going on."

"The house looks great, you look great Pat. You look well taken care of."

"I am. Bill treats me like a queen. I love him so much, he makes me feel so good and really great. We're planning to get married again to share our new love with everyone."

"Married, Pat! You and Bill?"

"Yes."

"When?"

"Next week." Pat replied.

"But why get married again? You guys are already married?"

"Bill wants to do this, so I'm going right along with him, whatever makes him happy. So now we've been planning for about one entire year and next week is it."

"How come you didn't tell me about this. You haven't even called me since you've been back."

"Well Joan, I've been too busy with my husband and I haven't had time. I did mail you and John a invitation to our wedding. You should be getting it soon."

"Well I'm happy for you Pat. I hope it works out for you and Bill this time. You look great. I have to keep telling you because you do. I had no idea what was going on here."

As pat listened to Joan she looked at the clock and worried. Bill had not called yet. He always calls at 1:00 p.m., she thought concerned. Pat sat waiting for the phone to ring. Instead, the doorbell rang and rang. She couldn't get to it fast enough. The person at the door was going crazy with the bell. As she opened the door, a delivery boy with 20 dozen yellow roses appeared at the door. He was struggling, trying to get them into Pat's house without dropping any of them because Bill gave him a big tip to deliver the flowers in one piece. The flowers included a lovely message of how much Bill loved her. The delivery boy sang a nice love song to Pat and she burst out in tears in front of Joan. They were happy tears, though. She closed the door and let the man go on his way.

"This explains why he didn't call. He really is a sweet person Joan. He's really

trying to please me in all ways."

Joan was shocked at what she saw and heard, "Bill sent you all those roses?"

"Yes, he's so wonderful and loving."

"Really, Pat?"

"He has really changed."

"Those are beautiful. Does he send flowers all the time?"

"No, he brings them himself. This is the first time he has had them delivered."

"Well, looks like everything is going great for you." Joan said not quite

believing what see was hearing and seeing.

After having lunch, Joan went home to tell John the news about Bill and how he had made a tremendous change. Pat returned to her wedding plans, getting excited as if it were her first time. As the days went by, people began calling to reserve their spot and congratulate Pat on her wedding. She started getting nervous as if it was her first time getting married. She answered all the questions that people were asking her, but most of all she was happy, very happy to share her love with others.

She and her husband were all ready to go the day before their wedding. Pat was preparing her eggshell dress with exquisite matching accessories. Once again she was getting married, getting ready to proclaim her love to her husband all over again. As Pat's family arrived they went to stay with her while Bill was in a hotel with his family. They were all waiting for that great moment, sharing an evening with their families whom they hadn't seen or spent any time with since they were married the first time. Pat became even more happy as she told them how much he really loved her. She dared not tell them that he beat her for a lot of years. She couldn't tell them that reason they were getting married again was to wipe away the years of abuse. She didn't want it to ever be brought up again. She would totally disown anyone who brought it up, and then clear them out of her mind.

She wanted to be happy for the rest of her life with the man she loved and knew since childhood. She was very happy and that was all that mattered to her. As their wedding took place, getting married for the second time was more precious than anything they had ever seen before. It was more like the first time around. Pat walked to her husband with smiles that would not disappear. He returned the smiles, unable to control his happiness. He waited until she reached him and he took her hand and they stared their love into each other eyes. Neither of them blinked as they were married once again for better and for worse. Pat married Bill in love till death parts them. Then they went to celebrate with their friends and family with food and drinks.

John and his wife Joan stared and watched, knowing Bill and Pat's past. They couldn't believe how they acted like nothing ever happened, like they never had problems. They knew something that no one else in the wedding party knew.

Bill and Pat celebrated with singing and dancing. Bill wouldn't let anyone touch his wife or have a conversation with her. Every time someone would talk to Pat, he would interrupt and take her to the floor to dance. He hoped she would not say anything about their past. Only he was allowed to dance with her. John watched every move that Bill made, waiting for him to make a mistake so that everyone would know the truth about him. John wanted them to see how Bill was not the sweet man that he claimed to be in front of his family and new friends.

The way Bill was acting became a problem for Pat. She wanted to share with everyone their marriage of love. Only with Bill's family could she share this love. He wouldn't let her dance with her own father, fearing that he might find out about their abusive past. Mike, their son, knew and he never said a word. Mike was happy for his mother and father because they were finally loving one another again. He was more than happy for them. Finally, it came time to thank everyone for coming.

Bill and Pat left and went to the airport, something Pat didn't know about. She didn't ask any questions. They went away on a long trip to the Islands, a place Pat had never been before. She was so happy she couldn't gain control over herself. She was nervously happy and kept a smile on her glowing face. Throughout the whole trip she was as happy as she could get. Bill made sure that she was happy. He gave her all she needed and more. Bill and Pat returned home from a long trip that lasted 3 weeks. The house was filled with gifts and flowers. People from all over were congratulating them. It was such a beautiful sight for Bill and Pat, serving in love for one another. They never got a chance to open and see all the lovely things people sent them.

Bill decided to have a welcome home party. This wasn't like Bill at all, so Pat planned a party for all her friends and family. It was a real delight, with catering like Pat had never done before.

Joan decorated the house in Pat's eggshell colors, the colors of her wedding. For the first time, Pat and Joan became close friends in happiness instead of pain and sorrow. Pain and sorrow had been in their life since they had first met. They became really close to a point where Bill couldn't brake up their friendship. The party was a success. People complimented them, then went their separate ways. Bill was pleased with what Pat had done. He knew she had it in her somewhere. He knew his wife was as lovely as he thought and it made him very happy.

Pat never had second thoughts about her marriage. One thing she knew is that Bill would never leave her or beat her ever again. She knew in her heart that this time their marriage was a success. Pat knew she could handle this because all the things that Bill said to her were true, especially about him falling in love with her and loving her forever and ever. All Pat could do was think about Bill day and night. She thought about how good he had been to her. Bill kept his promise. He kept control of his anger, which was the promise he made to Pat, he didn't let her down.

As time went on their love grew stronger and stronger. Bill maintained the same attitude about his wife and kept things under control at home. He was really possessive over her, though, and she was still locked inside without realizing it. It didn't matter to her as long as she was happy. Besides, she had nowhere to go anyway. Pat never went anywhere because she had to wait for him to call. That was his way of keeping up with her and knowing her every move. Pat didn't realize this because she had been sheltered for so long. It was no problem to her, but she had new friends now and they wanted to go places. They wanted to go out to lunch and have chit chats about their husbands and do different things. Pat couldn't attend because of the hold that Bill had on her. No one brought it to her attention because of what she went through the first time with Bill. Her friends were true friends. They understood Pat's problems, so they went to her house and brought lunch with them. It wasn't any problem for them as long as they could chit chat about their lives.

Pat was very happy with the decisions that they made, but

Joan had a problem with this. She didn't like the way Bill had control over Pat. Joan considered it another type of abuse. If Bill loved Pat then he should trust her. Joan thought about this over and over again. Every time she wanted Pat to have lunch outside the house she couldn't go because Bill was going to call. Pat would tell Joan that Bill loved talking to her whenever he got a break. Joan didn't understand Bill's way of love. She didn't understand anything he did. She thought he was out of his mind.

Joan tried to think of ways to get Pat out of the house. She decided to take her to a Duchess meeting. She began telling Pat about how women make money selling cosmetics and skin products. She said to her, "It's a great start for someone who has never worked before. The people are really nice. It will be a great job, Pat. Bill can enjoy you at home because you work at you own level and you are your own boss. I want you to give it a try Pat."

"Well, what time is the meeting Joan?"

"7:00 p.m. and it lasts for 2 to 3 hours. It all depends on how many people attend the meeting."

"Well Joan it sounds good, but I will have to ask Bill. He might have something planned for us tonight or maybe he would like to go with us."

Joan tried to explain to her that mostly women would be there, "John's not going."

"I'll have to call you back Joan after I talk to Bill. 7:00 is kind of late and he likes to cuddle up around that time."

"OK Pat, just give me a call before 6:00 p.m. I'm leaving around that time." Pat hung up and Joan began speaking to John about Pat, "She stays closed up like some kind of animal. She has to get permission for everything. I don't call that true love. I call that craziness. He's still abusing her mentally."

"Well as long as he's not hitting her, she's his wife. As long as she's happy he can do whatever he wants."

"It's not my problem, but John I still don't get this."

"He doesn't really trust her. That's the problem. He thinks she is going to run off and never come back."

"Well she has been gone a long time.  They have been having a lot of problems."

"He probably doesn't want things to get out of hand.  I guess that's his way of keeping her right where he wants her."

"Well she can't even go outside and that's not right.  I don't agree with that.  He might as well lock her up in the house."

"I don't think that's so, Joan."

"Would you want someone to lock you up in the house? No! That's why I'm trying to get her out of the house and away from him before she goes crazy being around him."

"Joan I think you should butt out before you cause some real serious problems for them.  I think he really loves her and wants to work it out.  You have to give the man a little credit, at least he is trying to do what's right."

"Okay, John.  I think you're right, but it doesn't look good at all."

Bill arrived home at his normal time and as usual Pat had dinner on the table waiting for him.  They sat down to eat and when Bill finished Pat asked if it would be OK for her to go with Joan to a meeting.

"What kind of meeting Pat?" Bill said, giving her a cold look as she nervously responded.

"A Duchess meeting, to sell make up for women."

"And when is this meeting?"

"Tonight."

Bill just looked at Pat like she was insane, "And where did Joan come up with this?"

"I think she sells the products."

"Well I guess you could go, but call me when you get there."

Joan called back to see if Pat was going.

"Hello," Bill answered.

"Is Pat there?"

"Yes, and what would you like with her?"

"This is Joan and I was wondering if she would like to go."

"Sure she would, she's getting ready upstairs."

"OK, tell her I'm on my way.  I'll be right there to pick her up."

After Joan hung up the phone John said, "It's not like what you think. She's not locked up after all."

"I guess he's letting her out. But I better go before he changes his mind." Joan ran out of the house and rushed over to pick up Pat.

As Pat and Joan were leaving Bill said, "Come straight home after the meeting. I'll be waiting for you."

"OK, honey!" Pat yelled. They took off. Joan pulled off quickly. She didn't want Bill to run out and change his mind.

As they were driving, Joan began to talk, "Don't you feel closed in, being in the house all the time?"

" hadn't thought about that. I love my husband and it doesn't matter to me, so why should it matter to you?"

"I just thought maybe you might need some air every once in a while."

"Well sometimes I need to get out, but it doesn't bother me."

"Well this will get you out of the house, at least part of the day while Bill is working. He won't have to worry at all."

Pat was enjoying the meeting. She was picking up a lot about cosmetics, things she never knew before. She liked it so much she joined the group to sell products without Bill's permission. She won a prize, a little package of makeup. She had never won anything before, so this made her feel really great. Besides, she liked what she heard about the company. She also wanted to win a car because she never had a car, at least her own car. Their car was always Bill's car. Everything sounded good to her. She knew Bill would love to hear about this information, since he loved anything that made her happy.

Pat took home everything she purchased, including tapes and the whole Duchess set. She had also forgotten to call Bill. After the meeting they went out to eat at the nearest restaurant. They sat and talked for hours. As time passed and Pat was having the time of her life, Bill was at home waiting on a call that never came. His wife didn't come home and it was getting really late. He started getting angry and worried about where his wife was. He was thinking about how he should not have let her run off with

Joan, because Joan never stays home to take care of her husband. As he was getting mad, Pat walked in. Bill was sitting up waiting, trying not to express his anger, but he wasn't very good at that. Whenever he got mad it showed everywhere, all over his face.

Pat stood in the doorway not knowing what to say.

"So where have you been and how come you didn't call me like I told you?" Bill demanded.

The meeting really took a long time and there wasn't a telephone in sight. There was a lot of people there, but look honey!" She began to explain to him about Duchess and showed him what she had purchased at the meeting and the prize that she had won.

All Bill could do or say was, "That's great. Who told you to buy this stuff? Who said that you could work?"

She began explain the concept of winning lots of prizes for selling a certain amount of products, "It all sounded great to me and I thought you would love to hear about this group."

"If you wanted a new car you should have told me. I would have bought us a new car."

Bill put down everything that Pat said. She felt very low. For the first time she wanted to do something with her life besides stay in the house. She wanted to get out like most women and have a job, but he didn't want her to work. He didn't want her out of his sight because he knew that she would always be gone.

"Bill you said that everything would be different, not like it was before. This is different. This is a start to a new life for us."

Bill didn't have anything to say. He got up and went to bed. He left her sitting in the living room alone with her Duchess products. She watched the film for hours and hours until he came downstairs and told her to come to bed. It seemed that she was going to watch the tape all night. Bill accepted Pat's new job as long as his dinner was on time and it didn't effect their relationship in any way. He was happy with the way she did her business because it seemed that she was always at home. It worked out for a while because she was just learning and she was at home when he called, so he learned to accept it and move on.

Pat was getting good at selling her products. She had a great business going on in her neighborhood. She sold so many products that she won a trip to a really nice meeting out of state. Bill wasn't invited. When she told Bill about the trip he wasn't too happy. He knew that Pat was leaving for a while. He felt she was becoming too independent. He told her she couldn't go.

Pat was very upset. "But Joan is going," she cried out.

"Forget about Joan, she doesn't live here and she not my wife! Do you think you could go everywhere she goes?"

"But I won this trip."

"Seems as if you're winning a lot lately. Are you sure you are winning these things? They're probably giving these things to you because of something Joan said."

"I've been working really hard on this job Bill. No one gives you anything."

They began to really argue about Pat's job like they had never argued before. They hadn't fought like this for long time. Bill and Pat were fighting but they were only fighting with words. Joan rang the doorbell, unable to hear what was going on inside. Even though Bill didn't want to see Joan at all, he let her in so she could hear the argument that was going on between him and Pat. He blamed Joan for their fight. If she would have kept her bright ideas at home it would not have gotten to this point. As Joan listened to Bill, she became angry at him for blaming her. She had not forced Pat into buying the Duchess products. Pat did it on her own. Bill didn't care, it was all Joan's fault.

Bill was very angry and started yelling at Joan too, "You drove Pat to this point where she wants our marriage go down the drain. You don't want to see us happy. Can't you see that Pat, or are you that blinded that you can't see what Joan is doing. We were happy before she came around. Every time her and her husband come around they bring trouble. Now look what is happening. You want to run off every time she blinks her eyes."

Joan was shocked at what she was hearing, what Bill was saying about her and her husband. She couldn't believe Bill was talking about John that way, after John helped Bill. Joan didn't say a word. She didn't want Bill to start taking it out on Pat when she left, so she kept quiet. Pat didn't say anything either. Bill did all the talking, he was angry and getting angrier at Joan. He decided to tell Pat that she could not go. He told her no and that was final. Then he asked Joan if she had something to say.

She said, "I think I'd better go home. Things are getting out of hand here."

"I think you better go home, too! I think you better stay away from my house and my wife. None of this would have occurred if you had never taken Pat to that stupid meeting. You just can't stop butting in our life."

"It's not a stupid meeting," Joan said. After defending the Duchess group she stormed out, slammed the door and rapidly drove off . She was mad at what Bill was saying about her and her husband when they were only trying to help them.

Bill decided that Pat wouldn't be selling anything in his house. He plainly told her, "If you ever sell anything or plan to go anywhere without my permission, you can just leave and never come back into my life again. It won't be a happy trip, I can promise you that Pat. I've only tried to make you happy and I went well out of my way to do that. If you can't accept the way I'm treating you then go where Joan is. She can't do anything for you because she can't help herself."

Pat started crying, "Why! Bill I thought you loved me?"

"I do love you and I will show you how much I love you. But every time Joan comes around things go bad. I don't want you talking to her ever again."

Pat begin to think about what Joan had said about Bill being too possessive over her. It was true but it kept them happy. "Bill I'm not going anywhere. I'm your wife and I will never leave you honey. That's why I came back. Because I wanted to be with you forever and if you love me you will not act like that toward my friends or my job. Joan was just trying to help. She was trying to be friendly by giving me something to do while you are at work. She was only trying to be helpful, that's all. She didn't mean any harm to our marriage. The only harm that can be done to us is you. I can make things better or worse, it's not her. So don't blame her for our actions."

Bill didn't have an answer for Pat. He went to bed and left her sitting at the table. He did not look back to see her reaction. He went straight to bed.

Pat called Joan to apologize for Bill's anger. She told her that everything was OK, "He understands now and I hope you are not offended by the way Bill was acting. He's just insecure right now and he has to learn to trust me. He will change his mind soon and I'll call you. Please Joan, don't call me while he's here. I don't want him to get upset again, at least not right now."

"OK, Pat. I won't call you. But you make sure you call me. I will be here for you. Bill can get out of hand sometimes and you can't control him."

"OK Joan, I'll call you, bye." Pat hung up the phone. She didn't want Joan to know the truth about how Bill felt about the situation.

Pat sat up all night drinking coffee, wondering if Bill was going to change back to his ways, if he was going to start beating her again. He promised her that he would never do that again. Pat never went to sleep. She stayed awake all night sitting at the table.

Bill woke up looking at Pat's side of the bed. It was empty. He jumped up, calling her. She didn't answer, she was still sitting in the same spot where he left her. Without a sound he ran downstairs and she just stared at him, not saying a word.

"Honey! How come you didn't come to bed last night?"

She began to cry, upset by the way he acted last night. So Bill sat down next to her and started hugging her, "What's the matter? Why are you crying?"

"Honey!" she began to say, "You promised me that you wouldn't act like this, that we were going to have a perfect marriage. We worked so hard to accomplish this love we have and I don't want to give it up. But you seem to be getting mad at everything I do outside the house. I'm only trying to do what's right. There is nothing bad about selling something. I'm not causing any problems Bill."

"Pat, it's not you at all. Some people are poison, like Joan. She doesn't want to see you happy. You think she's your friend, but she's not. If she was, she wouldn't be causing problems between us. She loves to make things worse and make you believe bad things about me. That's not a friend. I want you to see that. Think about all the things that she told you that are bad. They're not really all that bad. You need to find better friends, people who really care. I bet Joan told you that I don't really love you. That's because she doesn't know what goes on inside our house. You know for a fact that I love you, Pat. She doesn't live with us and she thinks she knows it all, but she doesn't and that's why I don't want her around you. All she brings is trouble and we don't need any more trouble in our life. Open up your eyes and see just what she's doing to you. She's not helping you at all. Just look at yourself Pat. Look at how you're acting. See, you are already thinking negative and we don't need that. So go upstairs and go to sleep, get some rest. I'll call you later and if you want to go somewhere I'll gladly take you. OK honey? Don't worry, we'll go to San Francisco and have dinner tomorrow. So go upstairs and get some sleep before you fall out. I'll take care of Joan."

"Bill, you need to call her and apologize."

"I'll do that for you."

As Pat went upstairs, Bill got dressed and went to work. He was very upset at what Joan was doing to their marriage. Anger flared up in him. He couldn't wait to call Joan to let her know how he felt about her being Pat's friend. Pat slept all day and he never called to wake her up, for he knew how tired she must have been after staying up all night worrying.

Instead of calling Pat, he called Joan. "Joan, this is Bill."

"What can I do for you Bill?"

"You can stay away from my wife. She doesn't need you around her causing problems. You are nothing but a problem in her life and I want you to stay away from her!"

"You know Bill, you really don't have a life. You keep your

wife locked up like some kind of animal. You get mad if she has friends. You need serious help Bill, so go and get a life." Joan hung up the telephone without giving Bill a chance to respond.

He called back, he had something else he had to tell her. Joan didn't answer the phone, though, she knew it was him and she didn't want to hear anything he had to say to her. John finally picked up the phone because Bill wasn't going to give up.

"Hello, Bill what is it?"

"I need to talk to Joan!"

"Bill say whatever it is, you can say it to me and I'll tell her."

"I want her to stay away from my wife and I don't want her to ever call my house again." Bill hung up on John and tried to clear his anger away ,like nothing ever happened. Joan tried to explain to John about everything that happened the night before, but he didn't have anything to say. He told her to stay away and stop butting into their business. She wouldn't listen to him. John already got a taste of Bill's anger when Jim called his house and he hadn't spoken to Bill since. He didn't want to hear what Joan had to say.. In fact, he left while she was talking. She was so mad she started throwing things at the door. It didn't work because he didn't look back.

Joan thought, "well if Pat wants to talk she can call me. I'm not ever going to call her again. If he starts beating on her again I'm going to ignore the situation and tell her to go somewhere else. Just when I was trying to be her friend she turns her back on me, listening to her abusive husband. She'll learn one day."

Bill sent yellow roses to Pat and they arrived an hour before he arrived home. She was so happy to receive these flowers. Her eyes showed a great deal of brightness. It let her know that he still wanted to be in love with her for good. Pat put the beautiful roses in a vase on the dinner table where they would be having guests, some new friends that she met at the Duchess meeting. She wanted to let Bill know that there was more to it than just selling. There were very nice people involved in this group. As she was preparing dinner, Bill walked in and saw the lovely table. All the china and crystal they received from their wedding was set out. Everything looked so beautiful. He couldn't believe his eyes. At least breaking up Pat and Joan's friendship didn't tear Pat apart. He started feeling good about her reaction towards the problem. He thought about how things can be worked out without anger.

"What's all this for?"

"We're having company tonight. You said find new friends, so I did and they're coming over tonight for dinner."

Pat didn't tell him that her friend belongs to Duchess. She told her friend not say anything. Helen and Tom arrived on time for dinner. Bill was pleased at their appearance Helen stood with her long wavy black hair shoulder length in colors of tan band brown to match her light brown suit with a multi-color tie to match as Bill stood smiling. Please! Come in, have a seat."

They had dinner then talked. Bill liked Tom, he was really pleasant. He liked his conversation. He asked him if they would like to join them for dinner in San Francisco.

"Oh that's quite a trip," Tom said. "but sure, we would like very much to join you."

The next morning Bill explained to Pat that they are the kind of friends she needed, someone who could help keep her positive about herself and their marriage.

She asked Bill, "If Helen is my friend, can I continue to sell the products?"

Bill said, "I have no problem. We'll have to see how they work out first. Then maybe so."

She finally told Bill that Helen sells Duchess.

After hearing this, Bill said "Sure that's OK, I like them and she seems really nice. She doesn't know anything about you and don't tell her. Keep things nice and it will be OK. We won't have the problems that we had with Joan. It won't ever get to that point again."

Pat accepted Bill's answer with a hug and a kiss. Finally it was Friday, time to get dressed up and go out for a nice ride. Helen and Tom rented a nice car for the drive to San Francisco. As Bill opened the door he was shocked at what he saw. He was shocked at the way they were dressed, they were all dressed up. So he went upstairs and completely changed his clothes so he wouldn't feel out of place. As they reached San Francisco, Tom asked what exit to take. He hardly ever went to San Francisco for dinner and this was a great treat for his wife. She had never been to San Francisco.

Bill told them, "We're going to the pier. We're going to ride the ferry."

"The ferry, we're having dinner on the ferry?" asked Helen.

"No, the ferry takes you to an island of restaurants, and that's where we are going for dinner and dancing," Bill explained.

Helen and Tom liked this idea. "Where did you get this idea?"

"Pat and I go all the time, only on Fridays.

They had a great time. Everything turned out marvelous and Bill was pleased. Helen talked about the trip all the way home and thanked Bill for a great time. He paid for the whole trip in advance.

"We'll have to do this again sometime," Bill.

Tom added, "It sounds good to me. Bill I'm ready whenever you are. We have to get together more often."

Pat was happy at the way Bill reacted to these people. She had never seen Bill act like this, especially around others. Did he really make a change she thought, when they arrived home. Pat decided to do something different, something she thought was special for Bill. As he went to take off his clothes and take a shower, she took the yellow roses and changed the bed linen. She spread the rose buds quickly all over the bed. She sprayed the bed with a rose scented perfume that she had gotten from her Duchess collection. She put on a white chiffon gown, Bill's favorite, and lay down waiting for him to return to the room. He looked shocked when he saw her. He had never seen anything like it before, especially from his wife. She looked so beautiful. She said out loud, "For you only, honey."

His stomach begin to rock from his wife talking sexy to him. He couldn't believe this.

"You make me so happy," she yelled out. "So I'm going to please you in any way I can. I want you to be happy because I want you to know I love you so much. I want to show you how wonderful I think you really are."

"Pat I don't know where you got this idea, but I like it. If this is what Duchess trains you to be like, then I suggest that you keep selling their products. Or if it's Helen or whoever is teaching you to be like this, then continue their process because I like this. This will make me happy. If you could do this for me all the time, it would make me happy and pleased."

After such a pleasant evening Bill left for work with a great big smile. He couldn't believe the way things were turning out. He knew for a fact that things could work for him and his wife. They didn't always have to live in anger, hating one another. The love they had was still somewhere in their hearts. He had faith in himself to bring it out. Later in the afternoon Bill called Pat as usual to make sure that she was feeling as good as he was. He was feeling more than good. It couldn't be explained how great he felt. He had no one to share it with but his precious wife Pat. As he talked to her he couldn't stop telling her how much he loved her and continued telling her how wonderful he thought the night was and how thrilled he was.

Pat was happy to hear that she could finally make her husband happy. It pleased her just as well. There was nothing like pleasing her husband. As time went on she continued her new job selling Duchess. He had no problems with it. She enjoyed this new job of hers. He gave her money to open up her shop in the house so she wouldn't have to travel much. People would feel more free to come to her house. Bill didn't have to worry about her leaving the house for anything but buying products. When Pat did leave, she would come back happy because Helen was a nice person and made Pat feel good about herself. Bill didn't mind her leaving with Helen at all. She was different from Joan, she didn't cause problems or tell Pat bad things about him. He was more than pleased. Pat became a positive thinker and they were happy with their new love and their new life.

# HAPPY
# FOREVER 8

As Bill and Pat began their new life together things began to change the future began to look a lot brighter. Even more lovely, their happiness finally came to life after all the darkness that came about in their lives. They put away all the old things and took a chance on all the new, and no one but Bill really knew if things were going to work. It was up to him to put away the horrible crimes that he was committing on his wife. He looked for brighter skies and a loving future with his wife, and when he searched for new things he found them.

They found new friends Helen and her husband Tom. They found life in these friends and began going out with them not only for dinner, but they would also just hit the town like never before. It brought happiness for Bill and Pat. Forgetting about the past even the trips became exciting for them. Helen and Tom knew nothing about Bill and Pat's past, which made their life even more simple. They were able to forget and not be reminded of how Bill used to treat Pat, or was treating her now. He became more free with her as long as she was with Helen, because she was a good wife to her husband and she showed him much love. Bill saw this as he watched Helen.

As time went on it paid off for him. It made his wife change. She became what he called sweeter and very loving to him. She became something he would not have dreamt of or even thought of. He accepted everything she did because she did it right. He showed he really did love his wife in spite of everything else. He also showed her in many ways possible that he loved her, it became the simplest thing in his life. Love became so simple and easy to manage. He wanted what he had, what he considered his, and that was Pat. She belonged to him forever and love kept them together in spite of all the unhappiness.

Bill worked on improving his attitude and controlling his anger. He tried to be nice to her in every way possible just to prove to her that he loved her and he was very sorry for his past actions. He had been wrong and he also suffered because of that. It didn't matter to Pat. She loved him. He was her only love. She sought to give it a second chance even if she wasn't really sure. She knew it would work because she had faith in his words. He was true and honest. When he said he was going to do something he would do it. She knew that for sure. He also gave her the option to leave if things didn't go the way he had planned; if he started beating on her again he would help her leave. Those were his true words and she believed him and went back home for love.

At one point Bill had gotten so angry at her that abuse was gradually creeping in, fighting anger showed his true love for Pat, he took control of himself. He refused to listen to his anger and went to bed and withheld his dangerous hand. He knew if he hit his wife that it would be over. She would never come back. He even instructed her to leave and never come back. He was true to his word and didn't want her to find another man to love. He wasn't going to let her leave and she wasn't going anywhere because she couldn't live without him. Bill knew that this love was very important, not only to him but also to her. He wanted to grow old with her. Love was important to the English family, and the way they treated one another made things work out for the both of them. Their son was happy to see his parents loving one another for the first time in a long time. Things went the way Bill had planned.

Things were going great until his friend John and his wife Joan started getting involved. In the event of helping it was creating more problems. Moments of hatred were soon returning back to reality for Pat not letting her forget the horrible hell Bill put her through, although she tried to clear it out of her mind and go on with her new life. John and Joan had no idea what life was like for Pat and Bill. They assumed that he was beating on her when all he was doing was loving her. He was giving her all he had, all that she deserved, all the love she had missed out on. He was giving her all he could and much more. Pat loved every bit of it, not complaining one bit or doubting Bill's compassion felt real good.

Pat's self esteem increased having patience and faith created a new and motivated person. He brought her back to life. Her appearance returned back to normal, Bill was her life. He was all she had and that completed her life. Pat knew Bill loved her. Insanity faded away hatred and animosity was no longer an issue. Strong aversion was needed for this person to move on with her life and become a new person. Bill gained respect for himself feeling of strong attachment capture his life a change of his unseen anger being able to control himself in all manners Bill's ardent affection was very important not wanting allow abuse to entered into his life ever again.

He took his marriage for what it was worth and treasured like precious as gold for all that it was worth to him. Disgrace fell upon the shelter of Pats return home her unbelievable heart after such horrible abuse, Pat was looked down on for returning back to her unconditional life style. Pat followed her heart and it paid off control had reconstructed her life.

John absent of their situation. He had Jim call and talk to Pat, upsetting Bill. Bill was very angry considering the extent of try-ing to keep his home a happy place to live. Joan had decided that Bill was keeping Pat locked up. In Joan's mind it was his way of treating her bad. Another system to over look his anger, pay back still in Bill's mind once again he's taking control (in Joan's eyes) so she decided to do something about it. This increased Bill's anger . Instead of curing the problem they were making life more miserable for Pat and especially for Bill, whom was learning to control his anger without involving Pat. It became a test of life, being able to prevent from flaring up Bill's vehement nature was definitely uncontrollable. He would constantly keep in mind the change he was supposed to be making.

He also remembered that anger is not a form of love or being sympathetic of you problems. The only way to control anger was to be happy and keep happiness throughout the family. He would have to get rid of the problem before it got out of hand and all problems would fade away.

Bill knew how to take care of his problem. Bill had to let their friendship go having no contact with John, although John was only trying to help. Bill didn't see things the same way. He sought to find new friends along with his new life, friends that might understand. He sought friends that didn't know anything about them or their situation, friends that could appreciate them one way or another. This is the decision that Bill made in order to keep happiness in his house. He felt that sometimes you have to let go of your friends or family, or whatever it is that causes the problem or brings bad memories into the open. Joan never called Pat. She sat around time after time waiting for Pat to call her. She wondered if she was OK, but Pat never called her nor had any intentions to call her. Bill didn't allow her to talk to Joan, he felt the same way about John too.

Pat listened to her husband in order to keep him happy. She went along all the decisions he made, whatever made him happy. She wanted him to trust her forever, so she never gave Joan a call. She went on as if she had never met Joan. She knew that one day Joan was going to call her. Not only did Joan call after she got tired of waiting, but she sent the police over to Pat's house. She had informed the police that Bill was abusing Pat and had her locked up like some type of animal. When the police arrived at Pat's house, they found that everything Joan said about Bill and Pat was not true. Joan was going crazy because she couldn't talk to Pat and sending the police didn't help at all. It made matters worse for Joan. Joan calling and interfering with Pat made Bill even angrier at Joan, especially after he told her to stay away from Pat.

Joan wouldn't give up. She felt there was a problem. She knew that Bill wasn't treating Pat right, regardless what Pat said. Joan still didn't believe what was going on. She felt no man could change the way he did, he had to be faking it. She finally got the nerve to call Pat while Bill wasn't home. Pat answered the phone while Helen was sitting nearby

"Pat, hi this is Joan I'm concerned about you."

"I know you sent the police over here; why did you do that Joan? It made Bill very angry with you!" Pat couldn't believe Joan was calling her again.

"I've been waiting for you to call me and you never did, so I wanted to make sure you were OK. You know how crazy Bill gets."

"I don't know Joan, tell me how crazy Bill gets. You seem to know more about him than I do. Things are not like you think they are, Joan, were getting along just fine. Bill decided that I shouldn't call you any more and I agreed it was a great decision. We're trying to live a new life and we don't need any problems. I hope you understand what I'm talking about. I really like you a lot Joan and you really helped me a great deal but we can't deal with the problems you are causing. I really trusted you but I have a new friend. I have company right now. It was nice of you to call and at this time we can no longer be friends, it's for the best. I'm willing to make my marriage work." Pat breathed heavily, wiping her forehead she hoped that Joan would finally understand that she had to move on.

"Well Pat, it's your life. I only understand that Bill is running your life, telling you who you can and cannot talk to. I was only trying to help, so I wish you good luck Pat. You really shouldn't stay in the position you're in, but if you ever need me or just need to talk, just call me and I'll always be here for you. Things could get out of hand you know. I don't have to tell you, you know already, like I said I wish you all the luck and good bye."

"Thanks for calling Joan and have a good life."

"You too Pat." Joan hung up the phone and burst out in tears. She no longer had Pat as a friend.

Pat placed the phoned down gently and looked across the room at Helen without really seeing her. Pat had to tell Joan the truth in order for her marriage to work. She had to let her know she was no longer wanted for a friend because she was too negative about her husband. Joan never had anything nice to say about Bill and it made things bad for Pat. She always had to listen to this. Joan would program her bad thoughts about Bill into Pat's head and she would actually believe what Joan was saying. It wasn't healthy for Pat, and it made matters worse and more confusing as she thought bad things about her husband. He was doing good things for her to please her in any way, so Joan had to go. Pat looked again at Helen and smiled, Helen is my true friend now, she is what I need she thought to herself.

Bill would be pleased when she told him about Joan, how she had the nerve to call after sending the police to the house. She was still trying to cause problems, thinking that problems exist in the house. When Bill arrived home, Pat told him about Joan and the conversation they had. It made him feel real good knowing that Joan didn't have any influences over Pat and that she finally let their friendship go. He was so proud of his wife that he gave her a nice kiss and a tight, long hug for a job he considered well done. He told her that he didn't think she had it in her to tell Joan to back off.

"You were getting so close to her like she was a sister, but why Pat, did you cut her loose?"

"Because I finally realized she was to negative when she talked about you. It wasn't going to work with Joan and I, our friendship wasn't any good at all. She really didn't know what was going on with us. She assumed and her assuming was wrong. I married you for better or for worse, and if this is considered worse then I have to deal with it."

Bill was touched by Pat's feelings. He had no words for her at all. He was happy that finally she put her troubles to rest. Bill and Pat are perfect examples that life can go on. It could be better if both parties really love one another and agree on both terms it could be worked out, but only if the woman loves the man and that love is returned. It can be worked out. It really takes two not blaming one another, but loving one another. If Bill didn't love Pat it would not have worked out. Their feelings were as one and they were able to put everything out in the open; how much they loved one another and wanted to be together. His apologies made a great difference in their life as he set guidelines. She followed them, which made things easier. It made life simple because they really wanted to be together and they were able to love one another again.

They got rid of all the bad rubbish, where no one else mattered to them. Their son Mike went on with his life, not involving himself in anything they had going. He wanted to have a family of his own, someone to love and cherish and to make very happy. Bill knew all he had was Pat and he wasn't going to let her go, not for anyone in the world. It made a great difference in their life. She made him happy by her presence and he made her happy with his love. Abuse will never take over their lives again as long as Bill controls himself from anger and does not let others put things into his wife's mind. They would have peace forever in love and happiness.

# HOW TO PREVENT A WAY OF ABUSE

**9**

For once Bill felt relieved that he no longer had to abuse his wife or see his son suffer from abuse. Bill felt pretty good, something he hadn't felt for a very long time. He felt clean because he hadn't had a drink in a long time. He was clean and was going to Alcoholics Anonymous Association three times a week at the church. He would talk about his drinking problem and how he felt. He looked at pictures of what happened to people who drank alcohol. He also studied the different effects of what it could do to the body and how it also harms the body liver and kidneys. He learned that it really affects the mind and drives people into doing things they wouldn't normally do. He learned that the alcohol made him act crazy toward his wife because he lost all feelings that he had for her. But once the alcohol cleared out of his mind he realized how much he hurt her and how much he really loved her. He realized how dear in his heart he held her.

Bill collected pamphlets on alcohol abuse and its harmful affects. He listened to tapes on drunk driving. Although he never drove while he was drinking, the study showed that a lot of people die from drinking and drugs. Bill was saying how lucky he was to overcome this abuse of alcohol. He no longer needed a drink and he could go to the bar and stare alcohol right in the face and it wouldn't affect him. He didn't have that urge to drink and he felt really great about it. He would have great conversations with Jim without any want of a drink. Bill learned a lot while attending his important AAA meetings. He never missed a day and he was always on time. He didn't want to miss a word of what they had to say.

Bill really wanted to cure his problem of abusing his wife

because he knew somewhere in his heart he loved her. He knew he was wrong about damaging her. He sought help to make his life better. He knew that things would get worse if he stayed in his drunken condition, his malevolence became reality and guilt took its course of abusing his wife. Clearing his mind of that nasty abuse over coming his alcohol problem gaining the understanding abuse is wrong. No one should be treated like an animal Bill was willing to give in to get rid of that demon that entered into his life unnoticed.

Bill felt so great about receiving help, ready to conquer the world by helping others with the same problem teaching that abuse is dead and happiness is what we should live for. Bill wanted to share his experience with every male by starting a men shelter helping those of an uncontrollable nature. His body was clean for once in a long time along with eating healthy which also help create a clean mind. Wanting to restore his health where alcohol destroyed it. While applying nutritional additives to his life creating his own recovery pamphlet "Better living for the disruptive male" hoe to cope with anger.

Bill was feeling great no alcohol and no abuse. The assurance of loving his wife over again, in spite of the way she had been abused. He felt alive! Once again it seemed that his life consumed with a clean mind. As Bill's life was taking a major change Pat's condition was worsening his feeling were mutual after viciously beating his helpless wife, He felt obligated to seek help Bill refused all distractions of getting better. Excluding the rubbish out of his system out of his mind. Searching for an answer of preventing this horrible nightmare from happening again, that we can only move forward and not making the past our future.

Bill attended a program for men that abused their wives. A lot of men attended this meeting men who were serious about getting their lives back in order, men who loved their wives and wanted to be with them. These men did as the women would do sat in a circle to discuss the horrible nightmare of being an abuser. Their confession were horrifying of the way they tarnished their wives, but they weren't judging one another the concept was to help kill the anger wasn't a pretty thing to hear about what these men did to their wives. Helping to cure their mental illness way the meeting went. No pity was spared, they were wrong and not ashamed to admit it. Expressing guilt to one another asking themselves "why"? repeating asking one another how important is family life, whom you supposed to love and cherish forever?" This meeting went on for a while. In order to prevent abuse, all problems should be discussed and brought out into the open. If abuse is not discussed, it will continue to exist in your life.

Shame forced through embarrassment everyone had the same problem excluding shame and all feelings. Bill benefited from these meetings. He knew the existing problem was serious and needed to be discussed in the open. It didn't matter what form opening up to others helps release pressure to advance in life.

Men that are abusive don't realize they need serious help. This group of men had a conscience and it had to be cleared. They were more than ready to seek help, more than ready to love their wives all over again. These were the smart men getting rid of abuse in their families. Regaining a peaceful life, like in the beginning when they put their family together in love. It takes a man to put a family together and a man to break it up. After destroying the very fundamental of love.

Therapy is needed in an abusive situation it only be express more than once. Abuse is very mental and it harms not only the family but also friends. Most men don't have a reason for abusing their family and sometimes it is not always drugs or alcohol. For these men, abuse began in their past. The key to solving problems is counseling. Abuse begins when it first enter into the mind, that's when its time to seek help, to help them realize their apprehensive thinking. Urgently seek help!

Bill knew that his family life was important. His was his only source beating his wife he missed out years of beautiful love. The abuse was uncontrollable for him, he became possessed with beating, Bill was like a demon. But now it was different his abusiveness was no longer present taking for granted the help which he was offered. His abusive ways, but had second thoughts about his ability to walk away from the situation when it occurred. Could he really seek help when it came his way? Was he strong enough to walk away from his wife when anger approached him? Could he get away from what he called disciplining her, pay back of the past thinking this would solve all past problems. According to Bill intention became criminal of hurting instead of reaching for out-side help. Bill sat the meeting while love pierced his heart of loving Pat again. Bill's feeling were active about Pat's return after hurting her so bad, wondering about his actions his bad feeling returning if he saw her again, in question if the meeting really worked? Could counseling be reconsider once Pat returned home.

Well, when Pat returned home in the condition she was in, his questions were answered. He beat her again. He was uncontrollable with his abusive ways. After continuing his abusiveness guilt over powered him, Bill felt terrible and loneliness took over his life. Time after time he wondered why he couldn't get over beating his wife. Constantly asking himself why it wont go away. My pledge, my commitment for so long. In the mist of not wanting to harm Pat without alcohol his anger was flared uncontrollable the lack of love in spite of Pat's problems Bill traded anger for love Abuse once again became a solution.

It took time for Bill to figure this out. his marriage the importance of control over mixed feelings. Preventing abuse isn't the easiest thing, it takes time and patience, quality time. Abusers that cannot gain control in time should leave the situation. Abuser should excuse them selves before someone gets hurts, before they destroy their family, family is a wonderful thing. Abuse can be prevented before it starts Both the abuser and the abused can walk away from abuse. There are plenty of places to go for help when upset.

In the case of child abuse, Pat abused her son thinking like Bill away of disciplining teaching a person a lesson in a disrupted way can cause serious damaged. Abuse follows its course it continues onto the next generation. Beating a child does serious damage to the mind. Kids become fearful of their environment, and they become unable to trust anyone. They become afraid to talk others about what is going on. Child abuse is not accepted. There is a way of spanking your children without seriously hurting them. There are ways of preventing child abuse. There are social services that can help people who abuse their children.

Pat in her furious ways viciously controlling her child refused to seek help to solve the problem fear crippled her thoughts for seeking help. Admitting her guilt her consuming lies led distrust and continuous abuse of her child. Child abuse is not a secret, you cant hid abuse, someone will definitely find out that you are beating your children, so get help,. Don't abuse your children, love them. Kids are to be loved, not abused.

There's always help for women. There are places to go and people to talk to assist you in the case of child abuse. Child abuse is harmful, it develop mental hatred if it seems complicated seek guidance there's various forms of information, people are willing to give a helping hand, kids are the future of the world and Abuse shouldn't be tolerated any aspect in which it is performed.

In this case, Pat feelings were mutual about abusing she continued to hurt Mike beating him like an animal which lead to fear not being able to alarm his or any one for that matter. Pat obnoxious treatment in-store fear that continued to worsen. Abuse really ly damages a child's mind. In order to prevent child abuse, talk the problem over in details with your child.

Discuss the problem if it doesn't work, consult a doctor. He can inform you how to get psychiatric help for your child. If your child is uncontrollable, then seek help from the local police department. They have a great deal of information on how to raise your child without harming them or getting yourself into trouble with abuse. Child abuse is not only beating a child, it is also leaving them by themselves without authority for months at a time. Child abuse is also leaving them without food or just leaving them out on the street, hoping that someone might find them. There are plenty of places for kids to go in the case of abandonment.

Abuse could have been prevented in the English family if only the situation could have been discussed by others. She could have prevented abuse  realizing that kids make mistakes, to distinguish the good from the bad. People cannot abuse children and expect them to do a lot better. Most times they get worse. Abuse is not discipline, it is a form of training the mind into something horrifying. Abuse is a form of damaging the mind, body and also the soul of a child. Their behavior becomes disorderly. No one wants to deal with them because of the fear that abuse brings about.

Punishing a child can be more simple than abuse. Abuse is a form of dislike. It is not training your child to be a perfect adult or to be a perfect parent. When they become parents they will also abuse, thinking that it is the right thing to do. Do not commit the crime of child abuse. Kids are to be loved and disciplined in the right manner. There are guidelines to follow without hurting your kids, it will effect you later. Abuse is wrong, it is cruel. To prevent abuse before it gets started, find someone to talk to. Get advice before it affects you. Don't be afraid to seek help, it is always available. If you can't handle the kids, send them to someone that can, someone that won't hurt them. Find someone to help. It is the best choice you could ever make. Your kids will love you just the same.

No one wants to be hurt or have that feeling of hurting. Seek before you abuse and you will win in the end. You will be the hero of non abuse and maybe you can help someone else. People helping people is a great form of killing the mind of the one who is abusing. You don't have to abuse to get the problem straight or even solve the problem. Abuse makes the problems worse because now you have to deal with getting over the fact that you hurt your kids and hurt them badly. Your mind will become abusive without anyone abusing you.

Abuse is a two way street. While you are abusing your loved ones, you are abusing yourself, hurting your mind as your mind is hurting. You will continue to abuse, thinking that it is right. You only hurt yourself worse. "Get help before it is too late:" So late that your family won't love you anymore, so late that you already start abusing your kids, hurting them, trying to kill them, showing them that you no longer care. It is too late when you make them fearful of their surroundings. It is too late when they are all bruised up, and you blame someone else instead of yourself. It is too late when children are afraid to tell why they have marks all over their body. It is too late when they are afraid to be around other kids, fearing the laughs and jokes. It is also too late when children fear the abuse from other children that is not done intentionally. Kids suffer more than adults in an abusive situation. So think!

## HAVING SELF ESTEEM

Self Esteem is the most powerful tool ever created in a lesson there for self esteem plays a great role in our lives it can either help us to be more gracious exploiting our qualities or reverse repugnance while anger strikes our every position in life the loser of life are those with less value vehement in our own ways. Our opinions come from within. The greatest on earth are valued for their self esteem not anger complaining with abuse. Not motivating to hurt or destroy but allow your self to be different having charter implementing in you life self esteem doesn't inflict pain it cures all sickness of the mind and can be contagious spreading like the flue angry one's the chance to experience some portion to recondition within themselves taste the great power of happiness which comes from having a sense of self esteem motivate your self away form abuse . In order to prevent abuse, one must have a great deal of self esteem and motivation. These factors are important in order to keep from hurting others. To keep a straight mind, you have to care a great deal about yourself. That care comes from value of one's self. People who don't have good feelings about themselves can't control abuse or prevent themselves from hurting others. In an abusive situation self esteem plays an important role. It gives us a sense of pride when it comes to loving our surroundings. We are able to stand ourselves, to love who we are as humans and also love the people that play the most important roles in our lives.

Without self esteem we tend to hate. We don't want to be liked by others. We lose sight of the person that we really are. Implying esteem brings a change throughout or surroundings. In an abusive situation our self esteem becomes low. People feel unwanted by others. In this situation, people become unbearable, and hard to deal with. There is no motivation to keep going. If you don't have self esteem, you can't gain motivation or a positive mind. You become a failure in your environment.

In an abusive situation we are no longer an individual. We become more of a character with unknown behavior, a character for whom no one has respect. In order to gain respect from others you must venerate your self. When you show love for your-self, others will have respect for you. Abuse doesn't show love. Disciplining in an abusive way is not a form of self esteem, it is a form of hating who you are. Cruelty takes over and your motivation becomes a form hatred. One way of preventing abuse is loving yourself.

If you live in an abusive situation, ask the abuser if he loves himself. Ask him what his motivation in life is. Find out how he can gain self control without anger. Finally, ask if what his values in life are if he does have values then he will gain some sense of self esteem. This provides a great impact in one's life towards preventing abuse or stopping abuse. Look back to when he had motivation in his life, when things were going great. Look back to a time when love was in the air. Self esteem brings back the great honor and pride that the abuser had when people thought highly of him. His honor and pride, the power he lost when he started to abuse. Remind him that it's not too late to return back to his great sense of self esteem.

People notice when self esteem is present because it brings a glow to your life that nothing can conquer or take away. Self esteem is important and should be looked upon highly in order to prevent abuse in your life. It brings a certain behavior, behavior of quality that no one can take away or destroy because it is inside you. If you abuse you don't have any self esteem at all. Focus on your intrinsic of what is causing failure while you are abusing the one you claim you love.

As for Pat, while she was abusing her son she didn't have any motivation. Nothing was going her way so she thought everything was downhill. Everything she tried to teach her son faded and she faded with it because she wasn't really teaching him, she was abusing him. Her value of respect were very low, in fact she didn't have any self esteem from the start. She gained hatred instead of love. From the first day her innocent son was born she forgot about her qualities putting all her attention towards her son, while applying abuse pushing anger before qualities was the start of anguish. As time went on her motivation to hurt increased even more. Things got worse for her and her baby. Self esteem to her was nothing.

She couldn't teach her son about having self esteem because she was too busy beating him. Teaching him way of learning respect. Abuse can never lead you the right way. Her son never gained the right kind of motivation. He never had a chance. When he tried, she shot him down with abuse. He was never looked upon with great honor because there was none. Pat didn't give her son honor but hated him for no reason at all. Her hatred came from her not having love for herself, or respect for her environment. Her self esteem was low. Even the poorest man couldn't touch what she had accomplished between her and her son, because she wasn't worth it. Her character was missing, her behavior was off. Adults have bad behavior as well and only they can straighten it out. With low motivation they can't be touched or even straightened out.

Children, on the other hand, can be straightened out. They can be taught without abuse, but Pat didn't think her son was worth anything. Her mind was fixed on abuse, whether or not everything he did was either right or wrong. This was due in part to having no self esteem. When abuse came Pat's way, the table turned and things got worse for her. She couldn't grab hold of herself because she was nothing. No self esteem, no motivation could get her out of an abusive situation. She was lost, she had no love. She forgot what love was when she started abusing her son. She never stopped to think about her character, about who she was and why things were happening the way they were. She knew something was missing, but had no idea what it was.

She didn't know what brought her into the cycle of abuse or why her behavior was so strange. She wondered why she felt down all the time and had no care for the world. All the time she thought she was doing the right thing. When she abused her son she didn't have any love for herself or respect. She was lost in her own world of abuse without any sense of control. All respect was lost and all her motivation gone when her self esteem faded away. Pat created an abusive relationship and it was hard for her to gain a winning streak about herself. She was all torn down and her abuser didn't have any bad feelings about what he was doing. She couldn't look herself in the mirror and say I am a great person with a great sense of humor because she had no sense of humor. She wasn't a great person. She was an abuser without love.

She couldn't pull herself out because she had no motivation, no way of gaining a new character. Her new world was deep in abuse. In an abusive situation you have to gain control of yourself. You have to find love within yourself in order to prevent abuse. You must show great admiration for yourself even if it is not there. What is lost, can be found. Pat couldn't find anything. She couldn't find a way of uncovering her self esteem. She was parched in all ways and it became a real problem for her later down the road when things got worse. She had nothing to look forward to but abuse. She couldn't look herself in the mirror.

She continued in an inactive way. Her esteem was too low to nourish, or to bring back to life. Her life was very dry and uncontrollable. Even her abuser couldn't pull her together. Even if he tried. If Pat had relied on self esteem she would have been much better off. Her life would have turned out differently. Abuse would not have entered into her life because her attitude would have been different and loving. She forgot what love was and how important it was to her.

In this abusive situation her husband caused her to lose her motivation and self esteem. He became like a demon of the worst kind. When he looked at himself in the mirror he no longer saw the happiness he used to see. He couldn't pull himself together like once before. Self esteem is very, very important. It keeps us going, it keeps us from falling apart, whether in an abusive situation or not. Where would we be without self esteem? Without self-esteem, we would be absolutely nowhere because all your happiness goes down the drain, your inner world becomes void and lonely. You lose out on important factors such as love.

Pat's self esteem would have prevented her from living in hell from the things she brought on herself. It would have prevented her from being unwanted by people who really cared and reached out to help her get out of the abusive situation. You really have to love yourself in order for others to help and love you. Respect plays a great role in our lives. It is a way of preventing abuse, because abuse only occurs if you let it. Abuse can't enter your world if you are alert. Self esteem helps you stay alert and be prepared for whatever comes your way. It keeps you wired and ready. Without it you can definitely lose out and harm yourself. Everything in your surrounding becomes empty, full of unwanted things such as abuse.

To overcome an abusive situation or even abusive thinking is to overcome low self esteem, a sense of not wanting to be loved. People who abuse dislike themselves, they are full of anger and hatred. They have no feelings for themselves or people that are in their environment. They cannot have feelings for others when they dislike themselves, so they abuse. They tend to abuse people who love them, not caring, rather hurting them or damaging their minds. They just create more of a problem of hatred.

Abuse is not pretty. It is an ugly sight whether it is verbal abuse or physical abuse. It just is not pretty. There are ways of preventing it before it gets started. Self esteem leads to motivation to love, it prevents abuse. If you love yourself then you will love your surroundings, which is one way of preventing abuse. Pat didn't love herself and her self esteem was very low, so she took it out on her son. There was no motivation for her to gain because abuse fell right back on her. The abuse began to affect her mentally as well as physically. Her self esteem didn't come until later when it was almost too late, when she was so badly beaten that she had no other choice but to gain self respect. She had to change her character into something she never before. It changed her life with her husband.

She learned how to be happy, how to love her surroundings. She started reaching out to others. Being around positive people helped her to be positive and get away from her nightmare. Then she began to see what abuse was about and how low her self esteem was while she was being abused. As she was going through this process things began to look brighter for her. She began to look better and feel better about herself, knowing that she didn't have to accept being abused. Being away from her husband for so long gave her motivation to look at things differently. She was able to see that what he was doing to her wasn't right. After gaining self esteem she accepted her husband. In love, she was happy. It led her back to the same situation, but things were different.

Her husband was able to control himself when he knew Pat had returned home for good. Returning home led her husband to see and experience that she was different. He was able to deal with what had happened and their love was once again put together. Self esteem does help bring change to life and it clears the memories of abuse. It helps solve abusive problems. It is a form of love and not hate. Loving yourself brings happiness and also helps you to reach out to others with a positive mind. Your attitude and personality has a great deal to do with the things that go on in your life, so make that change and don't abuse.

## SEEKING OUT OTHERS

In an abusive situation, the help of others is always a great cure for your problems. In this situation you should always seek others because this kind of problem cannot be handled alone. Refusing to seek out others can make the situation worse and it will create more of a problem for you and your family. Abuse is a closed circuit situation. The reason for this is because the problems are handled behind closed doors, where no one knows or can see what is going on. Seeking out others can bring the problem of abuse to reality. Expressing your thoughts to others can also kill the preexisting problem. You should seek out someone like a friend, relative, or even a stranger, someone that can give you a little feedback. They might be able to help you get rid of your problem.

Seeking others is a great step in preventing abuse. It is especially good to talk to someone that has been through it because they could coach you in what to do in this type of situation. If you don't feel comfortable talking about your abuse problem with a friend, try someone you don't know because families tend to make things worse. Sometimes families bring the problem to the point where it promotes anger between the two that are in the situation. Seeking out someone you don't know can get things more out into the open, without holding anything back. Holding information back isn't such a great idea when trying to solve your problems.

Working with someone you do not know can sometimes be beneficial, it can sometimes help. Strangers can give you advice that your family or closest friend can't give. They can probably give you the help you need and be honest about it, whereas family members tend to beat around the bush and try to say things to comfort you instead of helping you get out of the abusive situation. Seeking out a stranger helps your conscious be clearer because you won't have to continue to face the problem. When seeking out family members, you will always be reminded of what happened. It will never go away.

Seeking out a stranger, someone that's been through abuse,

can comfort you through the whole thing. This person knows what it is like to be hurt. If the person has experienced it, they can relate better to what you are saying than someone who hasn't been through an abusive situation. A stranger will take the time and listen and be a better guide you. This person will take the necessary steps to help you face your problem, or will show you how to get away from your problem. Some people leave rather than work things out. Someone that you seek out can help you get things the way you want them to be.

Seeking can help you find whatever it is that you are looking for. Just sitting around waiting for someone to come and help, when no one knows your situation, will not solve your problem. It will not even help you to realize that you have a problem. This is why you need to find help when you are in an abusive situation. No one knows what is going on unless you tell them. Telling someone is as simple as going through it. You have to reach out to others, no one knows what is going on behind closed doors. It is as simple said as done and no one will hate you for coming to them for help. Some people feel shame when seeking out help, fearing that abuse is private and should not be discussed, but it is not a private situation. You can't handle it alone. If it doesn't stop it will be too late for you and your loved ones.

Seeking out to others is not a hard thing to do when you are being physically abused. You are already hurting, so how much worse can it get? When you tell someone the problem seeking out can not only help you, but it can help the abuser realize what he or she is doing. It may help the abuser realize that it is wrong. No one likes pain or even verbal abuse. No one should be talked down mentally, it affects them. The verbal abuser doesn't see that there is damage. He or she doesn't see because it cannot be seen, but it is damaging to the mind. Of course we cannot see how badly the mind is bruised immediately, but later it will show. What is in the dark will always come to the light, mentally it will show. Mental anguish might show up years down the road. Eventually it will come out into the open and it won't be a pretty sight. People that are verbally abused need to seek out also. Just

because the abuse is not seen does not mean it is not damaging.
Any kind of abuse is damaging, seen abuse or unseen abuse.
No matter what kind abuse you are going through, you should
seek help. There is help for men, women and also children.
There is no excuse for not seeking out others. There are plenty
of places to go. There is always someone to talk to, but they are
only there if you seek them out. No one knows your problems if
you don't tell them. Eyes are blind to what they cannot see, but
words are reality. If you don't tell someone what is going on, then
no one will ever know, nor could they guide you to get you and
your family out of this abusive situation. That's why its important to seek out others. You deserve the best and abuse can be
conquered. It is harmful to your environment and most of all it
is harmful to you.

Abusers conception weighs he facts of not being  affecting,
that it only effects the one they are hurting. Abuser experience
mental harm by not being able to cope with society. Their cor-
rupt minds continues to  harm the one they claim to love more
than ever. . Inside they are going crazy and it is affecting their
mind. They don't realize that they are the one with the problem,
needing help. They also have a need to seek out, but they are
embarrassed to talk it over. They are full of shame because they
know that what they have done was wrong. It was wrong. But
seeking out helps solve whatever problems that existed. Once the
abuser seeks help a sense of happiness will appear.

People in abusive situations cannot get rid of the problem
unless both parties seek help. If the abused seeks out but not the
abuser, then what will it solve? It won't solve anything because
the problem still exists. In the situation of Pat abusing her son,
people were trying to help but she denied that she was abusing
him. She blamed it on something that didn't exist. The problem
of her abuse couldn't be solved, no matter how bruised up he was
or how bad he cried out for help. This uncontrollable anger took
place it didn't matter, because no one knew the truth about what
was going on. He was afraid that things might get worse if he
told the truth. Fear can drive you crazy and things get worse any-

way. She continued to beat him for worthless situations. She wasn't suffering physically, but mentally she was suffering. Often worried about her secret being exposed the tormenting anguishing of her abuse. If exposing the situation f abuse Mike's unexplained bruises.

When others were trying to find out why Mike was so bruised up, the problem would have been solved, but he refused to let others help because he was afraid of her. Seeking out is very important in this situation. Things are going to get worse anyway. Things got worse for Mike because he didn't seek out. When help came his way he refused to tell the truth about what she was doing to him. The abuse went on for most of his young life until she almost killed him. Unfortunately, that's what it takes sometimes. Sometimes someone must get hurt really bad in order to seek out. It shouldn't get to that point. Help is available in all forms. It was there for him. Don't let fear take over because the abuse will just get worse.

Pat was afraid that her husband might find out and leave her. The thought of being left alone crippled Pat's mind. Perhaps Pat should have sought help before abuse had taken over her life. The horror of living in an abusive world would have dissolved away. Instead she felt she was doing the right thing by abusing her son. She tried to make her husband believe that what she was doing was right. Her husband didn't see it that way and instead of seeking help for her Bill made the situation of abuse worse. He felt compelled to pay her back while revenge was on the table. She put herself in this situation. Where time was limited Pat had plenty of time to escape.

Pay back stuck on Bill's mind. He had no feelings about what he was doing to her, nor did he care when it came time for her to seek help. Living in hell of hatred and anger it was too late Pat owed Bill. She had no way out of her situation and no one knew. It was a closed circuit of abuse, with nowhere to go for help. Lost without friends or family members, for she cut them off when she got married. Excluding the hardship that people allow others to add to their lives leaving out family sometimes be the biggest mistake of your entire life. Pat had no one to reach out to when it became her turn to be abused. Mentally bruised as such was done to her son.

Bill had no intention of letting strangers revived their lives. Most women that go through abuse don't have any family or friends. Which shouldn't be the case always have one friend or that can be contacted at any time no matter what the situation is. When Pat sought out to talk to someone, The problem settled deep within locked in with no way out. It really doesn't pay to abuse. Anguish follows in all forms and fashion. If you are in an abusive situation seek help before it is too late. People who abuse appeared to be arrogance proud please, seek help! often feeling shame and embarrassment because they are hurting someone else but continues to abuse.

The abuse continued in the English family until Mike returned, still suffering from an abusive past. He was searching for answers, searching for help, trying to clear his mind. Mike was trying to seek out to others, to get over his abusive thoughts. He didn't want to fall into the cycle of abuse. He came back only to find out that abuse was much worse in his family. He didn't condemn his father for what he was doing, nor did he blame his mother. He went for help. He went seeking until he found someone who could help him and his family get out of their abusive situation. Mike's actions clearly show that if seek you will find just what you need to overcome your problems. He did just that, but the important thing is to release all your shame of the past. Now it was time for him to clear it out of his world and get a new start.

Bill and Pat tried to do that when others were helping, but the help Pat received wasn't enough to get over her abusive ways. Sometimes it take much more. She didn't have any motivation to get well nor did she know how to look at her problems. She created more problems and her situation got worse. After the abuse took place the last time it woke her up and she realized that no one really wanted to be bothered with that type of life. Either she must straighten up or things would get much worse.

The abuse did got worse for her, and it took a long time for her to come back to reality. When she did, the help of people who didn't know her, but who had been through the same thing, helped Pat. She was more open about her problems. She was able to talk about them without being looked down on. She was able to hold her head up high. She knew and felt this one last time that it was going to work because her self esteem level had risen. These people knew what she needed to get over her abusive ways. She was able to survive when she went back home. She was even happy once again, like never before. She was happy to hear from her once abusive husband.

Seeking out others is very important. Abusers and abuse victims that seek out are the ones who come out winning. Refusing to seek help can cause your problems to get much worse. The abused and the abuser must seek help in order for their situation to work. Men tend to think that they don't need to seek out help, they can solve their own problems. In reality they can't, they need help also. So seek help right away. If you don't like seeking out people you don't know then seek a friend or family member, someone you can talk to, someone who can help. Don't let the problem persist. It can get much worse. Seeking help is a great part of our life in order to solve our problems. Family members can't really coach you on how to solve your problems, but they can listen to what you are saying and try to give some advice on what they think is right. There are places to go for real help and real advice, but it's nice to have someone there when needed. Seek real help for an abusive problem that can be solved, "Seek out to others."

## ALWAYS BE GRATEFUL

Abuse can be prevented, the problem can be solved. Abuse can be worked out only if we can learn to be grateful to one another and have respect for our loved ones. We must treat one another like we are human and not like animals. Abuse can be solved. Being grateful is important. It is a form of politeness and wanting to be liked. Gratefulness could help prevent acts of abuse. How we feel about one another can play a great role in our lives. It shows a sense of caring and a great sense of love.

"Abuse is hated and unwanted." If you are in an abusive situation and can't seem to overcome it, a word of gratitude can sometimes throw a person off and get them on a different track. Being kind can also kill a person's conscious that is not thinking in that manner.

In the case of child abuse, it is hard for kids to show gratitude toward their parents because parents don't pay any attention to their kids. They ignore everything that comes out of their mouth in exchange for abuse. Abused kids seem to be more grateful than kids that are not being abused. They also tend to have a great deal of fear because of the beatings they receive. Gratefulness comes from abused kids. In order to prevent abuse, they try to show their feelings and give their parents unwanted love in order to prevent being abused. Being grateful is important and it plays a great role. If you tell your abusers that you love them, it could weaken that abuser's mind. Kindness may come out of the interaction. It also drains a person when they are being mean and can wake them up.

Most abusers never had love. They are lacking some type of love, so being grateful can bring that love back to life, back to reality. In the case of child abuse, the parent feels neglected and unwanted so they tend not to want their children. They can't seem to get rid of them, so they abuse them, hoping that they will go away. If they don't go away, they take all the love that they are not getting and replace it with abuse. Parents that abuse tend to have an empty shell, one that no one can seem to open. It takes a lot of love that they once lost to open that shell. Being grateful can sometimes replace that lost love in which abuse entered in without notice.

Abuse comes from not expressing oneself to it's opponent. The darkness can't seem to come to light. Once you go into this darkness you are stuck in the world without any light. Abuse is hard, it is not understood, but it can be cured and prevented. Being grateful has a lot to do with preventing and stopping abuse. When in an abusive situation you should really express yourself and have an open mind. You should be ready to listen to whatever you abuser has to say and respond in a manner of gratitude. Your response to an abuser can also play a great role in preventing abuse. Sometimes the things we say can get us into more trouble than not saying anything. Words can kill our mind, sometimes we tend to take talking for granted and regret the things we have said later. If things of gratitude are said, then there will be no regret, no worry and no abuse. It is all love, so being grateful has a lot to do with clearing evil thoughts and getting rid of all the ugliness that occurs when waking up the abusive situation and its ways.

Pat abused her son in many ways. He was so used to being abused that he had no grateful words for her, so the abuse continued. There was no way of preventing abuse. Her conscious was clear because her love was empty. With her husband gone all the time, she was lacking love and nothing could her abusing Mike. She took all her emptiness out on her son, replacing love for abuse. In child abuse situations, this is often the case. A woman who doesn't receive love replaces love with abuse. The kids suffer whatever it is that the woman is going through. In the case of Pat being battered, her gratefulness would have stopped her husband's abuse because he loved her. She continued to blame herself for the abuse and he continued to beat her.

Even if you are wrong, don't blame yourself. Find a way out. Abuse isn't nice and no one deserves to be abused. Everyone deserves love and being grateful can bring love into your life, it could end abuse. Abuse is dead, but being grateful can help you live again. Being pleasant is always a way out of a situation.

Pleasantness can also go to the heart of your abuser. Sometimes it takes a lot to be grateful. If your life depends on it, then being grateful isn't a bad way to go. No one really wants to be around ungrateful people and abuse can cause people to leave. It can cause them to stay away, not wanting to be in touch. If you are being abused you need people to be around to help you out of this situation.

As for Pat, she was ungrateful to the people who were trying to help her solve her problem. She only made it worse. She turned the other way, instead of the way they wanted her to turn. She was inconsiderate and her abusive situation got worse. It pays to be grateful and loving, with gratitude showing that you want to be helped. If help is there you should not take it for granted, you should take it for what its worth. People who are in abusive situations need to have lots of gratitude when being helped or the abuse will never go away.

Bill was grateful to John for helping him with his problem. He got better, he accepted whatever it was that could cure his problem with abuse. It worked for him. He gained a conscience about beating his wife. His attitude was well worth it when it came to accepting his wife the way she was. Because he was grateful to the people around him, it worked. He was no longer the abuser, he was the lover. It made him accept what he had, to go on with his life, and that's what he did. Gratitude sends you into the right direction, the direction of ending abuse. Being grateful helps prevent abuse.

Once abuse begins, it is hard to be grateful. It is hard to find love and trust in the person that is the abuser. It becomes difficult to survive with the same love in the same life because forgiving and forgetting takes more than simple words. Forgiving takes a lot of love and that's how we want it to be. With a lot of love, we can keep the attitude of wanting to be grateful no matter what the situation is or was. Being grateful shows a form of love and that's what a lot of abusers lack. They lack that kindness and politeness that one has to give. They also lack a sense of respect and integrity. In an abusive situation, being grateful is a way of communicating and solving an abusive problem. Being grateful can express how much you love that person and the thankfulness of being next to him. Being grateful can also make him realize that what he is doing is wrong and not accepted, especially if the abuser came from an abusive childhood. Being grateful shows some sense of love. It is a way of apologizing.

Abusers should feel guilty that the abused are being grateful and trying to help them. The abuser may feel bad that the abused is returning love and giving more love even if there is no love in sight of their abusive situation. One way of preventing abuse is being grateful, giving love and lots of gratitude.

## INVESTIGATE

Abuse begins before the sun goes down. The night appears and emptiness is all around. There is no way of controlling it. There is no way of stopping it and there is nowhere to hide. There is nowhere to run once abuse becomes serious. There is no way out and that's where investigation comes in. Investigating means overlooking the light and look directly into the darkness of a person. Everyone has a dark side to them, so investigate your love. See what that person is like at night when the sun goes down and the tables are turning. Investigation is easy, it is a way of observing and getting the truth out into the open so that later it won't cost you your life.

The things we find to be most apparent are not always what they seem. Seek that person's past to see if they have been in an abusive situation or if child abuse was present in their life. Prior abuse will definitely affect your life, it may not be in the beginning of your relationship, but later it will come out into the open. Search their family and their friends. Ask questions. Everyone has a past, this is not to say that everyone is perfect, but the good and the bad should be known. You should know these things if you plan to spend your life with this unknown love, a love that seems perfect, that almost never does any wrong. It is important to think of these things ahead because it takes time to get to know someone's dark side.

Investigating one's life is very important because you never know what you're getting into. If you investigate before entering into a relationship, then you would know whether or not it could cost you your life. If you don't investigate, then you could end up in a world of trouble. One thing about investigating your love is that it doesn't cost you anything. It is absolutely free unless this person really means a lot to you and you go to the extreme and find someone else to investigate for you. When entering a relationship, listen carefully to what this person is saying. They basically tell you everything about them, but it is up to you to listen and take everything under deep consideration and think about it. Serious conversations should be taken to heart. Some people go through identity changes in order to leave the past behind, and sometimes it is best for that person. However, what if this person was harmful in his past life? He could still be harmful. Once someone has abused, that person will always be an abuser unless the abuser receives help. That is why investigation is important. It could mean a lot when your life depends on it.

Get to know the people in his life by going to job functions, getting close to family and friends. Something will always slip out, whether it is in a joking matter or someone is just sitting around talking about that person's business. The way to gain knowledge is to listen carefully to what is being said and the jokes that are being told. These things could be saying something that could benefit you later. These people may say something you may not know or believe, but listen and take it into your mind. Think about it, because later it might be a bit of advice that you can use to your advantage.

Most people go into a relationship without investigating and later find out how bad the person was once, but it is too late. They then pay for that lack of knowledge with abuse. Sometimes, when people are bad they don't always remain the way they were. In abusive situations, it is important to get to know the situation you are getting into. Abuse is too serious to play around with. It has gotten out of hand and the only way to prevent yourself from falling into the same situation is to investigate your surroundings.

Parents who abuse their kids are easy to spot, they're usually nervous and hyperactive. They often tell lots of lies and never want their kids to be around other kids. Abusive parents make excuses for their actions and blame others. If you suspect child abuse, then it probably is abuse. It is clearly seen through the kids that are being abused. When kids are being abused they are afraid to seek out help. It takes a lot to catch a child abuser, a lot of investigating. Even the people that are close to this abuser tend to be shut out of this person's life. It is harder to investigate a child abuser because kids lie for parents. In turn, the parents go along with the lies until the kids are actually taken away where the parents can't get near them. Children are often taken away so that they are far from parents who threaten them for telling the truth about abuse. Abusive parents don't want their children to tell the truth about what is going on in their life, and why the child is being abused. Child abuse is hard.

Over a million kids are being abused, and most of this abuse is not spanking, but rather serious beatings. Many kids are dying from this horrible abuse. Their parents do not have a conscience about what they are doing. This happens in situations where no one took the time to investigate but they all suspected that something was going on. Situations where no one took the time to report it or tell someone who could report it. Because of this, that kid was beaten to death without anyone knowing. Abused children cry silently for help, afraid to scream out, fearing what will happen if they did. Abuse happened anyway because the investigation fell short, because they started with an open mind to help this child but believed everything the mother said. The people who did care went away, thinking the child was lying all the time. In reality, the child was only telling the truth. Because of this, the abuser got away with murder, set free, hiding from the truth of abuse. Many of these abusers go on to abuse other children. These other children end up in the same place as the first one because this child abuser is stuck on abuse. The abuser has no way out and no one to help because they believed everything that was said before and went away.

Child abusers should be investigated without any questions asked! You can't ask a child abusers if they are beating on their kids because they will get angry and deny it. They will then laugh like nothing ever happened or it was a joke that you said to them. Don't leave these kids in an abusive situation! If you see that they are being abused then help them. If you can't help them, then find someone who can. There is plenty of help out there. It takes investigation to cure abuse. The situation has to be looked over carefully because abuse can get out of hand. In order to solve or prevent abuse it must be examined. The parents that are abusing have to be tested mentally to find out whether or not they are really abusing their kids.

Pat abused her son, and people went along with lies without investigating. You could plainly see that her son was being abused by someone. People suspected that she was abusing and they knew something was wrong because of Mike's actions. He was full of fear when he was around others. The questioning started but never continued. Everyone who asked went along with whatever Pat said. The abuse went on and it got worse. Instead of sending someone to her house to examine her, they believed her lies. They believed her in part because of the middle class lifestyle she lived. Abuse can go on anywhere, whether you live in poverty or not. Abuse still exists in all walks of life, it has no prejudice to whom it falls on. Even her husband believed her because he thought he had the perfect wife. He too was fooled because he also failed to investigate why his son had so many bruises on him and ended up with so many broken arms. He had his doubts but they weren't good enough to help his child. Later, Mike thought his father was involved because he never asked any questions. Bill failed to seek the right information about abuse, thinking that it could never happen in his family.

Just when you think it could never happen, then it will begin. Pat was abusing his child in his house where it was easiest for him to investigate. She seemed so honest and right, though. She was always nervous and unable to answer questions about her son. His fear and that alone told people that something was going on. Even when her husband couldn't see it, others saw it. They began to investigate. The lies fell so fast that they were uncontrollable. Still they believed and still the abuse took place. The abuse continued because the abuser didn't have fear of what people thought. As long as no one found out the truth about what was going on the abuse continued to get worse. Someday it would come out into the light and then it wouldn't be a pretty sight. When everything came out, it wasn't pretty.

Investigation takes time, but it is worth it in the long run. It cannot always solve the problem, but it could alert you to what is going on. It can help you recognize the preexisting problem or the problems that may lay ahead. It could give some kind of idea of what an individual is like and help prevent some abuse in your life. Abuse is horrible and should not be taken lightly. There are plenty of ways to seek out a first impression of abuse: judge their reaction towards people you love, passiveness when out and about, their conversation around others, or their eye contact with others.

There are plenty of ways to search out information in order to prevent abuse. In our society we don't think about searching out information until it is too late and abuse has already begun. Sometimes people do not seek out information until someone has ended up dead or seriously injured. At this time we seek information and it never turns out good. It is always worse than if someone had asked questions before. That is why it is important to examine your love before it is too late and you put your life on the line.

If you are in an abusive situation already and you failed to investigate in the beginning, it is never too late to seek help before running away. Seeking help is best because you can't run from an abuser. You can help solve the problem in order to make things better in the future. There is always an answer out there somewhere.

Pat fell into a seriously abusive situation after her husband found out she had been abusing her son for many years. She knew he was going to do horrible things to her. If she would have sought help in the beginning, it wouldn't have gotten as far as it did. She failed to examine what he could do to her nor did she investigate how to solve her problem. She thought that it would go away. It took her son going out and seeking help for her to find out what to do in a situation such as the one she was in. He searched for information learned that was how he would find what he needed to get over abuse. All it took was a little investigation to clean his life of abuse.

The information he found was free information that anyone could get. This information included advice of how to make things better in your life. Investigation is important, especially if your life depends on it. Abuse falls into different forms and needs to be sought out before it is too late. Investigation is free of charge and doesn't hurt anyone. It is a red light to alert you to where your future will end up. It is up to you to take heed. Child abusers who are seriously harming their kids are not a pretty sight. Those children will grow up to hate their abusers. There is plenty of help out there, don't let the investigation fall on you. Seek help. Kids should be loved and not abused. There is a difference between discipline and abuse. There is a way of teaching your child to be the way you want him to be without abuse. So have yourself investigated.

## NEVER BE AN INSTIGATOR

Abuse should never be taken for granted, on the other hand it is clearly seen as well as heard. The darkness of an abusive situation will always be seen in the light of others. In functions it will always stand out like a shinning light that cannot be hidden. It plays a very bright role in an abusive life which require serious help. People who have never experienced abuse cannot understand the process. They cannot understand the meaning of trying to solve the problems of abuse. This is why instigators play a great role when involving themselves in the atmosphere of abuse. They seem to think they are helping with the problem, but they are only making the problem worse. They are hurting the person they claim they love and promoting a situation that just doesn't exist.

An instigator thrusts themselves in an abusive relationship where things are at their worst. They seem to not care and they aggravate the problem. They make the problem much worse and the person being abused tends to have more anger due to dealing with this instigator. People who instigate should be ignored and excluded out of the life of the abused in order for things to go right. A person that instigates is openly seen and loudly heard and their words are plainly and clearly heard when spoken. To prevent this way of abuse in your life is to get rid of the aggravation that one tends to cause in order to deal with abuse.

An instigator is a person who doesn't love himself and wants to see others unhandy. They love destroying what seems to be in good shape. It makes them feel as if they have something great, but deep inside their heart they know that what they are doing is wrong. They tend to overlook what is really happening because they are not suffering from the abuse. Instigating mostly comes when abuse has already occurred. Instigating comes from mostly a close friend or a relative who thinks that he is helping. In reality, they only end up hurting. This form of abuse could be avoided. They can become a source of a bad reality, a problem caused. This situation can easily be solved by totally dismissing this person from your life, even if there is love involved.

Abuse is dangerous and unwanted. A problem Caesar should be dismissed out your life in order for the abuse to vanish. It is a sick and mental disease for people to promote abuse where it has already begun.

An instigator has no love at all and likes to see others suffer. They will never experience this horrible fear that is being promoted by an unloved person. The instigators have a way of making things more miserable for both parties. They become very annoying and tend to cause many serious problems if they are not avoided. In order to prevent being abused by other people's aggravation, get rid of all the bad rubbish before it gets rid of you. It will take control of your life. In an abusive relationship there are ways a person can aggravate others, and these things can flare up a tremendous amount of anger and create more of an abusive problem. Then they will leave the scene as if nothing ever happened. The abused parties will feel as if they are being neglected and unwanted. To prevent this type of abuse is to go on without a response. It is called trading anger for some type of silence. It is giving that angry person time to explode without exploding on you, rather in their own world. In order to prevent abuse try ways not to aggravate the abuser so that they will not continue to abuse you the same way.

If you are in an abusive relationship you definitely know what makes that person tick or go off. It is important to know this kind of thing, so that when anger flares up you know the proper ways of avoiding abuse. Once abuse starts it is very hard to control, unless separation can occur between both parties for a short period of time. Teasing a person can also cause a conflict when the abuser does not like playing around. This can sometimes get serious. It can cause a bad impression which might make someone snap into something you might regret later, something you will definitely want to forget.

Instigating is dangerous. People have a tendency to strike, to want to get back at you. If you know that instigation is leading you to an abusive situation, then do not continue to let it go on or you will be sorry. Some abusers are easily intimidated by simple actions that people tend to spout out into the open. Words can easily insult abusers to the point where their anger is so uncontrollable. It creates a lack of communication. The abuser seems to lose trust in the people around him, especially the person being abused. Try to prevent aggravation in order to stop the abuser from doing his special thing. If you stop the aggravation, you won't have abuse in your lifetime.

If YOU are an instigator and living in an abusive situation, stop before it is too late. Think about what is going on. You could be the one promoting the abuse. Sometimes people tend to aggravate without a thought of what is going on in their relationship. Sometimes YOU have to move away to get rid of the bad rubbish, and if that is what it takes to make your life better, then move. You won't lose, you will come out better than if you stayed around instigating. Staying may cost you your life if you play up to it. Think before you lose out on your life and watch those who aggravate your situation.

Pat abused her son because she felt he was aggravating her in every way possible. She couldn't take his way of expressing a simple thought. When he was trying to express himself to her, Pat's anger grew out of control. She became furious with everything he did. Her anger led to serious abuse. She felt she had to teach him what she called a lesson, what she thought was right. Doing this, she only made things worse because she was hurting him. Pat had a problem, something she was bound to and could not control. She could not seek help for her problem and because she continued to abuse her son, she was later abused. Abuse fell worse on her by her husband who supposedly loved her. He was tearing her apart with abuse.

As she began her friendship with someone else, she couldn't see that it was causing a bigger problem in her situation. Her friend turned out to be an instigator. Just when things got better for Pat and her abusive husband, who was no longer sending the abuse down her way, that instigator came in, bringing them back to reality. She was instigating where problems didn't exist. She was flaring up anger. She became a bad influence for Pat, putting the old abusive memories back into her mind. She was really bad rubbish for Pat. In order to maintain good love with her husband Pat had to get rid of that rubbish. She couldn't stop her friend from promoting what she thought was bad. In order to get rid of it, Pat had to let their friendship go and find a new life. It was hard for Pat because Joan had helped her so much with her problems and she respected her for that. Sometimes people can be a real problem when trying to help. Instigating can lead to serious danger in a relationship that is just coming out of abuse and is trying to get off to a great start. So she let their friendship go and she was just as happy. Her life became more peaceful and loving.

Instigators have a way of making problems without staying around to solve them or seeing if any good comes out of it. They take off like a sky rocket so the blame won't fall on them. Instigation is a form of not wanting to have happiness. It promotes anger. Getting around an instigator is a hard and depressing because sometimes they can be telling the truth about your situation. The truth hurts and excluding that person from your life can be very hard. If you keep it in your life you will pay for whatever that person puts you through. So wake up and see who is helping you through your abusive ways and what you can benefit from. Your life may depend on this person and when you put your trust on the line you will know the results of that instigator later and they won't be in your favor. So think hard before abuse thinks for you.

## BUILD BRIDGES

In relationships we never think about the wall that can take over our lives. It can either make us or destroy us. It could ruin everything we ever worked for only because we forgot to build bridges and now we are living in complete destruction, unable to gain control of the relationship we started. All of this occurs because things didn't go right, the bridge that we built wasn't strong enough for the person we built it for. It is hard to see where it became weak and abuse entered in. Once the bridge became weak, we suffered and wondered what happened, how could abuse cross over when the bridge wasn't so solid? Did we let the other person tear it down? Once you build your bridge it becomes personal. It becomes a part of your life. No one can come in between it if it is strong and solid.

When love enters into our life, darkness overcomes the light and we can't see above it. We cannot see that it is important to build the bridge before love can take over its position. You become blinded when love enters into your heart. When falling in love, you should establish guidelines in order to prevent an abusive situation from flaring up, or getting out of control. Learning how to live in a marriage without someone falling for abuse, knowing how to draw the line before things fall to their worst point is difficult. Abuse can occur at any time and it is up to you to build a strong bridge, where nothing can tear it down. You must build something that a wild beast couldn't even touch.

When a relationship is headed towards marriage you want it to be a great walk as well as a bright future. You want it to be a bright future so when you make that walk it won't be the last walk that you make, it won't be the walk of abuse, it will be the walk of happiness. Building bridges alerts you to things to come and steers you in the right direction. Once the bridge is up, no one can tear it down. When you build your bridge it should be solid and strong, so strong that neither abuse nor anger could not even destroy it. Solid bridges last longer if you stand strong with them and tend not to weaken. If you do not stand strong, the bridge will definitely fail. Work hard on building your bridge. It takes effort and time. Building your bridge will cost you nothing at all but time. That time could be valuable if you are entering into a relationship because no one knows what they are getting until they actually get there. That is why building your bridge before you get there can be more than a safe start.

Learn to build a bridge in your life and abuse will stand so clear. You won't know it even existed because abuse comes unnoticed, when you least expect it. It often arises because you forgot to build your bridges. So think before entering into a relationship and later you won't be sorry for taking care of what comes first, you. You will be happy without abuse in your life. Build a strong bridge and no one will ever tear you apart or bring something into your life that you will regret later.

## ENJOY ONE ANOTHER

Abuse is not a form of love, it is a form of real hate. Hate comes from not loving yourself or the people around you, not being able to enjoy the things on the earth. Abuse takes away pride and self respect and most of all it takes away the enjoyment of one another that is in love and marriage. One way to prevent abuse is to find things or a way of enjoyment. Couples must find things that make them happy and feel great about themselves so that no one can conquer the happiness that they share or destroy what happiness brings. Enjoying one another is a part of life and a very special part of living. Enjoyment is something no one can take away unless you are not happy. It brings a form of love and self respect. It kills anger and softens hatred.

Enjoyment is a part of getting together and sticking where no one or nothing can tear you apart or take away your love. Getting to know one another once abuse has taken place is like starting over again. You must get back into the habit of dining out, taking long drives and whatever else it takes to bring love back into your household. You must do whatever it takes to cure that evil mind that was once brought into your life. Enjoyment is easy to accomplish in an abusive situation. Sometimes just watching television can be as much as enjoyment as going out. As long as two people are happy together it can sometimes bring back love that was once lost. That can be the beginning of enjoyment with one another. It also can help solve problems with joy and with laughter. Enjoyment also helps to exclude anger when unwanted problems do arise.

Enjoyment is like the savior of them all. It helps let loose what was once tight, getting rid of all anxiety with laughter. Laughter does a lot for us, it cures a broken and weakened heart. It tends to mend everything. Laughter is a part of life and it keeps us happy and healthy and leaves our mind open to enjoyment.

Bill abused his wife for many years. He was unhappy about the way she abused his son. He was angry and couldn't find away to overcome his anger. There was no way for enjoyment in his way of living. His life was destroyed with abuse and he lacked what he needed the most to cure his abusive ways. What he lacked was enjoyment. He missed out on pleasurable moments. Everything was downhill for him and his wife Pat. Enjoyment was dead meat, she had no way of living because she had no control, until one day life came into their house again. Bill was able to laugh again, he was able to see the light of happiness. He gained control of abuse and was able to bring enjoyment into his household which made a great and wonderful difference in their life. Bill and Pat began to go out and enjoy one another. Happiness entered into their life once again and it all came from the enjoyment of the pleasure of being able to live again. To prevent abuse find a way of enjoyment.

## NEVER MAKE THE PAST YOUR FUTURE

You must take life one day at a time. Life is not to be rushed. The past should not be lived again. Once something has occurred there is no way of changing what has happened. So why dwell on the past, why bring back those sorrowful memories and make them a part of your future? Why destroy your life because of something you cannot change or add to? Almost never look back on something you cannot control. Looking back keeps anger inside and promotes lots of unneeded anxiety. Looking back on a sorrowful past can cause serious depression. Anything that comes your way may cause you to stress out and be unlike by others. Recognize that the past has happened but do not dwell on it.

People tend to stray away from those who dwell on the past, who live in misery. No one wants to deal with you because all you do is cry over something that once happened. YOU have no control over what happened, so why dwell on it? Where does it help you, or where can you find peace in the past? Others don't want to deal with you because you dwell too much on the past and can't seem to get over what cannot be changed.

People who dwell on past abuse should seek serious help because the only way to get rid of an abusive problem is to erase the past from your mind. If you don't do this, it will definitely destroy your life and your surroundings. Things that previously existed with old friends can turn away new friends or new people in your life. Abuse should be let go of once it is over. Sometimes it is easier said than done, but this can be easily and quietly done. It is easy to just clear the bad out of your mind and think about the good things to come. You must get rid of all the old and bring in the new, as if you were bringing in the new year. All the existing problems will fade away. Coming from an abusive life, you don't want to carry a burden on your mind. The past should never be spoken of when not needed.

In order to release yourself from misery, never live in the past. Living in the past can cause you to miss out on a special love that may enter into your life. Someone may enter your life that you could probably benefit from later, but if you are dwelling on the past it just might run that person far away. You could be in serious trouble and your problems could escalate. You may begin to have problems with alcohol, some type of drugs or another kind of substance. Then you will be in much more trouble than you think because it is hard enough to clear your mind of abuse. You may add to your problems something that won't go away easily. You won't only be dealing with the past but your future won't look so great or as bright as you would like it to be.

Living in the past will chase others away. They will leave without looking back to see if you still exist. Once again no one wants to be unhappy because of dealing with someone else's problem who can't seem to get it right. Abuse should be let go of. It can cause you to be unloved and also steer you away from loving others. It can cause you to go into a shell with no way out and you could lose sight of help. If you can't overcome the past, how can you ask for help? No one will listen to anything you have to say because you cannot change what was done already in the past. The past can cause a mental problem which can be much more serious than the problem you had before. It can cause you to be less functional and your normal activities won't be as good as they were. When you are around a bunch of other people it can cause you to snap, and lose serious control. Your self esteem will most certainly hit ground level.

Never look back on the past when coming out of an abusive situation. You can be hard to deal with and it can destroy your life. It will never go away. You will never be free again and you could be unhappy until death. Misery loves company and that is not the type of company you would like to have. Once you dwell on your abusive past you will never get away from it. It is something you cannot control. If there is anything you could do, do it, but never live in the past.

Pat was abused for many years by her husband Bill while seeking help. She couldn't get over the fact that she had abused her son. Abuse fell on her much worse than anyone could have imagined. Pat would grow more miserable always having to discuss her past history of abuse. She could no longer contain or accept the love of others when they were trying to help. She was always miserable having to deal with the problem of what was done to her. The sessions went on. It was hard for her to forget, hard to clear it out of her mind and move on with her life. She could not go on being normal. Nothing could take away her abusive past. Pat's life didn't turn out right. She became hard to deal with, attacking others when she was drinking. She attacked people who were trying to help get over her abusive past. So after a while, people became fed up with her and could no longer help her. Friends even deserted her. While dwelling on the past, Pat became a mess. It sent back into her shell where abuse continued to fall on her and much harder than before. She had no other choice but to learn how to clean abuse out of her mind.

After she learned how to get rid of the past, she was able to live again. She was able to kill off her depression and live once again, happy with the one she loved more than anything in the world, her abuser. It brought life and she was able to love again and have better friends without living in the past. She got rid of what happened before it was spoken of again. As long as she wanted to be happy and live in peace then others were able to accept her for the new person she was. It was all because she learned not to live in the past.

## SET LIMITS ON HOW FAR TO GO

Getting off to a great start when entering a relationship can lead you into a positive life with the one you plan to love. That is why limits should be set at the beginning of happiness. Boundaries should have a way of clearing the path so that person will only go as far as you let them without crossing the line. So set the limits, draw the line. If you seek out before you get deeply involved then you won't regret it later. Lay down the boundaries that you want that person to follow. Let the person know what you can and cannot handle. Don't be afraid to draw the line. If you plan on having a serious relationship, speak out, say what hurts, because a person will never know unless you express yourself in a well liked manner. Don't let that other person cross the line. You know where your limit is. You know what you don't need.

The only way to overcome abuse is to lay down the law. Don't accept anything. Do unto others what should also be done unto you. If limits are set, then you have expressed where you want to go in your relationship. This way you won't end up caught in the cycle of abuse. An abuser will take charge if you don't have boundaries. He will gain complete control and then you will be in serious trouble, wondering what to do next with this abuser. You will have no one to blame because you didn't have a line and he felt free to do whatever he wanted. So limits are important. When limits are broken you can walk away clean, free of abuse because that line has been crossed and there is no way of mending it. It is very important to keep your word and let that person know that you can't change your limits, even if things are at their best. Don't go back on your word or that person will never believe anything you said. The abuser can then abuse you without having to listen to anything you say. So watch out, it is very important to set the limits on how far that person is allowed to go with you. This is one way to prevent abuse.

In the situation of child abuse, parents know what their limits are. They know when their kids have gone too far, but yet they tend to abuse them instead of letting them know what they have done was wrong. Child abuse is sick and very punishable for those who cross the limits of beating their children. Kids should be loved and they should also have rules of discipline. Some kids are very hard to deal with but there is help and it is free. It doesn't cost you your life to seek help with a child you can't deal with. But it can cost you much more if you abuse your child. Set the limits with your children before it is too late, and you have gone too far, abusing them.

After being abused Pat went home for the last time. She set the limits on how far to let her husband go, so she would not end up abused like once before. He gained control over himself so he wouldn't break the boundaries that would make her run away. He didn't want to be left alone so he reformed his life. When anger came out, she was more confused about leaving, hoping that abuse would not occur once again. So no matter how angry Bill got he still respected her limits and didn't cross the line. He did this because he didn't want to lose her for good. He wanted to maintain a peaceful life with his wife. Setting limits can set you off to a great start. When entering and leaving an abusive situation it is very important to let the person know how far they can go and what will happen if they cross the line. You won't be sorry and you will win in the end.

## MAKE SOME DIFFERENCE IN YOUR RELATIONSHIP

Falling in love is important. It is a way of living, getting to know your partner and putting your best foot forward. It takes love to have something good and a lot of hard work to keep it once it comes. Making some changes in your relationship can be very rewarding. It takes two to make one. Putting out what you might receive can make you very happy. In order to prevent abuse you have to make happiness. You have to put some effort in making things work for the better. Do things that make that person happy, conquer that person's heart even when anger occurs. Find ways to help overcome the sight of anger. Do things to get around making mistakes, and if mistakes are being made, solve them right away, don't go to sleep hating the one you love the most. Find ways to make that person smile, even if he hasn't smiled before. Making a difference is very important, especially if your life depends on it. Do things that the person wouldn't expect you to do, anything to kill abuse. It has to be wiped out of our lives. It is punishable in our environment and no one has to put up with it.

If you are in an abusive situation, go back to the old way of making that person happy before things got out of hand, before abuse occurred. Try everything to get rid of abuse so that you won't have to suffer with sleepless nights worrying about whether or not this person will snap. The thing is to not get abuse started, to try to prevent it in every way possible, because abuse is dangerous. It should be carefully watched in all aspects in which it exists. Making a difference in your relationships can cause happiness in your environment and your surroundings. Put your best foot forward and go for the good things and overcome that wall of abuse. Find love when it is hidden. Sometimes love is hard to find and abuse is always there, but when you find love it will conquer all that abuse has to offer.

No one should have to trade abuse for love, not even the abuser. He should also make a difference. It takes two to bring love into the hearts and it takes two to get rid of it. Abuse is not what we want to exchange love for. Some things cannot be avoided or settled, but making a difference can bring peace and joy with happiness. That is all that is needed to get abuse out of one's life and steer the abused into the right direction. It is something that should be at least tried before giving up, before vanishing or putting yourself into something you will regret later. So make a difference in your relationship and you will conquer abuse.

## In Need of Help?

WHEN IN AN ABUSIVE SITUATION A PERSON NEEDS HELP SERIOUS HELP. THEY NEED SOMEONE TO TALK TO AND SOME PLACE TO GO FOR SECURITY IN CASE OF SERIOUS DANGER. SOMETIMES FINDING HELP ISN'T ALWAYS EASY, BUT THERE IS ALWAYS SOMEONE WHO WILL LISTEN AND GUIDE YOU TO THE RIGHT PLACES. SOME OF THESE PLACES ARE UNKNOWN TO MOST OF THE PUBLIC. ABUSE IS SOMETHING THAT SHOULD NOT BE PLAYED AROUND WITH. WHETHER IT IS PHYSICAL, VERBAL OR CHILD ABUSE, NONE SHOULD HAVE TO SUFFER OR LIVE IN FEAR. ABUSE IS SERIOUS AND I HAVE LISTED DIFFERENT PLACES TO CALL IN CASE YOU OR SOMEONE YOU KNOW NEEDS HELP. IT MAY NOT BE THE RIGHT PLACE, BUT THEY CAN GIVE YOU GUIDANCE ON WHERE TO GO FOR HELP IN CASE OF EMERGENCY. ABUSE SHOULD NOT BE TAKEN FOR GRANTED OR PLAYED AROUND WITH. IT IS REALLY DANGEROUS AND IT COULD COST YOU YOUR LIFE. EVERYONE WANTS TO LIVE IN PEACE, EVEN THE ABUSER AND THERE ARE PLENTY OF PLACES TO GO FOR HELP, SO DON'T HESITATE TO CALL YOUR NEAREST POLICE DEPARTMENT FOR HELP IN THE CASE OF SERIOUS DANGER. YOU WON'T BE SORRY LATER. SO THINK BEFORE IT HAPPENS AND MAY LOVE BE WITH YOU. TRUST IN GOD.

BOX 63 500 W 4TH
HASTINGS, NEBRASKA 68902
402/461- 7181

ESSEX COUNTY
ARMANDO STREET
NEWARK, NEW HAMPSHIRE 07102
201/621-4105

BOX 1829
ALBUQUERQUE, NEW MEXICO 87103
503/768-4100

BOX 437 MAIN ST.
HILLSBOROUGH, NORTH CAROLINA
27278
919/745-3101

1002 A. SAGINAW ST.
FLINT, MICHIGAN 48592
31 3/224-2222

JUDICIAL BLDG.
SALEM, MISSOURI 65560
314/729-3241

FALLON COUNTY
BOX 899 10 W FALCON AVE
BAKER, MONTANA 59313
406/778-2879

CLARK COUNTY
400 E STEWART
LAS VEGAS, NEVADA
702/289-8800

NEW HAVEN COUNTY
BOX 200, 235 CHURCH ST.
NEW HAVEN CONNECTICUT 06510
203/789-7883
502/384-2776

ORLEANS PARISH
421 LOYOLA AVE., SUITE 403
NEW ORLEANS, LOUISIANA 70119
504/423-6143

911 PARR BOULEVARD
RENO NEVADA 89512
702/289-8808

ERIE COUNTY
BUFFALO NEW YORK 14202
716/858-7618

BROOKLYN
718/802-3542

NEW YORK COUNTY
NEW YORK CITY
212/374-8298

DENVER COUNTY
BOX 1108 10500 SMITH RD
DENVER, CO. 80201

KING COUNTY
SEATTLE, WASHINGTON 98104
206/296-4155

WYANDOTTE COUNTY
BOX 328, 204 South STREET
LEO, KANSAS 67861
313/375-2723

BENTON COUNTY
113 E. 3RD STREET
VINTON, IOWA 52389
319/291-2587

ADAIN COUNTY
COURTHOUSE, PUBLIC
SQUARE
COLUMBIA, KENTUCKY 42728

ORANGE COUNTY
BOX 1440, 701 SOUTH
ORLANDO, FLORIDA

ANDROSCOGGIN COUNTY
2 TURNER ST.
AUBURN MAINE 04210
297/784-7361
GARY W
701 KELLY RD
CUMBERLAND MARYLAND   21502
301/777-5959

CLACKAMAS COUNTY
2223 SIKAEN RD
OREGON CITY, OREGON
503/655-8281

ADAMS COUNTY
111 BALTIMORE STREET
GETTYSBURG, PENNSYLVANIA  15222
412/355-4700

WASHINGTON COUNTY
4800 TOWER HILL RD
WAKEFIELD, RHODE ISLAND 02879
401/782-4100

GEORGETOWN COUNTY
BOX 869 SCREVEN ST.
GEORGE TOWN, SOUTH CAROLINA
803/536-5101

AURORA COUNTY
BOX 333,402 N MAIN
PLANKINTON SOUTH DAKOTA 57368
605/942-7736

TENNESSEE
DAVIDSON COUNTY
506 SECOND AVE
ASHVILLE, TENNESSEE 37201
617/725-8200

AITKIN COUNTY
217 2ND FLOOR
AITKIN, MINNESOTA
218/927-2138

CHITTENDEN COUNTY
BOX 1426 410
BURLINGTON VERMONT 0542
502/863-4341
HENRICO COUNTY
BOX 27032
RICHMOND VIRGINIA 23273
804/672-4840

RAPPAHANNOCK COUNTY
BOX 487
WASHINGTON, VIRGINIA
703/675-3331

BEXAR COUNTY
200 N COMAL
SAN ANTONIO, TEXAS  78207
512-270-6010

METRO POLICE DEPARTMENT
9105 NW 25TH ST.
MIAMI, FLORIDA
305/471-2100

BROWN COUNTY
300 E WALNUT ST.
GREEN BAY, WISCONSIN 54301
414/448-4200

CHEYENNE COUNTY
1910 PIONEER AVE
307/778-3700

SUFFOLK COUNTY
COURTHOUSE, NEW BUILDING
BOSTON, MASSACHUSETTS
615/862-8170

SALT LAKE COUNTY
SALT LAKE CITY UTAH 84111
804/535-5411

DALLAS COUNTY
133 N INDUSTRIAL BLVD.
DALLAS TEXAS 75207 4313
214/653-3450

DUVAL COUNTY
BOX 2070, 501 E. BAY
JACKSONVILLE, FLORIDA
904/630-2120

HINDS COUNTY
BOX 1452 407 E PASCAGO
JACKSON MISSISSIPPI 39215
601/968-6700

ALABAMA
MOBILE COUNTY SHERIFF
BOX 113,101 GOVERNMENT ST.
205/690-8630

FULTON COUNTY
136 PRYOR ST. RM 108
ATLANTA GEORGIA 30303
404/730-5100

MAJOR ACT DIRECTOR
5700 E TUDOR RD
ANCHORAGE, ALASKA
907/269-5641

PUBLIC SAFETY DEPT.
111 1 ALAKEA ST.
HONOLULU, HAWAII 96813
808/548-4207

MARICOPA COUNTY
102 WEST MADISON AVE
PHOENIX, ARIZONA
602/256-1000

IDAHO COUNTY
320 W. MAINE
GRANGEVILLE, IDAHO 83530
208/983-1100

ALAMEDA COUNTY
1225 FALCON ST. RM 103
OAKLAND, CA 94612 4328
510/272-6878

COOK COUNTY
704 DALEY CENTER
CHICAGO, ILLINOIS 60602
312/443-6444

LOS ANGELES COUNTY
211 W. TEMPLE ST.
LOS ANGELES CA 90012
213/197-4211

MARION COUNTY
40 S. ALABAMA STREET
INDIANAPOLIS, INDIANA 46204
317/633/5181

## OTHER RESOURCES

CLEARINGHOUSE ON CHILD
ABUSE AND NEGLECT
INFORMATION
PO BOX 1182
WASHINGTON, DC 20013
(703) 385-7565

ACTION FOR CHILD PROTECTION
4724 PARK ROAD
UNIT C
CHARLOTTE, NC 28203
(704) 529-1080

AMERICAN ACADEMY OF
PEDIATRICS
141 NORTHWEST POINT BLVD.
P.O. BOX 921
ELK GROVE VILLAGE, IL
60009-0927
(800) 433-9016

AMERICAN BAR ASSOCIATION
CENTER ON CHILDREN AND THE
LAW
1800 M STREET, NW
SUITE 200
WASHINGTON, DC 20036
(202) 331-2250

AMERICAN HUMANE
ASSOCIATION
AMERICAN ASSOCIATION FOR
PROTECTING CHILDREN
63 INVERNESS DRIVE EAST
ENGLEWOOD, CO 80122-5117
(303) 792-9900
(800) 227-5242

CHILD WELFARE LEAGUE OF
AMERICA
440 FIRST STREET, NW
SUITE 310
WASHINGTON, DC 20001
(202) 638-2952

CHILDHELP USA
6463 INDEPENDENCE AVENUE
WOODLAND HILLS, CA 91367
HOTLINE: (800) 4-A-CHILD OR
(800) 422-4453

CLEARINGHOUSE ON CHILD
ABUSE AND NEGLECT
INFORMATION
P.O. BOX 1182
WASHINGTON, DC 20013
(703) 385-7565

C. HENRY KEMPE CENTER FOR
PREVENTION AND TREATMENT OF
CHILD ABUSE AND NEGLECT
1205 ONEIDA STREET
DENVER, CO 80220
(303 321-3963

AMERICAN MEDICAL
ASSOCIATION
HEALTH AND HUMAN BEHAVIOR
DEPARTMENT
535 NORTH DEARBORN
CHICAGO, IL 60610
(312) 645-5066

AMERICAN PUBLIC WELFARE
ASSOC.
810 FIRST ST., NE
SUITE 500
WASHINGTON, DC 20003
(202) 682-0100

NATIONAL ASSOCIATION OF
SOCIAL WORKERS
7981 EASTERN AVENUE
SILVER SPRING, MD 20910
(301) 565-0333

NATIONAL CENTER ON CHILD
ABUSE AND NEGLECT (NCCAN)
ADMINISTRATION ON CHILDREN,
YOUTH AND FAMILIES
ADMINISTRATION FOR CHILDREN
AND FAMILIES
DEPARTMENT OF HEALTH AND

HUMAN SERVICES
P.O. BOX 1182
WASHINGTON, DC 20013

NATIONAL CRIMINAL JUSTICE
REFERENCE SERVICE (NCJRS)
P.O. BOX 6000
ROCKVILLE, MD 20850
(301) 251-5000
(800) 851-3420

NATIONAL CENTER FOR MISSING
AND EXPLOITED CHILDREN
2101 WILSON BOULEVARD
SUITE 500
ARLINGTON, VA 22201
(703) 235-3900
(800) 843-5678

NATIONAL CENTER FOR THE
PROSECUTION OF CHILD ABUSE
1033 NORTH FAIRFAX STREET
SUITE 200
ALEXANDRIA, VA 22314
(703) 739-0321

NATIONAL COMMITTEE FOR
PREVENTION OF CHILD ABUSE
332 SOUTH MICHIGAN AVENUE
SUITE 1600
CHICAGO, IL 60604
(312) 663-3520

PARENT UNITED/DAUGHTERS AND
SONS UNITED/ADULTS MOLESTED
AS CHILDREN UNITED
232 EAST GISH ROAD
SAN JOSE, CA 95112
(408) 453-7616
NATIONAL COUNCIL OF JUVENILE
AND FAMILY COURT JUDGES
P.O. BOX 8970
RENO, NV 89507
(702) 784-6012

MILITARY FAMILY RESOURCE
CENTER (MFRC)
BALLSTON CENTRE
TOWER THREE NINTH FLOOR
4015 WILSON BOULEVARD
ARLINGTON, VA 22203
(703) 385-7567

NATIONAL ASSOCIATION OF
COUNSEL FOR CHILDREN
1205 ONEIDA STREET
DENVER, CO 80220
(303) 321-3963

NATIONAL COUNCIL ON CHILD
ABUSE
1050 CONNECTICUT AVENUE, NW
SUITE 300
WASHINGTON, DC 20036
(800) 222-2000

NATIONAL EDUCATION
ASSOCIATION (NEA)
HUMAN AND CIVIL RIGHTS UNIT
1201 16TH STREET, NW
ROOM 714
WASHINGTON, DC 20036
(202) 822-7711

NATIONAL NETWORK OF
RUNAWAY
AND YOUTH SERVICES
1400 J STREET, NW
SUITE 330
WASHINGTON, DC 20005
(202) 682-4114

PARENTS ANONYMOUS
6733 SOUTH SEPULVEDA BLVD.
SUITE 270
LOS ANGELES, CA 90045
(800) 421-0353 (TOLL-FREE)
(213) 410-9732 (BUSINESS)

The Child Abuse Prevention and Treatment Act was signed into law in 1974. Since that time, the federal government has served as a catalyst to mobilize society's social service, mental health medical, educational, legal and law enforcement systems to address the challenges in the prevention and treatment of child abuse and neglect. Child abuse and neglect is a community concern. No one agency or profession alone can prevent or treat the problem, the community has a legal, moral, and ethical responsibility to assume an active role. Child abuse and neglect is a widespread problem in the American society. A child of any age, sex, race, religion, and socioeconomic background can fall into child abuse and neglect.

To prevent and treat child abuse and neglect effectively, we must have a common understanding of the definition and the extent of the problem child abuse effects children under age 18 in which the child's health or welfare is harmed or threatened thereby. Producing any visual depiction of such conduct; in which physical abuse is characterized by physical injury which was indicated in the contents of this book. The forming of bruises and fractures resulting from punching, beating, kicking, biting, burning, or otherwise harming a child. Although the injury is not an accident, the parent or caretaker may not have intended to hurt the child. The injury may have resulted from over discipline or physical punishment that is inappropriate to the child's age or condition.

Specific life situations of some families can increase the likelihood of maltreatment, such as marital conflict, conflictual relationships with extended family, domestic violence, employment and financial stress, and social isolation. Child abuse can therefore be seen as a problem in parent child interaction with parental, social, and psychological factors playing contributory but not causal roles. Parent child interactions within the first days of life, particularly with premature and ill newborns specifically related to child maltreatment, studies have found that less parent-infant contact during early hospitalization was more likely to lead to abuse.

Within our constitutional scheme, each state has the power to enact laws that responsibility to protect the health, safety and welfare of its residents. The power to enforce such legislation termed "law enforcement," gives the States some control over the relationship between the child and its community. The Federal law recognizes that certain basic protections must exist to ensure a degree of equal treatment and basic service for all children regardless of the State of residence.

Principals, teachers, school counselors and other school-related personnel and early childhood educators play a critical role in the community child protection system. Their responsibilities include identifying and reporting suspected intrafamilial child abuse and neglect; recognizing and reporting child abuse and neglect occurring in the school system/early child care program.

What might be the cause in one family may not be the cause in another family, and the factors that may cause maltreatment in one family may not result in child abuse and neglect in another family. An incorrect conclusion from this finding, however, is that maltreated children will grow up to become maltreating parents. There are individuals who have not been abused as children, as well as individuals who have been abused as children, who do not subsequently abuse their own children. Characteristics identified in some maltreating parents are low self-esteem, low intelligence, ego deficiency, impulsivity, hostility, isolation and loneliness, anxiety, depression and apathy, rigidity, fear of rejection, low frustration tolerance, narcissism, fearfulness, immaturity and dependency, distrustfulness, neuroticism, drug or alcohol abuse, and criminal behavior. Alcohol abuse continues to be a common problem of parents who mistreat their children. While in the past alcoholism represented a family's only substance abuse problem, today alcohol has become a gateway drug used prior to or in conjunction with more highly addictive substances.

Certain children are more physically and emotionally vulnerable than others to maltreating behavior. Younger children, due to their physical size and development status, are particularly vulnerable to certain forms of maltreatment, such as the battered child syndrome, the whiplash shaken infant syndrome, and nonorganic failure to thrive. Also, infants with low birth weight may be at increased risk for maltreatment.

Physicians, nurses, and other medical personnel play a major role in the protection system in every community. Key functions of health care providers include identifying and reporting suspected cases of child abuse and neglect: providing diagnostic and treatment services (Medical AND Psychiatric) for maltreated children and their families.

Child Abuse has spread drastically throughout our nation and it has become a serious, uncontrolled problem. If child abuse is suspected in your community it should be reported right away for investigation. Sometimes it may not always be abuse but it can very well lead in that direction. Every state has enacted laws addressing this critical community responsibility. Communities can develop strategies to prevent abusive or neglectful patterns from happening. Prevention is commonly categorized as primary, secondary or tertiary. "Primary" prevention addresses a sample of the general population. It is a program administered to all students in a school district regarding how to prevent such abuse. "Secondary" prevention is targeted at preventing breakdowns and dysfunctions among families at risk for abuse and neglect. "Tertiary" preventing, or treatment, involves situations in which child maltreatment has already occurred. The goal is to decrease recidivism and avoid the harmful effect of child maltreatment.

Report child abuse. No-one should have to suffer. Together we can make a difference in someone's life.

IF YOU WISH TO ORDER ANOTHER COPY
OF THE' ABUSED AND THE' ABUSER
PLEASE SEND CHECK OR MONEY ORDER FOR
$22.00 TO:


PRINCESS LEE PUBLISHING COMPANY
P.O. BOX 72012
OAKLAND, CA.  94612-8212


NAME_____

ADDRESS_____

CITY_____STATE_____ZIP____

PHONE_____

PLEASE ALLOW 2-3 WEEKS FOR DELIVERY